At Our Best

A volume in
Current Issues in Out-of-School Time
Helen Janc Malone, *Series Editor*

At Our Best

Building Youth–Adult Partnerships in Out-of-School Time Settings

edited by

Gretchen Brion-Meisels
Harvard Graduate School of Education

Jessica Tseming Fei
Harvard Graduate School of Education

Deepa Sriya Vasudevan
Wellesley College

INFORMATION AGE PUBLISHING, INC.
Charlotte, NC • www.infoagepub.com

Library of Congress Cataloging-in-Publication Data

A CIP record for this book is available from the Library of Congress
http://www.loc.gov

ISBN: 978-1-64113-975-5 (Paperback)
       978-1-64113-976-2 (Hardcover)
       978-1-64113-977-9 (E-Book)

Cover art illustration by Alyssa Liles-Amponsah

Printed in the United States of America

To young people everywhere:
We (adults) are at our best—as educators, mentors, and caregivers—
when we listen, learn, create, and act alongside you.

CONTENTS

SECTION II

ON RELATIONAL PRACTICES

SECTION III

ON ORGANIZATIONAL PRACTICES

SECTION IV

ON THE COMPLEX ROLE OF ADULTS

SECTION V

LOOKING FORWARD

FOREWORD

INTERGENERATIONAL SOLIDARITY WHEN THE HOUSE IS ON FIRE

María Elena Torre
The Graduate Center of the City University of New York

In January of 2019, at the World Economic Forum in Davos, Switzerland, a gathering not designed for the presence or participation of young people, 16-year-old Greta Thunberg turned an opulent room of global leaders upside down as she called out their failure to address the rapid acceleration of climate change. Disgusted with their passivity, she made an urgent demand for action, ending with:

> Adults keep saying: "We owe it to the young people to give them hope." But I don't want your hope. I don't want you to be hopeful. I want you to panic. I want you to feel the fear I have every day. Then I want you to act. I want you to act as if you were in a crisis. I want you to act as if the house is on fire. Because it is.[1]

We are living in times of crisis. While Greta's action and continued organizing has captured global headlines, youth activists everywhere are making

At Our Best, pages xi–xiii
Copyright © 2020 by Information Age Publishing

similar demands and forcing public attention to the extreme structural inequalities that shape our lives, schools, and communities. Young people
in the United States are organizing against white supremacy, xenophobia,
cisheteropatriarchy, sexual violence, gentrification, the gun industry, the
criminalization of migration, racist policing, mass incarceration . . . and the
list goes on. These inequalities are not new, their roots are intertwined with
the colonization of this land, but the speed and magnitude of their contemporary manifestations call for our immediate response. In unprecedented
numbers, young people are taking to the streets, walking out of schools,
interrupting business as usual. They are reaching out and building new
solidarities—even at times after stumbling over traditional divisions—recognizing intersectional struggles, and insisting on new ways of being. Times
of crisis call for action, and today's urgency requires us to engage our most
radical imaginations.

Luckily for us, this is precisely the gift of this gorgeous collection of writings. Lovingly gathered by Gretchen Brion-Meisels, Jessica Tseming Fei,
and Deepa Sriya Vasudevan, the book you now hold in your hands offers
intimate and collective stories of intentional intergenerational organizing
and other forms of youth-adult solidarities and partnerships. Through poetic personal essays, theoretical and empirical studies, and reflections on
collaborative research, programming and activism, youth and adult authors
share honest insights into what it means to build, together, the just world
we are fighting for.

The youth–adult partnerships highlighted in this volume break apart
the kinds of youth–adult relationships that have too long been encouraged.
Youth are not innocent blank slates, in need of protection and education;
adults are not all powerful harbingers of knowledge. And neither group is
patronizingly sought by the other for their "pearls of wisdom," or as Greta
Thunberg rejects, their offer of "hope." Instead, the youth and adults in
these chapters represent passionate actors who have come together because of a deep recognition that each has invaluable knowledge born of
situated experience that is essential to creating the change they are mutually invested in. With their collectives, they build what Gloria Anzaldúa
called *nos-otras*, a "we" that holds us (*nos*) and others (*otras*) together with a
hyphen that insists on both individual recognition and mutual implication,
enacting a solidarity that holds at once the tension of/between history and
future imagination, of oppression and transformation.

This work is not easy—it is filled with the *choques*, or clashes, inherent
in *nos-otras*. Intersecting power and vulnerabilities that cut across age/
race/ethnicity/gender/sexuality/class/(dis)ability lines must be continually navigated and engaged. Tensions produced by the pain, frustration,
and outrage around the injustices being tackled—often differently experienced by members of the collective—must be attended to. None of these

important challenges are glossed over or swept under the rug in the pages that follow. Rather these tensions and *choques* are offered as generative gifts to the readers, grounded experiences for us to learn from, puzzle through, and be provoked by, as we engage these partnerships in our own contexts.

At Our Best: Building Youth–Adult Partnerships in Out-of-School Time Settings reminds us of the radical possibilities that emerge when differently positioned people come together, when youth and adults join forces and meaningfully engage each other's lives. Whether located in participatory research or collaborative organizing, each chapter offers us the necessary inspiration, reflection, creativity, and courage needed to respond, in partnership and solidarity, to the crises before us. The authors, young and old, open our imaginations to the power of collaboratively analyzing and theorizing the varying conditions of our lives and the systems and structures that shape them; of simultaneously reaching backwards and forwards, across time and generation, rooted in and at the intersection of our differences. Their stories incite us to see ourselves in each other and to see each other's struggles as our own. It is time to roll up our sleeves and join together with those younger and older, as we work, sing, draw, dance, research, and organize for justice.

NOTE

1. Greta Thunberg's full speech is available at https://www.theguardian.com/environment/2019/jan/25/our-house-is-on-fire-greta-thunberg16-urges-leaders-to-act-on-climate

ACKNOWLEDGMENTS

*We urgently need to bring to our communities the limitless capacity to love, serve,
and create for and with each other."*
—Grace Lee Boggs, Community Activist, Writer, Speaker

Over the past eight years, the three of us have shared the wonderful gift
of working together on a variety of educational projects and academic en-
deavors related to youth voice, community building, and out-of-school time
spaces. There is so much we have learned about the intersection of these
practices and contexts through our past collaborative work—from each
other, our students, and colleagues; many of these insights have found a
home in this volume. This book has become a meaningful meeting place
for our questions about issues of power and practice in developing youth-
adult partnerships in OST spaces, as well as an opportunity to bring multiple perspectives to the table. We are proud and excited by the range and
number of voices in this volume, and the lively conversations between youth
development scholars, youth workers, youth organizers, and young people
that have emerged on these pages.

Every part of this process was a collective endeavor, and we would like to
acknowledge the various individuals and entities who supported us along
the way. First, we are truly grateful to Helen Malone, Elizabeth Devaney,
and the Information Age Publishing OST Series Editorial Board, including Dale Blyth, chair of the Advisory Board, and Brenda McLaughlin and
Femi Vance, co-chairs of the Editorial Review Board. We are so grateful for

the opportunity to be a part of this book series. Relatedly, we would like to thank the members of American Educational Research Association's Out-of-School Time Special Interest Group and past book editors of the OST series—many of whom shared experiences that informed the direction of this book. We are also deeply thankful for a book development grant from former Dean James E. Ryan and current Dean Bridget Terry Long at the Harvard Graduate School of Education, which assisted with critical costs for copyediting, administrative coordination, and author contributions. A special thank you to Ellen Meisels and Amy Maranville, who assisted with chapter copyediting, as well as George Johnson and Lisa Brown at Information Age Publishing for supporting our vision for an edited collection that blends and bridges the worlds of research and practice, reflection and action, and writing and art through adult and youth voices.

We would like to extend our appreciation to all of our authors and contributors for their enthusiasm and dedication throughout the editorial process. From early idea-generating conversations to later rounds of revisions and feedback, your commitment to sharing your knowledge and experience is what makes this collection shine. Thank you, chapter authors and youth contributors, for making the topic of intergenerational partnerships in OST come alive through your engaging prose, poetry, and artwork. Because we held a selective process for youth contributions to this book, we would like to acknowledge *all* the young people who shared their work with us as well as our friends and colleagues who helped promote the opportunity for these submissions. We also want to make a special note of appreciation to Alyssa Liles-Amponsah, who beautifully captured an image of intergenerational solidarity through her artwork for our book cover. We must share our deep gratitude to our own multigenerational families for their timely advice, love, and support. Finally, to our past, current, and future students, you continue to inspire our work in innumerable ways. We are excited to share this book with you as we continue to engage in conversations about navigating intergenerational partnerships, in all of their beautiful complexity.

CHAPTER 1

INTRODUCTION

Gretchen Brion-Meisels
Harvard Graduate School of Education

Deepa Sriya Vasudevan
Wellesley College

Jessica Tseming Fei
Harvard Graduate School of Education

Youth from around the world have taken a frontline role in publicly addressing some of the most pressing social issues of our time: educational inequity, gun violence and reform, police brutality, racism, climate change, and more. Some of these youth-led efforts have gained attention from news outlets and social media as well as political traction among policymakers. Many have wondered what enables youth to step into the spotlight with such conviction, courage, and conscientiousness. How have young people implemented powerful strategies for change, despite the harm and trauma that so many have endured? What intergenerational ecosystems exist to support youth voice and leadership—and how can adults play a role in strengthening and sustaining this work?

Sitting at the intersection of education research, practice, and activism, we have been inspired by the wisdom and power of youth. We believe that adults can be advocates and partners for young people working towards social change within their programs, schools, and communities. We celebrate the oft-silent and taken-for-granted work of intergenerational partnerships, in which youth and adults envision and enact dreams for a better future together. From this standpoint, we have been troubled by news and media reports that fail to acknowledge the vast landscape of youth organizing and action, both within the United States and across the world, as well as those that erase the long history of intergenerational organizing and youth-led social movements (Ginwright, Noguera, & Cammarota, 2006; HoSang, 2006; Kwon, 2013).

Young people engaged in social change efforts have often asserted that their efforts are not isolated. For example, the young people who survived the 2018 school shooting in Parkland, Florida, and went on to lead marches and rallies that catalyzed a nationwide movement to end gun violence, have publicly recognized the longtime activism of youth of color for safety in their communities. Through building coalitions with longstanding youth organizations, such as Power U and Dream Defenders in Miami and Peace Warriors in Chicago, Parkland students highlighted the interconnected nature of the injustices that young people face, while also drawing attention to the ways in which these issues differentially impact communities due to social factors such as race and class.

Despite mainstream portrayals of recent political actions led by youth activists as unprecedented moments in time, youth-led movements for social change are not an invention of the modern era. Historians and education scholars have documented the instrumental role that young people have played in anti-colonial protests as well as movements for civil rights, democracy, and educational equity (e.g., Boren, 2013; Conner & Rosen, 2016; Franklin, 2014; Gordon, 2009; Kirshner, 2015; Sturkey, 2010; Tuck & Yang, 2014). Young people today are inheriting and extending these legacies of youth leadership, building upon the foundations of their predecessors as they work toward equity, inclusion, and justice in a changing world.

Throughout history, there have been many instances of adults mentoring, supporting, and standing in solidarity with young people who are fighting for their rights. For example, in the Newsboy Strike of 1899, young men refused to sell papers published by Pulitzer and Hearst, demanding higher wages and more equitable working conditions. Despite being relatively powerless economically and politically, the so-called "Newsies" developed a democratic process and drew on labor union strategies to win their campaign. Behind the scenes, the Newsies were supported by editors at competitor papers, who provided significant coverage of their efforts (Leavy, 2016). Almost half a century later, during the Mississippi Freedom Summer of 1964, the Student Nonviolent Coordinating Committee began Freedom Schools, alternative educational spaces where youth participated and engaged in Black print culture and discussed citizenship and freedom in ways that were profoundly limited in public school systems. In these schools, with the support of volunteer teachers, Black youth explored their intellectual and cultural heritage through the creation of youth-authored "freedom newspapers" (Sturkey, 2010). Sturkey (2010) notes that before Freedom Schools and freedom newspapers, Black youth activism "was limited to local civil rights campaigns where students played supporting roles to adult leadership" (p. 349). A few years later, in 1968, Chicanx students staged a series of walkouts in East Los Angeles to demand better educational conditions. Calling for bilingual education and ethnic studies, young people advocated to be reflected in the curriculum and respected in their schools. A small group of educators supported the efforts and the cause of these students, helping them organize and strategize their activism (Watanabe, 2013).

In recent years, youth of color have continued to drive grassroots efforts toward justice in their schools, neighborhoods, and communities. Campaigns, rallies, and marches have taken place across the country, with notable leadership by the Black Youth Project 100, a project coordinated by Professor Cathy J. Cohen. Across these historical and contemporary movements, youth–adult partnerships and intergenerational solidarity have been critical to building community power and engaging transformative work.

Recognizing the contributions of young people—in addition to the efforts of the adults who have stood behind and beside them—has been a major influence on our work in education research and practice. With combined experiences as critical educators, youth workers, mentors, and youth participatory action research (YPAR) facilitators in cities such as Cambridge, Boston, New York, and Philadelphia, the three of us have often witnessed the power of youth–adult partnerships occurring within out-of-school time (OST) spaces in particular—for instance, in youth programs, school-based extracurricular and co-curricular activities, community-based organizations, and through social justice education networks. In this volume, the fourth in a series on current issues in OST, we take up the theory and practice of youth–adult partnerships occurring in and through these programs.

This book provides research-based evidence and participant testimonials to help readers understand the power of intergenerational learning in OST spaces, while also responding to key questions that scholars, adult practitioners, policymakers, and youth navigate in this work, such as: What role can (or should) adults play in supporting youth learning, voice, and activism in schools and communities? What strategies of (and approaches to) youth–adult partnerships are most effective in promoting positive youth development and organizational transformation? What tensions and challenges arise in the process of doing this work? And what are the pressures of our contemporary era that influence youth–adult partnership in OST today?

We believe that building youth–adult partnership is a necessary component of developing high-quality OST programs for youth. It is also oftentimes the most meaningful and important work that adults can do with young people—especially with youth who are routinely minoritized, controlled, and patronized within existing systems of education.

In the following section of this introduction, we define youth–adult partnerships and explore the historical evolution of the concept. Next, we locate youth–adult partnership work within the broader context of research on quality youth programming in OST. We conclude by laying out the purpose and structure of this volume.

THE MEANING OF YOUTH–ADULT PARTNERSHIP

While the concept of youth–adult partnerships is not new, research and writing about qualities of youth–adult partnerships, and the factors that create them, is relatively recent. This research has been largely motivated by the Convention on the Rights of the Child (UN General Assembly, 1989), a document whose origins date back to the early 20th century. In 1924, the League of Nations adopted a Declaration of the Rights of the Child, which guaranteed children and youth five fundamental human rights, including a right to the resources necessary for healthy development, protection from exploitation, and significant relief in times of distress. In 1946, the United Nations built on this document, expanding it to include seven key points in 1948, and then 10 key points in 1959. The current version, which became effective in 1990, includes 54 separate articles and has been ratified by all eligible member states except the United States (Rothschild, 2017).[1]

In the United States, youth–adult partnerships have long been associated with the struggle for civil rights. In the early 1800s, several organizations were established to protect and advocate for abused and neglected children in the United States. In 1832, the New England Association of Farmers, Mechanics, and other Workingmen passed a resolution condemning child labor, and by 1836, Massachusetts had become the first state to pass a child labor law.[2] The same year, the National Trades' Union Convention adopted a recommendation to set minimum age requirements for factory work—a recommendation that was repeated without government action for over a hundred years, until the Fair Labor Standards Act of 1938. These early efforts to prevent the abuse and neglect of children and youth slowly gave way to more nuanced fights for civil rights. In 1851, Massachusetts passed the first modern adoption laws, and 2 years later, Charles Loring Brace founded the Children's Aid Society. Throughout the 19th and 20th century, youth and adults collaborated to advocate for the right to education, the right to food and housing, safe working conditions, rehabilitative justice systems, and equitable child welfare practices. The role of young people in these movements varied but often included publicly sharing their experiences and perspectives, pushing for more radical visions of change, building collective will and capacity, and supporting boycotts, marches or other forms of nonviolent direct action.[3] In similar ways, youth have contributed to national civil rights movements, anti-war movements, labor movements, socialist movements, anti-racism movements, and queer liberation movements.

Despite this long history, only in the last 50 years have educators, activists, and researchers endeavored to define and document what youth–adult partnerships entail. In 1974, the National Commission on Resources for Youth defined youth–adult partnerships as those in which there is "mutuality in teaching and learning and where each age group sees itself as a resource for the other and offers what it uniquely can provide" (p. 227). Two years later, that same commission added that, "youth participation can thus be defined as involving youth in responsible, challenging action that meets genuine needs, with opportunity for planning and/or decision-making affecting others, in an activity whose impact or consequences extends to others—that is, outside or beyond the youth participants themselves" (p. 25).

Building on these ideas, as well as on Articles 12–15 of the Convention on the Rights of the Child, researchers have outlined fundamental aspects of youth participation that underlie youth–adult partnerships. Checkoway (2011) describes 10 elements of youth participation, which actively involve young people in the institutions that affect their lives. Mitra, Serriere, and Kirshner (2014) define youth participation as, "a series of rights, including access to information, expression of views and freedom to form collective organization" (p. 292). Shepherd Zeldin and colleagues at the University of Wisconsin-Madison have put together a variety of resources—research articles, an open access guide, and a website—devoted to building youth–adult partnerships and fostering organizational cultures that support youth engagement in leadership, decision-making, and community change.

Two frameworks about youth–adult partnerships are particularly essential to the design of this book: Hart's (1992) ladder of youth participation and Zeldin, Christens, and Powers' (2012) components of youth–adult partnerships.

The Ladder of Youth Participation

In 1992, after spending 3 years studying young people's participation in environmental projects, Hart wrote an essay for UNICEF in which he described the tension of participation in work with youth. Defining participation as "the process of sharing decisions which affect one's life and the life of the community in which one lives" (p. 5), Hart (1992) describes a typology of the ways in which adults interact with children and youth in school- and community-based projects. His ladder of participation includes eight levels at which young people are often invited to participate in civic and social life. The bottom three rungs of the ladder—manipulation, decoration, and tokenism—are considered "nonparticipation"; they do not actually count as an integration of young people into the decision-making processes that affect their lives. The top five rungs describe typologies of young people's participation that range from "assigned but informed" to "child-initiated, shared decisions with adults." Hart's (1992) ladder provides a typology through which we can understand participation in youth–adult partnerships across dimensions of power and context (see Figure 1.1).[4]

The Components of Youth–Adult Partnership

Zeldin and colleagues have spent the last 20 years investigating examples of youth–adult partnerships and illuminating the mechanisms through which these partnerships lead to positive outcomes. Zeldin's work has been seminal in considering processes and practices of youth–adult partnership, specifically in drawing attention to the role of youth–adult partnerships in community empowerment and in OST settings beyond the U.S. context. Zeldin, Christens, and Powers (2012) define youth–adult partnerships as the practice of: "(a) multiple youth and multiple adults deliberating and acting together; (b) in a collective [democratic] fashion; (c) over a sustained period of time; (d) through shared work; (e) intended to promote social justice, strengthen an organization and/or affirmatively address a community issue" (p. 388). The authors note that youth–adult partnerships are distinct from other forms of youth–adult relationships, in part because they focus on collective development and transformation. In other words, rather than focusing on individual-level outcomes for youth—in the way that mentoring or coaching might—youth–adult partnership work typically is designed to "support youth (and adults) as agents of their own development... [who are] expected to collaborate, choosing objectives, and making commitments on issues that matter to both parties" (p. 389).

In this same piece of work, Zeldin, Christens, and Powers (2012) identify four core elements of youth–adult partnerships: (a) authentic decision-making, (b) natural mentors, (c) reciprocal activity, and (d) community connectedness. Authentic decision-making is defined as the active participation of youth in decisions that affect their everyday lives, including the opportunity to deliberate with those in power. Natural mentors are defined as nonparent, non-peer support figures (Rhodes, Ebert, & Fischer, 1992).

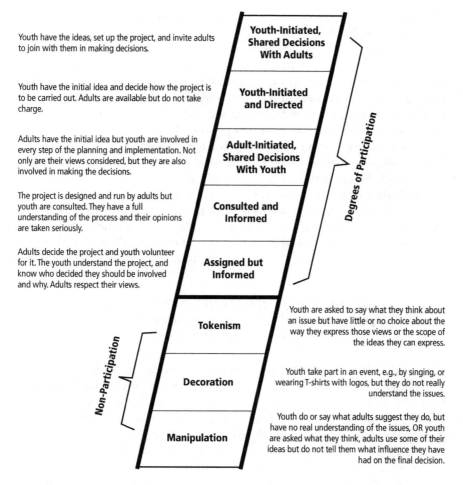

Figure 1.1 Ladder of youth participation (recreated from Hart's 1992 ladder of children's participation).

Unlike more formal mentoring, "natural mentoring occurs without a defined program, and by the mutual consent of those involved under conditions of more equal power" (Zeldin et al., 2012, p. 391). Reciprocal activity is built on the principle of mutuality, and demands that adults and youth act as both teacher and learner. In reciprocal spaces, "there is an emphasis on creating structures and norms for collective reflection and critical thinking among intergenerational groups" (Zeldin et al., 2012, p. 392). Finally, community connectedness refers to the strength of social networks among members of a community, which can provide both social capital and social support. These aspects of youth–adult partnership work in tandem to nurture collective development.

Zeldin and colleagues' definition of youth–adult partnership, and the examples that accompany it, resonate deeply for us. We believe that in addition to being reliable, reciprocal, and responsive, youth–adult relationships must be: (a) strengths-based, (b) committed to cultural humility, (c) partnership-oriented, and (d) praxis-oriented (Brion-Meisels, Fei, & Vasudevan, 2017). In these relationships, adults provide the scaffolding and the tools that enable youth to critically analyze and act upon the world around them. We recommend that in order to best support these positive relationships between adults and youth, settings should include or feature: (a) nurturing physical spaces, (b) the space and time to build trust, (c) joy/fun, and (d) a commitment to explicitly address institutional equality (Brion-Meisels et al., 2017). These types of settings typically adopt democratic and participatory decision-making processes, as well as a set of humanizing practices that center individual and collective transformation.

AUTHENTIC YOUTH–ADULT PARTNERSHIPS: A VERTEBRAE OF QUALITY YOUTH PROGRAMMING IN OUT-OF-SCHOOL TIME

Out-of-school time (OST) programs vary widely in their curriculum (e.g., media arts, political education, health and wellness, outdoor education), in their processes (e.g., maker spaces, organizing spaces, youth on boards, arts-based spaces, athletic spaces, youth radio and television) and in their cultures (e.g., spaces defined by identity, or geography, or ideology, or interest). Yet across programs, OST work is highly relational: Many providers see their roles as working *with* youth rather than *for* youth (Chávez & Soep, 2005; Jones & Deutsch, 2011; McLaughlin, Irby, & Langman, 1994). In OST programs, youth and adults are often partnering to change dominant systems, like schooling or corporate policies. In addition, OST programs themselves tend to be settings of community and collaborative decision-making, from the initial design of programs to the development of activities and projects, and their evaluation (Deschenes, Little, Grossman, & Arbreton, 2010). Historically, OST programs have met a set of youth-driven demands that include access to: informal learning spaces (Halpern, 2002; Mahoney, Larson, Eccles, & Lord, 2005; Malone & Donahue, 2017); information about cultural identities and histories (Akom, Cammarota, & Ginwright, 2008; Cabrera, Meza, Romero, & Rodriguez, 2013; Pozzoboni & Kirshner, 2016); key social, emotional, and civic tools (Lerner, Almerigi, Theokas, & Lerner, 2005); and sites of resistance and disruption of educational inequities and sociopolitical consciousness building (Baldridge, Beck, Medina, & Reeves, 2017; Ngo, Lewis, & Maloney Leaf, 2017).

In the first volume of this edited series, *Current Issues in Out-of-School Time* (Malone & Dohahue, 2017), Karen Pittman (2017) makes the argument that the OST field must shift its focus from the *where* and *when* to the *what* and *how*. Pittman (2017) writes that researchers and youth workers should

> embrace sharper, cleaner criteria that describe and differentiate...[OST] programs not only based on where and when they operate, but also on what skills, behaviors, and capacities they hold themselves accountable for developing, which groups of students they best support, how they create environments that support predictable growth for these populations, and how well they monitor and manage their performance. (p. 295)

Pittman (2017) suggests that this shift is critical if we are to help K–12 educators understand the specific ways in which context-driven, personalized learning can successfully nurture holistic development and equity in educational spaces. By articulating the *what* and *how*, OST programs can provide significant insights for school-based educators on the strategies that underlie context-driven, personalized learning. Indeed, according to Pittman (2017), the *what* and *how* of effective youth programs may, in fact, be the *what* and *how* of effective learning spaces across time-of-day and context.

Through highlighting authentic youth–adult partnerships as a central component of quality youth programs, this fourth volume of the IAP series on OST aims to sharpen the field's understanding of positive, intergenerational relationships—an essential *what* of OST programming. In addition, we aim to articulate *how* positive youth–adult partnerships are nurtured, such that educators across school and community-based contexts can better enact context-driven, personalized learning, while also enabling processes of healing, empowerment, and transformation.

In their work on OST programs, researchers at the David P. Weikart Center for Youth Program Quality (CYPQ, n.d.) offer a framework for understanding the set of factors that influence the quality of youth programming.[5] The CYPQ uses a pyramid to illustrate the multitiered nature of factors of safety, support, positive interactions, and engagement; factors which combine to create environments in which youth can gain essential skills, thus affording opportunities for positive youth development. In 2012, Akiva proposed adding youth program governance (YPG) to the CYPQ's pyramid. This, Akiva (2012) notes, "may include providing opportunities for youth to lead activities, to participate in advisory boards, and to be involved in decisions about how the physical space is arranged, the activities offered, field trips, how money is spent, and even staff hiring" (p. 1).

Prior volumes of this IAP series provide evidence of the ways in which social-emotional learning (SEL; Devaney & Moroney, 2018) and equity

(Hill & Vance, 2019) are essential to quality OST programs. In some ways, both SEL and equity can be seen as core elements forming the base of the CYPQ pyramid. In order for youth to be safe and supported, OST programs must build a climate that is healthy and health-promoting for all youth. The skill-building and conflict resolution skills found in the second tier of the CYPQ pyramid are explicitly rooted in the fields of SEL and equity. At the same time, it is hard to read the CYPQ pyramid without acknowledging the overlap among its tiers; in other words, each subsequent tier rests squarely on the foundation of the tiers below. In this way, SEL and equity not only form a base on which quality youth programs build; they are, in fact, vertebrae of a backbone that steadies quality OST programs and enables them to promote positive youth development.

In this volume of the *Current Issues in OST* series, we argue that another, equally important, vertebrae is the quality of the relationships between youth and adults in a program (see Figure 1.2). We refer to quality youth–adult relationships as partnerships because we believe that these relationships are only truly authentic when they exist outside of traditional power hierarchies and negative constructions of youth. In using the phrase "youth–adult partnerships" to describe the intergenerational relationships that facilitate high levels of youth participation and power, our work intentionally builds on the work of Shepherd Zeldin and his colleagues, whose research on the quality of youth–adult relationships has been a core part of our own learning.

Returning to the CYPQ's Pyramid of Youth Program Quality, one can identify myriad ways in which youth–adult partnerships impact each of the tiers of programming quality. The strength and quality of youth–adult relationships is directly related to young people's feelings of safety in an OST setting, as well as their ability (and willingness) to access support. Given the dangers of hierarchical adult–youth relationships, which often recreate structural violence, we argue that high-quality youth–adult relationships are partnership-oriented. These relationships allow young people to feel seen and valued in their full humanity, enhance young people's sense of agency to pursue their individual and collective goals, and ensure the scaffolding needed for youth to experience success of many kinds. They also demand of adults an equal willingness to grow—to learn, to build capacity, to stretch themselves in new ways—which is critical for long-term, reciprocal relationships. By building partnership-oriented spaces and relationships, OST programs can foster safe and supportive settings where young people's developmental and relational needs are given priority. These settings allow for restorative and humanizing responses to harm, often providing a model quite different from that of school.

In addition to baseline considerations of safety and support, the CYPQ model suggests that youth programs must foster high quality interaction

Figure 1.2 Factors influencing the quality of youth programming (with content adapted from the David P. Weikart Center for Youth Program Quality).

and engagement. In the Youth Program Quality Assessment (PQA) overview, high quality interactions are defined as a peer culture where youth "support each other," "experience a sense of belonging", participate in small groups as members and as leaders, and have opportunities to partner with adults (Smith et al., 2011, p. 6). High-quality interactions occur both among youth, and between adults and youth. They are characterized by trust, a shared sense of purpose, agency, and authentic collaboration. The YPQA defines quality engagement as settings in which young people feel safe and included such that they can "assert agency over their own learning." Quality engagement requires that youth have "opportunities to plan, make choices, take on responsibilities, reflect and learn from their experiences" (Smith et al., 2011, p. 6). And, they encourage programs to provide youth with choices and opportunities to reflect on the decisions that they have made in the past. Youth–adult partnerships foster high-quality engagement by providing the scaffolding and safety within which flexible engagement can occur. In addition, youth–adult partnerships often draw on adult expertise in ways that have been chosen by youth. That is, although adults have a clear role and purpose in the work, youth pick the central goals.

Evidence from across the fields of education and youth development has begun to illustrate the impact of youth–adult partnerships on the outcomes of participants. Across a study of 198 programs, Deschenes, Arbreton, Little, Herrera, Grossman and Weiss (2010) found that OST programs that were most effective in engaging older youth were ones that included leadership opportunities focused on: volunteering, having input into designing activities, designing and leading activities for peers or younger youth, conducting community service activities, and shaping program rules, among others. Additionally, through hierarchical linear modeling, Akiva, Cortina, and Smith (2014) found that especially for older youth, different youth–adult partnership practices were positively associated with young people's motivations to attend programs as well as their skill-building, further confirming these kinds of partnerships between adults and youth as foundational for positive programming.

We also know that the power of youth–adult partnerships goes beyond their impact on individual youth. As Zeldin and colleagues (2012) note, youth–adult partnerships can lead to mutually transformative experiences for both youth and adults, inspiring ongoing efforts in community advocacy, participation, and coalition-building for all involved. Other scholars (e.g., Camino, 2000; Ginwright, 2005) have suggested that youth–adult partnerships can be healing for adults who have themselves experienced marginalization, exclusion, and trauma. For these reasons and others that will be discussed through the chapters in this volume, youth–adult partnerships not only represent a core element of high-quality OST programming, they also constitute a key aspect of OST pedagogies from which school-based educators might learn.

We entitled this book "At Our Best: Building Youth–Adult Partnerships in Out-of-School Time Settings" because our authors and contributors reveal how youth–adult partnerships necessitate that both adults and young people bring their best selves to their work. The chapters in this volume explore, in varied ways, how youth–adult partnerships can enable people and programs to develop toward their full potential. In this way, building youth–adult partnerships helps us expand our collective capacity to achieve transformational change in our organizations, schools, neighborhoods, and communities.

Out-of-school time programs have the power to model new paradigms of learning, creating, and being. In OST spaces, adults and youth have the opportunity to re-envision learning and build social consciousness without the scripts of the classroom. However, OST spaces can also reproduce the adultism, misogyny, and racism from which youth seek refuge, if these systems of oppression go unchecked (Baldridge et al., 2017). When adults partner with youth in driving the mission, approach, and outcomes of learning, OST settings can become sites of resistance and transformation for all involved. Thus, we believe that it is imperative to address both the possibilities and the challenges of engaging in partnership work in OST, and we see these youth–adult partnerships as representative of the work we can do *at our best.* It is our hope that as educators begin to draw more readily from the best practices of the OST field, the power and promise of youth–adult partnerships become kernels from which they build.

OVERVIEW OF THIS BOOK

In this volume, we bring together the voices of over 50 adults and youth who have thought deeply and critically about youth–adult partnerships, and whose unique perspectives enable us to think in new ways about the theory and practice of youth–adult partnerships in OST. The book is anchored by 14 chapters that represent a mix of empirical research, theoretical and conceptual studies, and engaged dialogue on what it means and looks like to engage in partnership work. Of these 14 chapters, several are co-written by intergenerational collectives of youth and adults, or people who began collaborating with one another in the context of a youth–adult partnership; their chapters are a direct reflection of the many opportunities for learning and knowledge-building inherent in positive youth–adult relationships. In addition, throughout the book, we have incorporated short essays, poetry, and artwork by 11 young people who offer insights based on their lived experiences of partnership with teachers, youth workers, counselors, family members, and other caring adults in their lives. Through these varied works of creative expression and storytelling by young people, readers can engage in the practice of listening to the voices of youth and learning from the wisdom they have to share. For adults, we consider this practice to be the starting point of building solidarity with young people and creating space for young people's stories to be heard.

The intention of this book is to lift up the stories, experiences, theories and knowledge of authors with multiple positionalities. We focus on amplifying the experiences of young people who have been traditionally marginalized by structures of—and institutions with—power, including young people of color, young people with disabilities, young people from opportunity-constrained environments, immigrant and refugee youth, gender nonbinary youth, and sexual minority youth. The chapters that follow are organized into four sections: "The Foundations of Partnership," "On Relational Practices," "On Organizational Practices," and "On the Complex Role of Adults." Each of these sections addresses theoretical frameworks in addition to concrete strategies and approaches for building youth–adult partnerships in OST. Section I, "The Foundations of Partnership," establishes three fundamental aspects of effective youth–adult partnerships, each of which plays out at both interpersonal and organizational levels. In Chapter 2, Aisha Griffith and Xue Jiang theorize a process of trust-building in youth–adult relationships, based on interviews with youth and adults at a number of different project-based OST programs. In Chapter 3, Luis-Genaro Garcia takes readers into his practice as a teacher, researcher, and artist in Los Angeles, describing how he draws from Paulo Freire's problem-posing methodology to collaborate with youth in processes of community change, working together to challenge oppressive and limiting circumstances. In Chapter 4, Juan Medina, Bianca Baldridge, and Tanya Wiggins explore a set of key tensions that present challenges to authentic youth–adult partnerships, with a focus on the sociopolitical contexts that shape programming in community-based youth organizations. Ultimately, Medina and colleagues highlight the importance of creating organizational cultures that are humanizing, critically reflective, and grounded in an asset-based approach to supporting youth of color. We view such spaces as guided by the principles and aspirations of democratic participation, wherein all members of a community—including those with the least power and privilege—can assert their voices and exercise their rights to shape the conditions of their lives.

In Section II, "On Relational Practices," we zoom in on youth–adult relationships—what we consider the underpinning of effective partnership work. These chapters help us think about what it takes to form, sustain, and leverage positive relationships that are based in shared values and driven by shared goals. In Chapter 5, Marcellina Angelo and Deborah Bicknell reflect on how they cultivated a 10-year relationship through their involvement with the Maine Youth Action Network (MYAN). Through a steady exchange of love, care, communication, and laughter, their relationship grew to allow each person to be their authentic self as they grappled together with racial difference, cultural issues, and personal hardship. In Chapter 6, Donté Clark and Molly Raynor juxtapose and interweave their stories of growing up, finding poetry, and ultimately co-developing and co-directing a youth arts program in Richmond, California. In addition to acknowledging the contrasts in their identities and backgrounds, their chapter explores how they collaborated across differences of power and privilege to create healing-centered, youth-driven spaces in their local communities. In Chapter 7, Amanda Torres and Anna West, former mentee and mentor as well as longtime collaborators in youth arts organizing and education, dive deeply into the intricacies and complications of forming reciprocal and transformative relationships between adults and youth. They highlight the paramount importance of critical reflection and individual healing in ensuring that the relationships formed between adults and youth do not perpetuate the often exploitative conditions of under-resourced youth organizations, and can effectively provide shelter against systems of oppression in society at large. Within this section, youth authors and artists Kelsey Tonacatl-Cuatzo, Sylvia Boguniecki, Arie Dowe, and Arianna Ayala share their visions and experiences of times when adults supported them to pursue their passions and interests, fostering relationships that honored their unique gifts as young artists and writers.

All together, these authors and contributors help us see the challenges as well as the hope inherent in youth–adult relationships. Perhaps unsurprising for a volume on intergenerational partnerships, these works signal that adults should be viewing younger people as not only worthy of a seat at the table of community change, but also as co-leaders, co-facilitators, and co-directors with valuable contributions to share. Moreover, they illuminate how the quality of youth–adult relationships fundamentally shapes the work that adults and youth can do in partnership with one another.

Section III, "On Organizational Practices," continues to emphasize the importance of positive youth–adult relationships while turning focus to the settings that support youth–adult partnership work. In this section, we include poetry and essays by Tianna Davis, Yohely Comprés, and Latifat Odetunde—young people who describe their involvement in affinity spaces for women of color, student organizations focused on experiential learning and social justice activism, and youth–adult collaborations that amplify youth voice. The chapters in this section further examine the structures, routines, and curriculum that not only foster positive youth–adult relationships, but also center them within the context of OST programs and community-based organizations. In Chapter 8, Pegah Rahmanian advances a model for youth development in which partnership with adults intentionally moves young people through a continuum of adult-led to youth-led participation. Based on her experiences with Youth in Action, a youth development organization in Providence, Rhode Island, Rahmanian contends that differentiation in curriculum, opportunities for personalization, and community-building experiences can help individuals and organizations offer the best versions of themselves to the world. In Chapter 9, Sarah Zeller-Berkman, Mia Legaspi-Cavin, Jessica Barreto, Jennifer Tang, and Asha Sandler—all members of an intergenerational research collective addressing issues concerning justice-involved youth in New York City—describe practices that are grounded in the principles of democratic participation and power-sharing. In addition to providing readers with theoretical grounding in critical participatory action research (CPAR), Zeller-Berkman and colleagues share examples of ways to name and address power, scaffold roles and responsibilities, establish common goals for action, and engage in group reflection on the progress of shared work as well as on the influence of current events on their everyday lives. In Chapter 10, Erica Van Steenis and Ben Kirshner examine the literature on youth media arts and hip-hop as an entry point to youth–adult partnerships. Drawing from their research on a youth media arts organization in the San Francisco Bay Area, Van Steenis and Kirshner discuss how youth workers have engaged hip-hop music production as a curricular tool to foster equity and collegiality in their relationships with youth. In Chapter 11, volume editor Jessica Tseming Fei presents a conversation between Rush George, Nayir Vieira Freeman, Allyn Maxfield-Steele, and Ash-Lee Woodard Henderson—community organizers who have occupied various roles as leaders and staff members at the Highlander Research and Education Center, founded in 1932 in Tennessee. These contributors cast light on practices such as developing group rituals and norms, learning about the historical and global context of resistance and movement-building, and creating structures of governance that nurture and support younger leaders. Moreover, their stories reveal how intergenerational organizing can help build communities defined by lifelong commitments to mutual learning and collective liberation.

In Section IV, "On the Complex Role of Adults," our authors take a close look at the tensions that emerge in youth–adult partnership work. The chapters in this section surface the ways in which partnership work asks for adults to take on different roles and responsibilities than they traditionally do when working with youth; they also illustrate how educators, organizers, and activists have interpreted the call to partnership in different ways. In Chapter 12, Melissa Kapadia, Anika Kabani, and Nudar Chowdhury discuss tensions that they wrestled with in their roles as organizers and former participants within a summer program for South Asian, Diaspora, and Indo-Caribbean youth. Using the Zeldin, Christens, and Powers (2012) framework for youth–adult partnerships as an analytical lens, they show how even in radical spaces that are designed to be nonhierarchical and healing-centered, youth and adults still need to work actively to recognize and transform hierarchical relations, to balance a sense of comfort alongside the push to grow, and to invest in long-term collective healing that transcends the bounds of any one space and time. In Chapter 13, Samantha

Rose Hale, Heang Ly, Nathaniel McLean-Nichols, and Carrie Mays—authors who first began collaborating as youth and adult staff at Teen Empowerment in Roxbury, Massachusetts—unpack an intergenerational conflict that arose in the process of planning for a community dialogue on racism. Hale and colleagues identify several contributing factors—such as histories of oppression, cultural differences, biases and assumptions, and limited time and resources—that give rise to these tensions between adult and youth, and detail the tools they used, such as debriefing conversations, consensus-building around goals, and shared facilitation practices, to recover from the harm caused by adults in the group. In Chapter 14, Kristy Luk, Noah Schuettge, Keith Catone, and Catalina Perez reflect critically on their collaboration with young people in planning a regional youth-organizing conference. Describing the ways in which this experience revealed tensions of power and manifestations of adultism and white supremacy in an OST space, the authors advance an approach to fostering authentic youth leadership that asks adults to confront their own perfectionism and feelings of shame and failure. Luk and colleagues also share tools for assessing levels of youth participation and power in youth–adult partnership work. Finally, in Chapter 15, Thomas Nikundiwe speaks on the tensions that adults experience around when and how to exercise their own voices in youth-led and youth-run organizations. Drawing lessons from a past conversation between adults and youth involved in the Baltimore Algebra Project, Nikundiwe argues for the importance of fostering strong relationships with and among young people and providing opportunities for youth to take the lead from the beginning stages of youth–adult partnership work. Nikundiwe's chapter adds depth to our understandings of trust as a foundational aspect of youth–adult partnerships, and provokes thought on the many ways in which adults and youth might "flip the script" of hierarchical relations and power dynamics in their contexts. Section IV includes artwork and writing by Emmylou Nicolle, Gassendina Lubintus, Noelis Tovar, and Eduardo Galindo—young people who raise up the need for adults to hold high expectations of youth; create sanctuary spaces that include and honor young people's cultures, families, and communities; and share their own wisdom in order to support young people towards their goals.

We conclude this volume with a chapter written by the volume editors. Brion-Meisels, Fei, and Vasudevan explore connections across the chapters and sections of the book, and describe four core principles of effective youth–adult partnerships that were outlined by our authors and contributors: (a) trust, (b) problem-posing methodologies, (c) democratic participation, and (d) collective action. These principles of partnership represent a synthesis of our learning from the book, and underlie a dynamic mix of strategies that practitioners can use to build authentic youth–adult partnerships in OST contexts and beyond. As a diverse group of authors and contributors show through this volume, youth–adult partnerships have the potential to profoundly impact not only the lives of individual youth and adults, but also the many places and communities in which we live, work, and play. We recommend that scholars, practitioners, and policymakers expand the discourse around quality youth programming to include youth–adult partnership as a critical mechanism for transformational change in the broader systems and settings of which we are all part.

NOTES

1. While there are varying perspectives on why the United States has refused to ratify the Convention on the Rights of the Child, several key conservative lobbies are opposed to the treaty.
2. This early law required children under 15 to attend school for at least three months of the year, if they were to work in factories.
3. For more on contemporary youth activist movements, see: Ginwright, Noguera, & Cammarota, 2006; Barrett, 2015; Conner & Rosen, 2016; Hogan, 2019.
4. Although Hart (1992) focused his ladder on a typology of children's participation, we believe the same typology can be applied to the participation of all young people. We reflect this in the language around "youth" that we use in Figure 1.1.
5. For a visual and for more information about this framework, please see http://cypq.org/about/approach.

REFERENCES

Akiva, T. (2012, April). *Involving youth in running youth programs: How common and what might it do for youth?* Presented at 2012 AERA Biennial Meeting, Vancouver, Canada.

Akiva, T., Cortina, K., & Smith, S. (2014). Involving youth in program decision-making: How common and what might it do for youth? *Journal of Youth and Adolescence, 43*(11), 1844–1860.

Akom, A. A., Cammarota, J., & Ginwright, S. (2008). Youthtopias: Towards a new paradigm of critical youth studies. *Youth Media Reporter, 2*(4), 1–30.

Baldridge, B., Beck, N., Medina, J., & Reeves, M. (2017). Toward a new understanding of community-based education: The role of community-based educational spaces in disrupting inequality for minoritized youth. *Review of Research in Education, 41*(1), 381–402.

Barrett, D. (2015). *Teenage rebels: Stories of successful high school activists, from the Little Rock 9 to the class of tomorrow.* Portland, OR: Microcosm.

Boren, M. E. (2013). *Student resistance: A history of the unruly subject.* New York, NY: Routledge.

Brion-Meisels, G., Fei, J. T., & Vasudevan, D. S. (2017). Building positive relationships with adolescents in educational contexts: Principles and practices for educators in school and community-based settings. In M. A. Warren & S. I. Donaldson (Eds.), *Positive Psychology of Relationships: New Directions in Theory and Research* (pp. 145–178). Santa Barbara, CA: Praeger.

Cabrera, N. L., Meza, E. L., Romero, A. J., & Rodriguez, R. C. (2013). "If there is no struggle, there is no progress": Transformative youth activism and the school of ethnic studies. *Urban Review, 45*(1), 7–22.

Camino, L. (2000). Youth-adult partnerships: Entering new territory in community work and research. *Applied Developmental Science, 4*(1), 11–20.

Center for Youth Program Quality. (n.d.) *Approach.* Retrieved from http://cypq .org/about/approach

Chávez, V., & Soep, E. (2005). Youth radio and the pedagogy of collegiality. *Harvard Educational Review, 75*(4), 409–434.

Checkoway, B. (2011). What is youth participation? *Children and youth services review, 33*(2), 340–345.

Conner, J., & Rosen, S. M. (Eds.). (2016). *Contemporary youth activism: Advancing social justice in the United States.* Santa Barbara, CA: ABC-CLIO.

Deschenes, S., Little, P., Grossman, J., & Arbreton, A. (2010). Participation over time: Keeping youth engaged from middle school to high school. *Afterschool Matters, 12*, 1–8.

Deschenes, S. N., Arbreton, A., Little, P. M., Herrera, C., Grossman, J. B., & Weiss, H. B. (2010). *Engaging older youth: Program and city-level strategies to support sustained participation in out-of-school time.* Cambridge, MA: Harvard Family Research Project.

Devaney, E., & Moroney, D. (2018). *Social and emotional learning in out-of-school time: Foundations and futures* (Current Issues in Out-of-School Time book series). Charlotte, NC: Information Age.

Franklin, S. (2014). *After the rebellion: Black youth, social movement activism, and the post-civil rights generation.* New York: New York University Press.

Ginwright, S. (2005). On urban ground: Understanding African-American inter-generational partnerships in urban communities. *Journal of Community Psychology, 33*(1), 101–110.

Ginwright, S., Noguera, P., & Cammarota, J. (2006). *Beyond resistance!: Youth activism and community change: New democratic possibilities for practice and policy for America's youth.* New York, NY: Routledge.

Gordon, H. R. (2009). *We fight to win: Inequality and the politics of youth activism.* New Brunswick, NJ: Rutgers University Press.

Halpern, R. (2002). A different kind of child development institution: The history of after school programs for low-income children. *Teachers College Record, 104*(2), 178–211.

Hart, R. A. (1992). *Children's participation: From tokenism to citizenship.* Florence: UNICEF International Child Development Center.

Hill, F., & Vance, S. (2019). *Changemakers! Practitioners advance equity and access in out-of-school time programs* (Current Issues in Out-of-School Time book series). Charlotte, NC: Information Age.

Hogan, W. C. (2019). *On the freedom side: How five decades of youth activists have remixed American history.* Chapel Hill: University of North Carolina Press.

HoSang, D. (2006). Beyond policy: Ideology, race and the reimagining of youth. In S. Ginwright, P. Noguera, & J. Cammarota (Eds.), *Beyond resistance: Youth activism and community change* (pp. 3–20). New York, NY: Routledge.

Jones, J. N., & Deutsch, N. L. (2011). Relational strategies in after-school settings: How staff–youth relationships support positive development. *Youth & Society, 43*(4), 1381–1406.

Kirshner, B. (2015). *Youth activism in an era of educational inequality.* New York: New York University Press.

Kwon, S. A. (2013). *Uncivil youth: Race, activism, and affirmative governmentality.* Durham, NC: Duke University Press.

Leavy, E. (2016, May 25). Labor history lesson: The "Newsies" strike. [Blog post]. Retrieved from: http://aftct.org/story/labor-history-lesson-newsies-strike

Lerner, R. M., Almerigi, J. B., Theokas, C., & Lerner, J. V. (2005). Positive youth development: A view of the issues. *Journal of Early Adolescence, 25*(1), 10–16.

Mahoney, J. L., Larson, R. W., Eccles, J. S., & Lord, H. (2005). Organized activities as developmental contexts for children and adolescents. In J. L. Mahoney, R. W. Larson, & J. S. Eccles (Eds.), *Organized activities as contexts of development* (pp. 3–22). Mahwah, NJ: Erlbaum.

Malone, H. J., & Donahue, T. (Eds.). (2017). *The growing out-of-school time field: Past, present and future.* (Current Issues in Out-of-School Time Book Series). Charlotte, NC: Information Age.

McLaughlin, M. W., Irby, M. A., & Langman, J. (1994). *Urban sanctuaries: Neighborhood organizations in the lives and futures of inner-city youth.* San Francisco, CA: Jossey-Bass.

Mitra, D., Serriere, S., & Kirshner, B. (2014). Youth participation in US contexts: Student voice without a national mandate. *Children & Society, 28*(4), 292–304.

National Commission on Resources for Youth. (1974). *New roles for youth in the school and the community.* New York, NY: Citation Press.

Ngo, B., Lewis, C., & Maloney Leaf, B. (2017). Fostering sociopolitical consciousness with minoritized youth: Insights from community-based arts programs. *Review of Research in Education, 41*(1), 358–380.

Pittman, K. (2017). Securing the future: Pivoting from where and when to what and how. In H. J. Malone & T. Donahue (Eds.). *The growing out-of-school time field: Past, present and Future* (pp. 293–308). Charlotte, NC: Information Age.

Pozzoboni, K. M., & Kirshner, B. (2016). *The changing landscape of youth work: Theory and practice for an evolving field.* Charlotte, NC: Information Age.

Rhodes, J. E., Ebert, L., & Fischer, K. (1992). Natural mentors: An overlooked resource in the social networks of young, African American mothers. *American Journal of Community Psychology, 20*(4), 445–461.

Rothschild, A. (2017, May 2). Is America holding out on protecting children's rights? *The Atlantic.* Retrieved from https://www.theatlantic.com/education/archive/2017/05/holding-out-on-childrens-rights/524652/

Smith, C., Akiva, T., Jones, M., Sutter, A., Hillaker, B., Wallace, L., & McGovern, G. (2011). *Program quality assessment handbook: School age version.* Ypsilanti, MI: Forum for Youth Investment.

Sturkey, W. (2010). "I want to become a part of history": Freedom summer, freedom schools, and the freedom news. *The Journal of African American History, 95*(3/4), 348–368.

Tuck, E., & Yang, K. (2014). *Youth resistance research and theories of change* (Critical youth studies). New York, NY: Routledge.

United Nations General Assembly. (1989, November 20). Convention on the rights of the child. *United Nations, Treaty Series, 1577*, 3. Retrieved from https://www.refworld.org/docid/3ae6b38f0.html

Watanabe, T. (2013, April 15). Sal Castro, teacher who led '68 Chicano student walkouts, dies at 79. *Los Angeles Times.* Retrieved from https://www.latimes.com/local/lanow/la-xpm-2013-apr-15-la-sal-castro-teacher-who-led-68-chicano-student-walkouts-dies-at-79-20130415-story.html

Zeldin, S., Christens, B., & Powers, J. (2012). The psychology and practice of youth–adult partnership: Bridging generations for youth development and community change. *American Journal of Community Psychology, 51*(3/4), 385–397.

SECTION I

THE FOUNDATIONS OF PARTNERSHIP

CHAPTER 2

TRUST FORMATION IN YOUTH–ADULT RELATIONSHIPS IN OUT-OF-SCHOOL TIME ORGANIZATIONS

Aisha N. Griffith
The University of Illinois at Chicago

Xue Jiang
The University of Illinois at Chicago

Supportive youth–adult relationships are essential for promoting positive development in youth organizations because they positively impact the experiences of young people in these contexts, their developmental outcomes, and the outcomes of the programs themselves (Li & Julian, 2012; Vandell, Larson, Mahoney, & Watts, 2015). One type of supportive youth–adult relationship is the youth–adult partnership, in which youth and adults collectively move toward a shared goal (Zeldin, Christens, & Powers, 2013).

At Our Best, pages 25–39
Copyright © 2020 by Information Age Publishing

Interpersonal trust is a foundation of many different types of youth–adult relationships, including youth–adult partnerships (Brewer, 2012; Donlan, Mcdermott, & Zaff, 2017; Hammond, 2014; Rhodes, 2005; Taft & Gordon, 2018). A youth–adult partnership can be challenging to foster and maintain because it requires a shift away from the typical hierarchy expected in intergenerational relationships (Conner, Ober, & Brown, 2016; De Lissovoy, 2010). This shift requires adults to be especially attuned to several essential components of their relationships, such as trust. Trust is especially critical if youth and adults seek to engage in authentic collaboration, often a central goal of youth–adult partnerships.

Different fields have identified interpersonal trust as a critical construct that is largely influenced by someone making assessments of another person over time (Hammond, 2014; Hoy & Tschannen-Moran, 1999; Lewicki, Tomlinson, & Gillespie, 2006; Mayer, Davis, & Shoorman, 1995; Rhodes, 2005; Rotenberg, 2010). In our work, we conceptualize interpersonal trust as confidence that someone has your best interests in mind (Rotenberg, 2010).

In this chapter, we propose a model of how young people's trust in adult staff develops in youth programs based on our research in project-based programs. We define project-based programs as youth programs in which participants gain new skills by working on short- or long-term projects with their peers and adult staff. After describing our model of how trust forms, we discuss several implications that our findings have for youth–adult partnerships. We hope this chapter encourages readers to consider trust as a central element of the youth–adult partnerships discussed in this book.

RESEARCH CONTEXT

To understand the role of interpersonal trust within youth–adult relationships, we draw upon research conducted by the first author as part of the *Pathways Project* (conducted during 2012–2013) led by the principal investigators Reed Larson and Marcella Rafaelli and funded by the William T. Grant Foundation. The Pathways Project sampled 13 high-quality project-based youth programs serving high-school aged youth in Chicago, Central Illinois, and Minneapolis-St. Paul. Programs were identified as high-quality based on criteria that included low youth and staff turnover, staff having three or more years of experience, and a focus on youth development (McLaughlin, Irby, & Langman, 1994). The majority of programs served low income and working-class youth. Seven programs were primarily comprised of Latinx youth, two programs were primarily comprised of White youth, two programs were primarily comprised of African American youth, and two programs were relatively diverse. In each program, youth engaged in either multiple small tasks or a large task focused on science, technology, engineering, and math

(STEM), leadership, or the arts. These tasks had some level of complexity and offered youth a sense of ownership over the project.

Semi-structured interviews were conducted with 108 youth and 25 adults across the programs. Each adult interviewed was a part-time or full-time staff member who ran program activities. In this chapter, we refer to these staff as "adult leaders" or "leaders" of the programs. Youth were asked whether they trusted an adult leader in the program and, if so, how that trust formed and whether that trust impacted them. A subset of youth also drew graphical representations of how their trust in a leader grew over time before answering the interview questions on their trust in that leader (see Figure 2.1). Adult leaders were asked how they built trust with youth. They were also asked to provide advice for novice leaders on how to build trust.

We analyzed interviews using constructivist grounded theory to capture how participants made meaning of their experiences and to identify processes that unfolded to promote trust development (Charmaz, 2006). After open coding data, we developed data-driven focused codes. From there, we engaged in an iterative process of analyses that included coding, memoing, refining focused codes, connecting codes, constant comparison of data excerpts, and generating categories. We analyzed youth and adult leader data separately and have discussed these findings in a number of articles (Griffith, 2016; Griffith & Johnson, 2019; Griffith & Larson, 2016; Griffith, Larson, & Johnson, 2017). Finally, we generated a theoretical process model to represent trust formation in the youth program context more broadly by connecting the aforementioned findings to extant literature on interpersonal trust (Mayer et al., 1995;

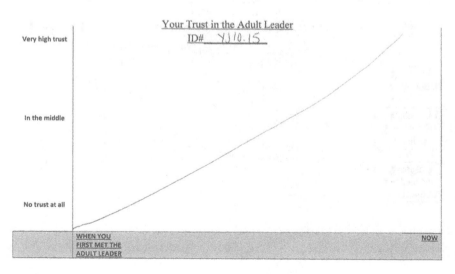

Figure 2.1 Sample youth representation of their trajectory of trust in an adult leader.

Rotenberg, 2010). This exploratory model is based on our research; however, extant literature allowed us to represent the findings in a way that we believe can be applied to many contexts. This model has not been tested.

The co-authors wrote this chapter because of their experiences and interests. Aisha N. Griffith is a former middle school teacher and a professor in a graduate program in youth development who has researched out-of-school time (OST) programs for a number of years. As a teacher, she became interested in OST programs because her students excitedly talked about these programs, and she believed OST programs had greater flexibility to support development than schools. Her research focuses on relational processes that promote positive development.

Xue Jiang is a doctoral student who situates her work within attachment theory, with a focus on how children from different communities develop a sense of security with caregivers. Her focus on security-building in child-caregiver relationships shapes her thinking regarding the role of trust within youth–adult relationships.

THE PROCESS OF TRUST FORMATION
IN THE YOUTH PROGRAM CONTEXT

In this section of the chapter, we discuss our research within the framework of our proposed model of trust formation in youth program contexts (Figure 2.2).

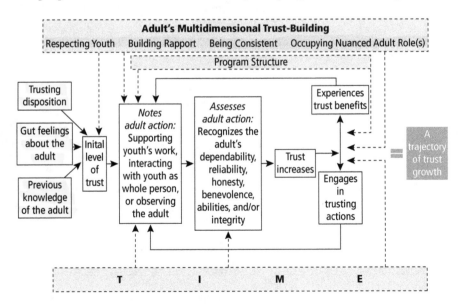

Figure 2.2 Proposed model of trust formation in youth program contexts.

We will first discuss the gray boxes in the model that represent contextual factors, focusing primarily on multidimensional trust-building. We will then describe the white boxes in the model from left to right, which represent a youth participant's experiences. This part of the model begins with a youth's initial level of trust in a leader. The model then represents how transactions in the program increase a youth's trust, especially when an adult is able to demonstrate trustworthiness to the youth. Next, the model shows that an increase in trust leads to benefits for the youth and leads to the youth behaving in ways that demonstrate they trust the leader. Finally, we show that these two outcomes provide the context for a subsequent action by the leader that the youth then assesses. The model concludes by showing that, over time, this process facilitates the trajectory by which a youth's trust grows across program participation.

Approaches Adults Use to Build Trust: Multidimensional Trust-Building

The contextual factors that shape youth trust include how adults approach building trust, the program structure, and time. In our research, we found that when asked about how they built trust, adult interviewees provided detailed and comprehensive responses that pointed to four core approaches to building trust (Griffith & Johnson, 2019). One approach for building trust was to respect youth; this approach required a concern for how one treats youth and a commitment to remain cognizant of how youth perceive that treatment. What "respect" entailed varied, but the majority of leaders emphasized that it was important. The second core approach to building trust was building rapport by getting to know the youth and sharing appropriate personal information so that the youth could get to know the adult. This created a connection between the youth and adult. The third approach to building trust entailed being consistent—for example, always being available, being fair, and following through on what one said. Finally, leaders built trust by occupying a specific type of adult role in young people's lives, which tended to be distinct from other adults. Interviewees, for instance, described how they built trust by being an "adult friend" or by playing multiple roles in a youth's life like a coach, advocate, and social worker (Griffith & Johnson, 2019).

In our model, we refer to these distinct yet related approaches as multidimensional trust-building. We argue that these four approaches are interconnected (Griffith & Johnson, 2019). We speculate that they are interconnected because each core approach complements the others. For instance, showing respect to someone and building rapport with someone can be closely linked. Additionally, some approaches require that an adult effectively engages in another approach. For instance, an adult who plays a nuanced role in a youth's life is meeting the needs of the participant. In order to know the youth's needs and fulfill this role, that adult would have also likely shown respect for that participant, built a rapport with them, and been consistently available. Given the importance of multidimensional trust-building, we emphasize it across the model. The two other contextual factors—program structure and time—are shown across the model; however, multidimensional trust-building is particularly important because one may expect it to be present across various program structures with differing program dosage.

Youth's Initial Trust in an Adult Leader

Generally, a youth's trust in a leader begins at an initial and temporary level, based on various factors, such as the youth's trusting disposition, positive or negative gut feelings about the leader, and whether or not the youth has previous knowledge about the leader (Griffith, 2016). In our research, we found youth interviewed described their trusting disposition influencing their initial trust. For example, one noted, "I'm not a very trusting person." Another shared, "I don't trust no one the first time I see them—it's pretty common sense."

Another factor that influenced initial trust was a youth's gut feelings about the leader based on how they looked or a vibe they got. Gut feelings were unique to the individual. For instance, two of the youth interviewed reported completely different gut feelings about the same adult leader. One said, "First thing when I got in [the program] and I saw [the leader], he has a mean face. So I was like he's probably going to be screaming at me." In contrast, the other said of the same leader, "Well, I met [the leader], and I don't know, he seems like as soon as you look at him, he just looks so friendly." This variability in trusting dispositions and gut feelings across youth suggests that leaders should anticipate youth may come in with different levels of trust, and, as a result, will likely engage with each adult in different ways.

Finally, a young person's initial levels of trust in the adult were influenced by whether they knew the leader before starting the program. For instance, we found that second-hand knowledge from a family member could influence initial trust. One youth who had an initial medium level of trust stated that since his siblings knew the leader, "I already kind of knew her... they've told me to trust her and stuff like that. So, I already kind of trusted her." Although having previous knowledge of the leader seems to be a factor outside of the adult's control, one could imagine leaders being able to shape this factor by engaging participants' family members in the beginning of a program.

Regardless of the initial trust level of each youth, we suspect that a leader's multidimensional trust-building process emphasizes the approaches of respecting youth and building rapport at the beginning of the program. These components of trust can set a foundation for the relationship and establish the atmosphere of the program.

Transactions That Increase Youth Trust

Next, our model depicts the following sequence: A leader engages in an action that is meaningful to the youth, the youth makes a positive assessment of the leader based on that action, and this assessment increases (or decreases) their trust. In our research, youth described three categories of actions that increased their trust: (a) experiencing the leader supporting their work, (b) experiencing the leader interacting with them as a whole person, and (c) positive evaluations of the leader based on observations (Griffith, el al., 2017). Within the program structure, project tasks (e.g., using software to edit video footage; putting together a play) enabled adults to meaningfully support youth in their work. Interviewees reported their trust increased when leaders demonstrated confidence in their capabilities, entrusted them with responsibilities, provided instrumental guidance in the face of both emotional and technical challenges, and offered specific feedback in a respectful and honest manner (Griffith et al., 2017). For instance, one youth said his trust increased because the leader's respectful critique illustrated, "He's actually trying to teach me how to do something [and that] shows me that he actually cares about what I'm doing."

Youth also reported that their trust increased when leaders acknowledged and respected them as whole people. Youth valued moments when leaders discussed shared interests, as well as times leaders noticed youth were upset and asked if everything was okay. One youth recalled a leader doing the latter as "the sweetest thing ever." The leaders' multidimensional trust-building and the informal nature of the youth program structure likely fostered such exchanges. Finally, some youth increased their trust because they liked how a leader interacted with others, managed the program, or carried themselves. Youth could make such observations because programs were structured such that multiple youth worked with a few adults. The category of actions youth considered most meaningful to increasing trust varied by the young person. We believe the most meaningful category or categories of actions fostered "positive expectations of trustworthiness" (Fulmer & Gelfand, 2012, p. 1171).

Theoretical frameworks across disciplines argue that assessing whether one will be trustworthy involves judging the person across various dimensions (Hoy & Tschannen-Moran, 1999; Mayer et al., 1995; Rotenberg, 2010).

Thus, we suggest that when youth evaluate adults on one of these three categories of actions, they assess the extent to which the adult is reliable, benevolent, capable, honest, compassionate, or other dimensions that are critical to an adult's trustworthiness. A positive assessment of a dimension increases youth trust.

The Outcomes of Trust

Our model illustrates how increases in trust lead to two outcomes, which we propose have a bidirectional relationship: trusting actions and trust benefits. In our study, youth reported benefits from trusting an adult leader that seemed to amplify what youth gained from the program, because it led them to engage with the leader and the leader's strengths (Griffith & Larson, 2016). Leaders reported that they believed youth began engaging in certain actions when youth developed trust in them (Griffith & Johnson, 2019), aligning with Rotenberg's (2010) discussion that people who trust another person engage in behavior indicating they trust the individual. We summarize our findings by listing the outcomes of young people's trust from both the young person's and the leader's perspective (Griffith & Larson, 2016; Griffith & Johnson, 2019) as program-related changes and personal changes.

In our study, increased trust between youth participants and leaders[1] led to the following program-related changes:

- *Increased use of leaders' guidance in program activities (reported by youth and leaders).* Youth reported that having trust in a leader made them more likely to listen to that leader's instructions, more likely to follow suggestions, and more likely to apply advice. Leaders reported that they perceived youth trusted them more when they started asking for feedback on their work.
- *Increased motivation in the program (reported by youth).* Youth reported having trust made them care about a project more, made them work harder, made them more confident in their own abilities, and lessened how worried they were about taking risks in putting together the project.
- *Sharing more opinions regarding the project (reported by leaders).* Leaders reported that they perceived youth trusted them more when youth began giving more input on the direction of a project or the program.
- *More "willing to help" with activities that help the program (reported by leaders).* A few leaders believed some youth developed trust in them because the youth began engaging in actions that benefited the program. For instance, a young person would volunteer to participate

in an event that promoted the organization to sponsors, or a young person would join a committee.

- *Increased experience of program cohesiveness (reported by youth).* A few young people described how their trust in the leaders, combined with others' trust in the leaders, fostered a positive program climate.

Overall, the outcomes associated with program-related changes suggested that youth trust made them more invested in their programs and enhanced their experiences in the programs. Increased trust also led to the following personal changes:

- *Increased use of leaders for mentoring on personal issues (reported by youth and leaders).* Youth said trust helped them open up to a leader more generally or use them as a sounding board. Leaders also described an indicator of trust being that youth engaged in more personal disclosures. Youth said trust helped them ask for advice in their personal lives. Leaders also saw that youth asking for advice on personal matters was a sign that youth trusted them.
- *Provided a model of a well-functioning relationship (reported by youth).* Youth said that trusting a leader created a relationship in which they learned relationship-building skills. Frequently they then applied this to other relationships beyond the one with the leader. This relationship also changed how they perceived adults in other contexts, often beginning to give other adults the benefit of the doubt.

Overall, the outcomes of trust associated with personal changes suggest youth trust fostered natural mentoring relationships within the youth program context between youth and leaders. Given that trust is key to mentoring relationships (Rhodes, 2005), it makes sense that increases in trust led some youth to seek out adult leaders for support in their personal lives.

One may ask: *Did the way trust grew determine the domain in which trust then existed?* For example, if a youth reported receiving support on their work increased their trust, was the outcome of that trust only a program-related change? In our research, this was not the case. This is why our model collapses all leader actions rather than linking any category of actions with a specific outcome.

Hypothesized Feedback Loop Between Outcomes and Transactions That Increase Trust

To explain how trust grows over time, our model includes a feedback loop between the outcomes of trust and transactions that increase trust. Although this feedback loop is not empirically driven, considering our analysis in tandem with Mayer et al.'s (1995) proposed model of trust from human resources leads us to speculate that as time passes in the program, the outcomes of trust create an opportunity for another transaction that increases trust.

One example of such a feedback loop could be a young person valuing a leader noticing that they are upset. The leader is seeing the youth as a whole person, recognizing and responding to an emotional need. The youth then makes a positive assessment of the leader, which then increases their trust in that adult. As a result of this increased trust, the youth may begin asking the leader for help on the project, thereby becoming more focused on the leader's guidance. Focusing on the leader's guidance on the project and asking for help sets the context for the leader to support the youth's work by giving specific feedback in a respectful and honest manner. This leads to the youth positively assessing the leader and increases their feelings of trust. The feedback loop is likely to ebb and flow based on the day-to-day experiences youth and leaders have in the program; however, we believe the accumulation of transactions that increase trust across time through this feedback loop leads to higher levels of trust in leaders.

In our research, we found that most youth graphically represented their trust as gradually increasing over time, a few youth graphically depicted specific events that spurred significant growth in trust, and a few depicted their trust growing with decreases of trust along the way (Griffith, 2016). We argue that what occurs during this proposed feedback loop can explain variations in the trajectories of young people's trust across time. We suspect a feedback loop that regularly reinforces a youth's positive assessments of the adult leads to a gradual increase in trust over time. We suspect that significant growth in trust after specific events may be caused by a feedback loop moving more quickly such that a positive assessment of a leader's action quickly benefits the youth; and this benefit immediately facilitates another leader action that youth positively assess. We suspect a decrease of trust along the way indicates that there are breakdowns in the feedback loop. A particular leader action may lead to a negative assessment of the leader that then decreases the young person's trust; there may be less time spent in the program, such as a youth not attending; or perhaps the leader is not balancing their approaches to building trust in a way that fits the needs of a particular youth. In our sample, these dips in trust recovered such that youth reported having high levels of trust in the leader at the time of the interview. We imagine this may be because the optimal feedback loop was restored. Being consistent may have been critical for overcoming barriers to increases in trust and resolving conflicts that decrease trust.

IMPLICATIONS FOR YOUTH–ADULT PARTNERSHIPS

The model presented in this chapter suggests two takeaways relevant to youth–adult partnerships. First, the model suggests trust in adults can positively impact youth's work, as well as their personal experiences, in a program. Second, contextual features of a program, time, and adults' approaches to building relationships all foster varying opportunities for trust to grow from a relatively low level to a high level. In this section, we consider these takeaways through the lens of youth–adult partnerships.

The first takeaway from our model is that trust in adults can positively impact youth's work and their personal experiences in a program. In youth–adult partnerships, high levels of trust may enhance young people's experiences, adults' experiences, and the work being done together in the partnership. In our research, one outcome of trust was that it increased the likelihood that youth actively engaged with a leader's guidance on project activities. In the case of youth–adult partnerships, we imagine that trust might foster young people's willingness to utilize adult scaffolding and support in decision-making and managing tasks. This active engagement may then open up opportunities for intergenerational communication and exchanging of experiences that are valued in youth–adult partnerships (Zeldin et al., 2013).

One aspect critical to fostering youth–adult partnerships that is missing from the research reviewed here is how we understand an adult's trust in a young person. An adult's trust in youth may influence the extent to which youth feel seen in the organization, which may in turn influence the extent to which youth are able to trust adult partners. An adult's trust in youth also may lead to adults actively engaging with young people's guidance on activities. In other words, trust could lead to adults seeing youth as experts with knowledge that could improve their own work. Thus, one can imagine that the benefits resulting from adults trusting youth are central to the type of reciprocity essential to youth–adult partnerships (Zeldin et al., 2013). Taft and Gordon (2018) state that mutual trust can enhance how well activists in youth–adult partnerships foster equity and positively impact youth and adults because, "trusting relationships not only encourage young people to express themselves but also require that adults take those voices seriously and allow young people's views on the world to potentially change their own understandings of the issues at hand" (p. 234). In our work, we found that one outcome of trust was youth's increased motivation to engage in program work. If we consider mutual trust leading to a similar outcome, one would expect mutual trust to increase the partnership's motivation, ultimately fostering perseverance for both youth and adults.

More generally, trust can foster a context that is psychologically safe and supports "radical healing," both of which are important to the work of youth–adult partnerships (Ginwright, 2015; Krauss, Kornbluh, & Zeldin, 2017). Partnerships focused on radical healing through the process of healing centered engagement would be supported by the presence of mutual trust because trust can build empathy, a critical link between youth and adults in spaces that involve partners risking vulnerability (Ginwright, 2018). Feeling trust and safety with one another can set a foundation for sharing vulnerabilities, collectively engaging in healing, and authentically supporting youth.

The second takeaway from our model is that contextual features of a program, such as time, organizational structures, and adult approaches to relationship-building, all foster varying opportunities for trust to grow from a relatively low level to a high level. When collaborating, it is likely that adults and youth support each other's work in the same ways described in this research; this support then nurtures trust. Our research found that adult leaders built trust by incorporating respect, building rapport, being consistent, and occupying a nuanced adult role in participants' lives. Adults attempting to authentically partner with youth are likely to be guided by a desire to treat youth like active agents in the relationship and the organization (Brion-Meisels, Fei, & Vasudevan, 2017). In the same way that project-based programs offer varying opportunities for adults to support young people's trust development, youth–adult partnerships provide opportunities for adult partners to support young people's work. Authentic partnership requires that adults recognize, value, and validate youth's involvement in meaningful decision-making (Zeldin et al., 2013). This aligns with our research finding that some interviewees increased their trust when adults demonstrated confidence in their abilities and gave them responsibility. When youth perceive that their knowledge and skills are valued, trust not only grows, but youth also experience psychological empowerment (Watts & Flanagan, 2007). Another contextual factor found in youth–adult partnerships that likely fosters trust is the emphasis on having youth take on leadership roles that build civic competence. Entrusting youth with responsibilities is one way that leaders in our research fostered young people's trust.

Given that youth–adult partnerships typically center around issues that both adults and youth care deeply about, adults in these partnerships also may be likely to engage with youth as whole people. Jointly addressing a civic concern, the management of an organization, or a cause fosters shared personal interests. In our research, discussing a mutual interest was one way that youth experienced leaders engaging with them as whole people. Like in project-based programs, there is likely to be informal time in which adult partners can become attuned to the needs of the youth with whom they work. If adult partners show they are responsive to these needs, it can increase trust. As a result of the interactions within the larger community that are often inherent in youth–adult partnerships, youth have many opportunities to observe the adults they work with interact with others. Finally, we believe that the sustained and significant amount of time that youth and adults contribute to a youth–adult partnership is likely to foster the feedback loop that increases young people's trust in adults and adults' trust in youth.

CONCLUSION

The youth–adult partnerships in this book present an opportunity for interpersonal trust to grow that is not found in many other contexts in the United States, because youth are often "isolated from . . . adults—spatially, socially, and psychologically" (Zeldin et al., 2005, p. 1). The separation of youth from adult society leaves youth with limited opportunities to develop the types of trusting relationships with nonfamilial adults that are associated with beneficial developmental outcomes (Luthar & Brown, 2007; Werner & Smith, 2001). We have presented an exploratory model of trust formation in youth programs to encourage readers to consider how trust may underlie the work of the programs described in this book. Even if an organization does not emphasize trust, trust is indispensable to partnerships between youth and adults that exemplify authentic collaboration. Thus, youth and adults in effective organizations are working within structures in which they can do the foundational work needed to foster trust.

NOTE

1. When we say "increased trust between participants and leaders," we are referring to a youth's trust in an adult. Our research does not yet assess an adult's increase in trust in a youth because of the nature of our interview questions.

REFERENCES

Brewer, A. M. (2012). Positive mentoring relationships: Nurturing potential. In D. Springer (Ed.), *Positive relationships* (pp. 197–214). Dordrecht, Netherlands: Springer. https://doi.org/10.1007/978-94-007-2147-0_12

Brion-Meisels, G., Fei, J., & Vasudevan, D. (2017). Building positive relationships with adolescents in educational contexts: Principles and practices for educators in school and community-based settings. *Toward a positive psychology of relationships: New directions in theory and research* (pp. 145–177). Santa Barbara, CA: Praeger.

Charmaz, K. (2006). *Constructing grounded theory: A practical guide through qualitative analysis*. Thousand Oaks, CA: SAGE.

Conner, J. O., Ober, C. N., & Brown, A. S. (2016). The politics of paternalism: Adult and youth perspectives on youth voice in public policy. *Teachers College Record, 118*(8), 1–48.

De Lissovoy, N. (2010). Rethinking education and emancipation: Being, teaching, and power. *Harvard Educational Review, 80*(2), 203–221.

Donlan, A. E., Mcdermott, E. R., & Zaff, J. F. (2017). Building relationships between mentors and youth: Development of the TRICS model. *Children and Youth Services Review, 79*, 385–398. https://doi.org/10.1016/j.childyouth.2017.06.044

Fulmer, C. A., & Gelfand, M. J. (2012). At what level (and in whom) we trust: Trust across multiple organizational levels. *Journal of Management, 38*(4), 1167–1230. https://doi.org/10.1177/0149206312439327

Ginwright, S. (2015). *Hope and healing in urban education: How urban activists and teachers are reclaiming matters of the heart.* New York, NY: Routledge. https://doi.org/10.1080/00131946.2016.1231684

Ginwright, S. (2018, May 31). *The future of healing: Shifting from trauma informed care to healing centered engagement* [Web log post]. Retrieved from https://medium.com/@ginwright/the-future-of-healing-shifting-from-trauma-informed-care-to-healing-centered-engagement-634f557ce69c

Griffith, A. N. (2016). Trajectories of trust within the youth program context. *Qualitative Psychology, 3*(1), 98. http://dx.doi.org/10.1037/qup0000049

Griffith, A. N., & Johnson, H. E. (2019). Building trust: Reflections of adults working with high-school-age youth in project-based programs. *Children and Youth Services Review, 96*, 439–450. https://doi.org/10.1016/J.CHILDYOUTH.2018.11.056

Griffith, A. N., & Larson, R. W. (2016). Why trust matters: How confidence in leaders transforms what adolescents gain from youth programs. *Journal of Research on Adolescence, 26*(4), 790–804. https://doi.org/10.1111/jora.12230

Griffith, A. N., Larson, R. W., & Johnson, H. E. (2017). How trust grows: Teenagers' accounts of forming trust in youth program staff. *Qualitative Psychology, 5*(3). https://doi.org/10.1037/qup0000090

Hammond, Z. (2014). *Culturally responsive teaching and the brain: Promoting authentic engagement and rigor among culturally and linguistically diverse students.* Thousand Oaks, CA: Corwin.

Hoy, W. K., & Tschannen-Moran, M. (1999). Five faces of trust: An empirical confirmation in urban elementary schools. *Journal of School Leadership, 9*(3), 184–208.

Krauss, S. E., Kornbluh, M., & Zeldin, S. (2017). Community predictors of school engagement: The role of families and youth-adult partnership in Malaysia. *Children and Youth Services Review, 73*, 328–337. https://doi.org/10.1016/j.childyouth.2017.01.009

Lewicki, R., Tomlinson, E., & Gillespie, N. (2006). Models of interpersonal trust development: Theoretical approaches, empirical evidence, and future directions. *Journal of Management, 3*(6), 991–1022. https://doi.org/10.1177/0149206306294405

Li, J., & Julian, M. M. (2012). Developmental relationships as the active ingredient: A unifying working hypothesis of "what works" across intervention settings. *American Journal of Orthopsychiatry, 82*(2), 157. http://dx.doi.org/10.1111/j.1939-0025.2012.01151.x

Luthar, S., & Brown, B. (2007). Maximizing resilience through diverse levels of inquiry: Prevailing paradigms, possibilities, and promising for the future. *Development and Psychopathology, 19*, 931–955. https://doi.org./10.1017/S0954579407000454

Mayer, R., Davis, J., & Schoorman, F.D. (1995). An integrative model of organizational trust. *Academy of Management Review, 20*(3), 709–734. https://doi.org/10.5465/AMR.1995.9508080335

McLaughlin, M. W., Irby, M. A., & Langman, J. (1994). *Urban sanctuaries: Neighborhood organizations in the lives and futures of inner-city youth.* San Francisco, CA: Jossey-Bass.

Rhodes, J. (2005). A model of youth mentoring. In D. L. DuBois & M. J. Karcher (Eds.), *Handbook of youth mentoring* (pp. 30–43). Thousand Oaks, CA: SAGE.

Rotenberg, K. (Ed). (2010). *Interpersonal trust during childhood and adolescence.* Cambridge, MA: Cambridge University Press. http://dx.doi.org/10.1017/CBO9780511750946

Taft, J. K., & Gordon H. R. (2018). Intergenerational relationships in youth activist networks. In S. Punch & R. Vanderbeck (Eds.), *Families, intergenerationality and peer group relations.* Singapore, Singapore: Springer. https://doi.org/10.1007/978-981-287-026-1

Vandell, D. L., Larson, R. W., Mahoney, J. L., & Watts, T. W. (2015). Children's organized activities. In M.H. Bornstein & T. Leventhal (Eds.), *Handbook of child psychology and developmental science, Volume 4: Ecological settings and process in development systems* (7th ed.; pp. 305–344). Hoboken, NJ: Wiley. https://doi.org/10.1002/9781118963418.childpsy408

Watts, R. J., & Flanagan, C. (2007). Pushing the envelope on youth civic engagement: A developmental and liberation psychology perspective. *Journal of Community Psychology, 35*(6), 779–792. https://doi.org/10.1002/jcop.20178

Werner, E., & Smith, R. (2001). *Journeys from childhood to midlife: Risk, resilience, and recovery.* New York, NY: SAGE. https://doi.org/10.1542/peds.114.2.492

Zeldin, S., Christens, B. D., & Powers, J. L. (2013). The psychology and practice of youth-adult partnership: Bridging generations for youth development and community change. *American Journal of Community Psychology, 51*(3/4), 385–397. https://doi.org/10.1007/s10464-012-9558-y

Zeldin, S., Larson, R., Camino, L., & O'Connor, C. (2005). Intergenerational relationships and partnerships in community programs: Purpose, practice, and directions for research. *Journal of Community Psychology, 33*(1), 1–10. https://doi.org/10.1002/jcop.20042

CHAPTER 3

ART EDUCATION AND THE PROBLEM-POSING METHODOLOGY

A Critical Approach to Learning From and Working With Students and Their Communities

Luis-Genaro Garcia
Sacramento State University

During my first year teaching, a student came to me and handed me an invitation to her quinceañera. I was extremely flattered, but also conflicted at the thought of going to a social gathering where other students would be present. But then I recalled the time that one of my teachers brought his family to our senior class fundraiser. When we saw him outside of his teaching element and met his family, the barrier between him and us became more transparent, both inside and outside of the school setting. So I went to my student's quinceañera, where I danced in an enthusiastic crowd of students and I conversed with various parents about their childrens' performance in

At Our Best, pages 41–60
Copyright © 2020 by Information Age Publishing

class. The following week, I saw students become more receptive of me on campus and become much more active as participants in class. From that experience, I understood that the best engagement you can get from students is by interacting with them outside of the school setting. Since then, I have made my own efforts to develop opportunities in which my students and I collaboratively engage in learning about their communities.

This chapter highlights a framework for working with students—both in schools and in out-of-school time settings—by drawing on Freire's (1970) problem-posing model and on the concept of *creative resistance* (Darts, 2004; Garcia, 2015, 2017a, 2017b). I begin by discussing my positionality to anchor the way my experience informs my teaching, and then elaborate on how I draw on the critical pedagogical approaches I use in my work. I share examples from my own practice as an educator, focusing on two community mural projects through which students responded to the negative portrayals of their neighborhood in the mainstream media. In addition, I include students' own narratives about their experiences of completing these art projects. I conclude this chapter with suggestions on the collaborations and lessons that can be developed in out-of-school settings.

POSITIONALITY

In this chapter, I draw from my previous research that examines how a critical approach to art education benefits marginalized students from under-resourced arts programs (Garcia, 2012, 2015, 2017a, 2017b; Yokley, 1999). My methods are informed by my own experiences of marginalization and from working with marginalized youth as an educator. As a teacher, scholar, and artist who is an alum of the school and community that I now teach in, it is difficult to consider my position as anything else but personal. My previous experiences as a student at the school I teach in have influenced my teaching approach and they have provided me with a unique understanding of the emotional, political, social, cultural, and academic needs of students from marginalized communities. This section introduces my positionality through what Delgado Bernal (1998) and other Chicana scholars (e.g., Delgado Bernal, Burciaga, & Flores Carmona, 2012; Malagon, Huber, & Velez, 2009) identify as *cultural intuition*. Although I am a male scholar, I recognize the importance of drawing on my cultural intuition. I find this concept valuable and important for the field of education research and especially for supporting communities of color.

According to Delgado Bernal (1998), cultural intuition draws from the personal experiences that we have embodied through our upbringing. Delgado Bernal identifies legends, *corridos*, storytelling, behavior, and studies as resources for developing community knowledge with youth. As a teacher and scholar, my cultural intuition is rooted in the home-based knowledge of marginalized students and the art education I experienced as a student. Based on lived experience and academic research, I know that students in marginalized communities do not have the same art education resources as schools in high-income areas. For this reason, I make an effort to draw from the historical knowledge, experiences, understandings, and stories that my students articulate through their artwork. I do this in order to develop a critical analysis of art education research, and to foster pedagogical approaches that center the needs and interests of marginalized students and communities.

In part, my own activism as an artist-educator developed through my involvement with the Cesar Chavez Foundation. From 2007–2009, the Cesar Chavez Foundation provided students and educators with resources and professional development training to develop service learning projects for local communities. The service learning projects were student led—with facilitation and support from educators—and showcased during the yearly Cesar Chavez Walk in downtown Los Angeles. During these years, my students and I engaged in dialogue with students and educators from other schools, thus joining our community advocacy efforts. We were trained to understand the Cesar Chavez core values, such as nonviolence, service to others, and community-driven education. Alongside students, I developed my art-based approach to service learning projects that focused on addressing relevant community needs. Thereafter, I worked closely with students to develop independent service learning projects, and continued building advocacy with the community by joining critical education support groups focused on social justice education.

BACKGROUND AND CONTEXT

The student narratives presented in this chapter come from three students who wanted to be identified as Resistencia (Resistance), Familia (Family), and el Revolucionario (the Revolutionary).[1] Our collaboration took place at Eastside High School,[2] an urban high school that serves a predominantly working-class population. In the 2015–2016 academic year, the student body of Eastside High School was 28% English language learners. Its ethnic population included 88% Latinx students, 10% African American, 0.1% Pacific Islander, 0.1% Native American, 0.1% Filipino, and 0.3% White, non-Hispanic. Eighty-six percent of Eastside High School students were classified as "socioeconomically disadvantaged." The graduation rates that met University of California (UC) and/or California State University (CSU) certification were 40% for African American students and 60.3% for Latino students.[3] According to the Department of Education, Eastside High School was in the lowest 5% of performing schools in the state in the 2015–2016 school year.

During my first year of teaching in 2005, Eastside High School was being blamed for a series of "race riots" between Black and Brown students that spread to other local campuses. The media—with a long history of portraying the Eastside neighborhood as gang-ridden and violent—did not lose a beat in bringing local, state, and national attention to the circumstances created by institutionalized class and racial inequality. Long before the uprising following the Rodney King case in 1992, the media had perpetuated stereotypical depictions of the Eastside community and failed to highlight the families, scholars, and leaders who had developed the positive conditions of the community. The Eastside community is far from being perfect, but there are plenty of community advocates and students who are working toward its improvement. Further, the Los Angeles Unified School District's (LAUSD) partnership with the Cesar Chavez Foundation from 2007–2009 developed many teacher activists who continue to work in their communities.

As an educator of color who experienced growing up in the community I now teach in, I understand that the struggles for liberation that begin in our classrooms are extensions of the neighborhoods, political climates, and home environments that students navigate in their everyday lives. To think critically about these circumstances requires that students and educators reflect upon and consider approaches to liberating education. In teaching for social change through service learning, Hicks-Peterson (2009) suggests a critically conscious praxis of community engagement. She suggests that the community be seen and treated as an equal partner in the exchange of knowledge, service, time, and resources. Like Hicks-Peterson (2009), I believe that students, community members, and professors should be in relationships where there is reciprocity, a perspective that is shared by other scholars of color that have worked in communities (e.g., Calderon, 2004; de los Rios & Ochoa, 2012; Gonzalez, Moll, & Amanti, 2005; Huerta & Rios-Aguilar, 2018; Kiyama & Rios-Aguilar, 2017; Moll, Amanti, Neff, & Gonzalez, 1992; Morrell, 2013; Pizarro, 1998).

PROBLEM-POSING METHODOLOGY: A COLLABORATION BETWEEN STUDENTS AND EDUCATORS

If educators are to meet the needs of working-class students, we must acknowledge the limiting socioeconomic circumstances they live in, and co-create ways to transform those environments. According to *Pedagogy of the Oppressed* (Freire, 1970), we must unveil the reality of oppression and commit to social transformation through the process of praxis. Praxis allows students and educators to constantly reflect and act upon forms of oppression. A critical pedagogy, which should include a critical and liberating dialogue as an act against oppression, needs to be co-facilitated between students and educators in order to achieve social transformation. As Freire (1970) writes:

> It is only when the oppressed find the oppressor out and become involved in the organized struggle for their liberation that they begin to believe in themselves. This discovery cannot be purely intellectual but must involve action; nor can it be limited to mere activism, but must include serious reflection: only then will it be a praxis. (p. 65)

Once social transformation takes place, this pedagogy can result in permanent liberation that challenges the media's dominant culture through the ongoing process of action and reflection.

Critical pedagogy and liberating education are structured through the problem-posing methodology, which entails processes of praxis, dialogue, and *concientización*—critical consciousness that allows us to recognize and challenge the limiting social, political, and economic circumstances of oppressive environments (Duncan-Andrade & Morell, 2008; Freire, 1970; Solorzano,1989). According to Freire (1970), a problem-posing methodology involves the constant unveiling of the sociopolitical realities that exist for students, pushes for the acknowledgement of limiting factors, and co-produces a resistance to those limitations. The first part of problem-posing methodology requires communication between students and educators to identify the problem. The second part requires analyzing and understanding the problem. Lastly, the third part requires finding solutions to the problem by taking action and reflecting on the action taken.

As a teacher, I first involve students in this process by developing Art and History units that engage them in understanding how historical and systemic forms of racism, classism, and sexism in our academic, social, and judicial structures continue to affect their communities today. Through these art lessons and units, I have students question and expand their understanding of how the historical effects of race, class, and gender continue to affect communities of color like their own. It is through these classroom activities that I developed service learning projects that took place in out-of-school time spaces with students—projects that allowed us to question and examine the issues affecting their home and community spaces. One such project, taking place in 2009, included a walking mural that addressed issues of environmental racism, gentrification, and the school-to-prison pipeline (Garcia, 2015). In 2011, a group of students decided to represent their own immigrant narratives on picket signs by participating in the May Day march as a way to show their opposition to Senate Bill 1070[4] (Garcia, 2012). Both of these community projects were extensions of community knowledge that we developed in our art class; by drawing from students' community knowledge in class, we connected art-making to the real life experiences of their communities.

In both circumstances, my students expressed the agency they felt in voicing, engaging, and challenging some of the issues affecting their communities; they valued how what began as a classroom dialogue evolved into an exchange of community knowledge in other environments. Freire (1993) conceptualizes the exchange of *dialogue* as "a horizontal relationship of trust between individuals founded on love, humility, faith, and commitment to the liberation of the oppressed" (p. 91). Engaging in dialogue with students initiates a humanistic approach to education that accounts for students' knowledge, their existing worlds, and the collaborative exchange of ideas for social transformation. It is an approach that recognizes the individuality and wisdom of those engaged in dialogue as an act of love and a commitment to the liberation of the oppressed. Dialogue "requires a faith in humankind, faith in their power to make and remake, to create and recreate, faith in their vocation to be more fully human (which is not the privilege of the elite, but the birthright of all)" (Freire, 1993, p. 90). It is through this act of love for students in marginalized environments that I challenge the banking model of education that diminishes the cultural knowledge students possess.

Connections to Critical Art Education

Connecting problem-posing methodology and the arts provides the opportunity to (a) unveil the sociopolitical realities of students through the creative process, (b) generate the ability to recognize limiting factors through visual literacy, and (c) co-produce a resistance to those limitations through art collaborations and investigation. Because resistance is generated through the creative process, the realities of oppression are recognized and challenged through what I call *creative resistance* (Darts, 2004; Garcia, 2015, 2017a, 2017b).

I define creative resistance as "any practical art form, visual or performing, that contests or challenges systematic-oppressive structures, actions, misconceptions, stereotypes, political agendas, or inequalities that diminish the development of a group of people or community" (Garcia, 2015, p. 140). More specifically, what I define as creative resistance (Garcia, 2015, 2017a, 2017b) is the way that high school students use the arts to develop what Delgado Bernal (1997, 2001) refers to as *transformational resistance*. Drawing on her concept of transformational resistance, I combine the theoretical frameworks of critical pedagogy (Camangian, 2010; de los Rios & Ochoa, 2012, Darder, 1995; Duncan-Andrade, 2010; Duncan-Andrade & Morrell, 2008; Freire, 1970; McLaren, 1994; Morrell, 2013), critical race theory in education (Delgado Bernal, 2001, 2002; Solorzano,

1998; Solorzano & Delgado Bernal, 2001; Yosso, 2005; Yosso, Smith, Ceja, & Solorzano, 2009), and the funds of knowledge (Gonzales & Moll, 2002; Gonzalez, Moll, & Amanti, 2005; Huerta & Rios-Aguilar, 2018; Kiyama & Rios-Aguilar, 2017; Moll, Amanti, Neff, & Gonzalez, 1992; Moll & Greenberg, 1990; Rios-Aguilar & Kiyama, 2012; Rios-Aguilar, Kiyama, Gravitt, & Moll, 2011), to develop an understanding of resistance through the visual arts (Garcia, 2012, 2015, 2017a, 2017b). Critical art education develops students' understanding of oppressive circumstances, encourages action to change those circumstances, and eliminates the dependency instilled through banking models of education.

The purpose of introducing a critical approach in art education is to develop the consciousness of students through a subject that must be seen as equally valuable as the other core subjects we teach. We must think of the arts as the visual component to the sciences, mathematics, history, language, reading, and writing. In other words, when we are building knowledge in other subjects, there are visual components that help us develop understanding. In the sciences, we have illustrations that help us understand cell structures, anatomy, biological organisms, and so forth. In mathematics, we look at the composition of formulas and equations to help us solve problems. When we learn about history and the social sciences, we analyze photographs that document the historic circumstances of specific periods. When developing language, students often analyze visual images for understanding. Additionally, when we read and write, we are using our visual perception to develop an understanding of communication.

We must understand that the arts provide opportunities to develop ideas and possibilities through imagination, and therefore the objective of the arts should be to build the consciousness of students through an imagination of possibilities. Once students have developed the ability to analyze and critique their social limitations through a visual perspective, students can apply these methods to other subject areas. Their ability to think visually and creatively could be applied to other classes that they will no longer see as courses they need to pass, but rather as opportunities to learn collaboratively and share their cultural knowledge. Further, it is important to recognize that when we teach students of color in marginalized communities through European perspectives in art, we are not liberating them from the reality of their oppressive conditions; we are assimilating them. In contrast, a critical art education develops a student's critical consciousness to see the world through a creative and critical perspective. In this way, marginalized students of color can view their realities no longer as limiting situations, but as ones they can creatively transform through praxis.

A Process of Developing Community Murals to Challenge Dominant Perspectives

During the 2014–2015 school year, one of the culminating class projects provided students the opportunity to challenge the misconceptions of their community by creating murals in their neighborhoods. For this, we drew on Yosso's (2005) concepts of community cultural wealth and counter-narratives, concepts that highlight the experiences and perspectives of racially and socially marginalized people. According to Yosso, "counterstories reflect the lived experiences for People of Color to raise critical consciousness about social and racial injustice" (p. 10). By drawing on student knowledge, and counter-storytelling methods in education (Delgado, 1989; Delgado Bernal, 2001; Solorzano, 1997; Solorzano & Yosso, 2001; Yosso, 2005), students and educators can not only resist misconceptions about their own local communities, but also use the arts to challenge dominant and deficit perspectives that do not account for the histories of marginalized populations (Garcia, 2017a, 2017b; Pérez-Huber & Solorzano, 2015; Solorzano, 1989, 1997).

During the spring of that school year, my students and I engaged in an intense and transformational dialogue related to the movie *End of Watch* (Lessher & Ayer, 2012). I had opened up a discussion about dominant narratives and highlighted the media's portrayals of the South Central community since the 1992 uprising following the Rodney King verdict. We discussed films like *Boyz n the Hood* (Singleton & Nicolaides, 1991) and *Menace II Society* (Hughes et al.,1993) as films whose narratives came from African Americans, and compared them to *End of Watch*, which was written and directed by a White director who had not experienced growing up in the community. Although marginalized communities in places similar to South Central usually have higher crime rates, the film portrays a hyper-violent narrative of South Central reflected through shootouts, high-speed chases, and street fights between the police and gang members—incidents that are hyper-realized by the film. The discussion prompted students to consider counter-narratives to explore and challenge the negative portrayals of their neighborhood that were being told by a White director who had not lived there. The discussion developed on its own to a point where I stepped out of the facilitation. I believed this discussion to be transformational because it was one of the times when students independently engaged in a critique of a film which some students believed was an accurate representation of their community, while others challenged their perspectives by making equally valid arguments about their experiences.

The culminating project was something that enabled students to draw from previous knowledge in order to challenge community misconceptions and develop community counter-narratives. It required students to identify some of the major issues and concerns affecting them or their communities. After a series of in-class discussions concerning their neighborhood—which included the misconception of students dropping out of high school, graffiti, cleanliness, homelessness, lack of art in the community, safety, and the lack of motivation in the neighborhood—one of the concerns that students voiced repeatedly was, *how do we show students and kids in the community that what they see on TV is not what our community is like?* Having developed a vast quantity of ideas, the class felt that there weren't murals in the neighborhood that made students like themselves feel inspired. The class decided they wanted to create murals to beautify the community and inspire students in the neighborhood.

When they decided they wanted to beautify their community, I saw the opportunity to share the experience and process of being a community artist.[5] I worked with them to submit art proposals to the three elementary schools closest to our own school. Before contacting any of the elementary schools, I showed students what it was like to submit an art proposal in order for them to understand how to clearly articulate their ideas for community art projects. This gave them the opportunity to draft, write, design, and submit proposals before the school year ended. After 2 weeks of editing proposals and planning, I had six groups of students, each with a complete proposal that included an introduction of the group, the context behind creating their mural on campus, and the goals and objectives of completing the mural with elementary-age students.

Although only one school responded to the mural proposals, site administrators and parents were eager to have local students create murals on their site. In the summer of 2015, after the school year ended, a number of students volunteered their mornings to complete the murals that were chosen by the principal and parents. It took approximately two weeks to complete the murals from start to finish. While on site, I guided students step-by-step through the process of setting up a mural—starting from the original mural design they completed on a gridded paper, to transferring their design onto a wall, using a similar grid method. Despite the similar goals of the murals, each had its own individual design and message.

The first of the murals (Figure 3.1) showed four student silhouettes surrounded by a number of objects, all related to school engagement. It included the overarching message, "You're braver than you believe, stronger than you seem, and smarter than you think." This particular design was inspired by a birthday card that was given to a student by one of her close family members. She felt it was an encouraging message to share with other students through this mural.

The second of two murals was taken from a project that many students felt deeply connected to. The class project introduced students to Tupac Shakur's (1999) "The Rose that Grew From Concrete," with the goal of

Figure 3.1 Mural A at Local Elementary, Summer of 2015.

developing the understanding that even the difficult environment they live in is what helps them grow (Duncan-Andrade, 2009). For this mural design, the group focused on reflecting that students in the community are roses that not only grow from concrete, but also from the knowledge that they receive in school. The mural (Figure 3.2) depicts a radiating rose that is growing out of an open book, and blooming graduating students. The book sits

Figure 3.2 The rose that grew from knowledge. Local elementary, Summer of 2012.

over a desk that has a pencil and sheets of paper, surrounded by a colorful background with the message, "I am the rose that grew from knowledge." The goal of this mural was to encourage elementary students to view themselves as living beings that need love and nourishment to develop their full potential. Students also discussed the idea of younger students using the murals as a backdrop for their graduation pictures.

Throughout the processes of creating these murals, there were plenty of interactions between the participating high school students, elementary students, the principal, and parents. Because the projects were being completed during a summer school program, elementary students were able to engage closely with the high school students and helped to paint the murals. One thing I did not anticipate was how parents brought more of their children to the summer program so they could participate in painting the murals. I also thought about this engagement as an authentic exchange of learning capital and what I truly feel community engagement should be: students of different ages, parents, teachers, and administrators exchanging knowledge to complete these community murals. I saw the enthusiasm of my high school students grow as they took on the role of educators—directing younger students and teaching them painting techniques. I felt their enthusiasm when they eagerly communicated with me late at night, or as early as six in the morning, to see if I could pick them up.

In the following section, I share and reflect upon student narratives about their experiences in the mural projects described above. Through their own words, I show how effective it can be to engage with our students by drawing on the community as a space of learning.

STUDENT NARRATIVES AND REFLECTIONS

As the students and I collaborated in facilitating the completion of the murals, we had many conversations about how they thought and felt about the process. At the later stages of the project, I found that when they talked about the murals, they engaged in reflection through a transformed and socially conscious perspective—an end result of the problem-posing methodology we had used. This became even more evident through post-mural interviews that I conducted with the students. The process of social transformation that develops from problem-posing methodology is explained by El Revolucionario, one of the students in the project. When I asked how he thought the mural project changed the way in which he thought about the community or his aspirations, El Revolucionario said:

> Our neighborhood is often associated with having a poor education, and the only way to change that is to encourage students to find an interest in reading

and learning. This project was the beginning of me changing my mind about not going to college and made me realize that I love art, and I'm thinking about pursuing a career in art education. I used to think art wasn't a big part of our curriculum. This project helped me see how wrong my perception of art was and now I want to help others realize that as well... I am a product of this community, and it is my responsibility to make sure it keeps improving.

El Revolucionario was able to challenge the perception of education in the community through his participation in the mural project (Figure 3.3). The process of action and reflection that El Revolucionario engaged in is the process of praxis (Freire, 1970). At the time of his interview, El Revolucionario was a sophomore going into his junior year. Art was one of his favorite classes, but he had no interest in thinking about college. However, through our collaborative work, he engaged in a process of reflection that ultimately became part of his liberation from deficit thinking. He also reflected his empowerment by acknowledging his commitment to changing his community.

Familia's narrative mirrored that of her classmate, El Revolucionario, but Familia also emphasized the importance of dialogue (Figure 3.4). To

Figure 3.3 El Revolucionario working on Mural A.

Figure 3.4 Familia working on Mural A.

Familia's, dialogue helped build the trusting relationships that then contributed to the community building she did with her classmates and other participants in the mural project. Recall that Freire identifies the exchange of dialogue as a "horizontal relationship of trust between individuals founded on love, humility, faith, and commitment to the liberation of the oppressed" (p. 91). When asked whether the mural project made her feel connected to her community, Familia responded in a way that clearly reflects this practice:

> During this project, I definitely felt a connection with everyone involved and everything around me. But even before this, the connection was already built. With my classmates, I realized we were quite similar, and what brought us together was our community and our daily struggle, how we lived our days, at school and at home. We had similar challenges and goals. A challenge was seeing our parents struggle to give us a better life through our education, and our goal then would be going to college. Having each other really motivated us to pursue everything we wanted, that our community didn't seem to reflect for us. We talked to each other about our hopes, ideas, and everything that moved us.

It is important to understand and process the reason why we must make connections between our classrooms and the communities we work in. Through shared engagement, advocacy, and struggle between students and community members, we develop circles of trust and motivation to move through struggles and aspirations. This is why it is essential for educators working in marginalized communities to draw on the knowledge that students possess about their environments, and take on the responsibility of creating opportunities to connect the community to the curriculum. If we do not develop such opportunities in our learning spaces, then we are sustaining a culture dominated by the banking model of education, and we are failing to prepare our students to change their social circumstances.

Another narrative that reveals a transformative reflection comes from Resistencia (Figure 3.5). Resistencia is a student who experienced anxiety episodes while being by herself, and who shared how the role of artistic collaborations supported her and helped her through anxiety. She also shared feeling enthusiastic about motivating students and feeling like she made a difference in their community. Resistencia explained:

> When I was painting, and we let some of the kids paint with us, I felt proud of myself and them. It made me feel like a role model and that has inspired me to paint more murals around my community. While painting the murals one of my classmates casually told me that if he wasn't doing this right now, he would probably be messing with drugs somewhere else. It made me feel glad that we were focused on the mural together. I also didn't feel lonely, I felt like I was where I was supposed to be and that gave me an intense empowering feeling.

Resistencia feels a sense of empowerment and pride in being engaged in her community and with younger students. Dialogue has served the purpose of developing social consciousness and generating opportunities for students to analyze their communities and themselves, as independent

Figure 3.5   Resistencia showing a younger student how to paint.

individuals. Through problem-posing methodology and creative resistance, there is trust built between students, and between students and their educators as well.

Within the school year, there were many instances in which students expressed their trust in each other and in me. There were moments in which I understood that the trust we exchanged in class contributed to the relationships we developed outside of the classroom setting; there were instances in which students expressed how our out-of-school activities made them aware of the unique relationships we had built. For example, on one occasion, El Revolucionario and I were the only ones working on the mural one Saturday morning. As we worked on the mural, El Revolucionario randomly asked what school I would recommend for him if he wanted to teach "art through a political perspective." He shared that although he was not interested in college, teaching art was something that he would potentially be interested in doing. I explained that a political perspective really came more from the individual rather than the institution, and in my case, my own identities and experiences influenced me to teach art through a social justice philosophy. While talking with El Revolucionario, I learned that our personal talks and projects enabled him to trust me more. As El Revolucionario explained:

> Because I figured with the way you've been teaching, this might enhance my learning more because I don't have this type of relationship with my teachers because I really don't care for them. I thought you were a really good teacher, so I got into art because of you. Since this is about art I took the opportunity to learn more about it and that's why I am here. I feel I can talk to you and open up to you and with my other teachers I can't. I can't talk about some of the things I've done, some teachers will judge me, but with you it's not like that. That's one of the reasons I feel I have a more open relationship with you.

Talking with El Revolucionario about his aspirations and circumstances was something that drew us closer together, and it was the same case with many of the students in class (see Figure 3.6). In this way, my teaching was not limited to the confines of my classroom; it extended to the environments of the students and developed relationships that could transcend the boundaries of physical space and time.

CONCLUSION

I would like to close this chapter by revisiting the process of praxis that Freire (1970) and other critical pedagogues draw on, and encourage educators to continue taking action and reflecting on the current work they are doing with students. As a practitioner of critical education, I do not want to close this chapter by providing a summary of how to draw on the

Figure 3.6 Eastside students after completing the murals at Local Elementary.

problem-posing methodology through art education, nor do I want to leave the reader with a set of instructions on how to do this. What I will suggest is for educators, cultural workers, and advocates for youth to develop their own problem-posing methods, drawing from students' own knowledge and understandings of communities. It could be through the arts, ethnic studies, the sciences, mathematics, or other subjects. What matters is that you draw on interdisciplinary subjects to enhance the subject you teach.

Students in marginalized schools and communities need educator allies who are critically conscious and who understand the circumstances, the dreams, the wishes, the knowledge, and the needs of the communities they serve. In marginalized communities, there are plenty of topics that need further attention, such as gentrification, environmental racism, housing discrimination, immigration, the school-to-prison pipeline, and educational resources. In order to become allies for students and communities of color, each of us must acknowledge the privileges we have and take action toward our own learning and growth. This could mean joining social justice education teacher support groups or attending local social justice curriculum fairs where you can engage and collaborate with other educators and develop ideas for projects, units, and lessons. I call on arts educators to remove ourselves from teaching traditional art courses that focus solely on art techniques and art periods; instead, we must create opportunities and experiences where students can use the problem-posing methodology, develop their own forms of resistance, and apply their knowledge towards changing their current social climates and begin transforming their communities. This is what I have identified as creative resistance.

My intention for this chapter was to show an approach to critical art education that draws on the problem-posing methodology to develop the creative resistance of students in a high school setting. Through a community mural project that illuminated and drew from students' cultural knowledge, I sought to support students in linking their understanding of community issues to broader social circumstances, and in using art to motivate them to challenge the inequality of their communities. Through the creative process, students transformed their social consciousness through their real-life experiences and became driven to improve their communities.

Creative resistance—and critical art education, more broadly—represents an asset-based and culturally relevant approach to art education that is overdue and necessary in marginalized schools. I advocate for a meaningful and relevant art education for students—a critical art education that nurtures their creativity, dreams, hopes, and hearts. I hope that practitioners acknowledge this perspective as not only coming from the expertise of an experienced teacher who developed meaningful relationships with students, but also as coming from a person who lacked opportunities to act upon his own schooling conditions when he was a student of Eastside High School. This comes from a former student whose potential creativity was ignored, but who now, as an educator, draws upon his students' hopes—as well as his own—to imagine and develop forms of *creative resistance.*

NOTES

1. These are pseudonyms that students chose for themselves in the original dissertation study (Garcia, 2017a).
2. Eastside High School is used as a pseudonym and refers to the region of the Los Angeles Unified School District (LAUSD) schools, located east of downtown Los Angeles.
3. "To ensure all LAUSD graduates have the option to enroll directly into a university and be prepared for a career, the district has implemented a College and Career Readiness through A–G initiative." (https://achieve.lausd.net/Page/2114)
4. Arizona Senate Bill 1070 became a law that allowed law enforcement to demand "legal documentation" from people whom they "reasonably suspected" were "unlawfully present" in the United States.

5. Being a community artist is what I have defined as dedicating my time as an artist and educator to working with students and communities. As someone who came out of this neighborhood, I genuinely draw on my experiences and dismiss academic notions of "social practice." I also recognize the privilege that I have as an artist, researcher, and state-employed educator. My interest in improving communities began when I was a student of the South Central community—that is, before I became an educator and a researcher.

REFERENCES

Calderon, J. (2004). Lessons from an activist intellectual: Participatory research, teaching, and learning for social change. *Latin American Perspectives, 31*(1), 81–94.

Camangian, P. (2010). Starting with self: Teaching autoethnography to foster critically caring literacies. *Research in the Teaching of English, 45*(2), 179–204.

de los Ríos, C. V., & Ochoa, G. L. (2012). The people united will never be divided: Reflections on community, collaboration, and change. *Journal of Latinos and Education, 11*(4), 271–279.

Darder, A. (1995). Bicultural identity and the development of voice: Twin issues in the struggle for cultural and linguistic democracy. In J. Frederickson (Ed.), *Reclaiming our voices: Bilingual education critical pedagogy and praxis* (pp. 36–52). Covina, CA: California Association of Bilingual Education.

Darts, D. (2004). Visual culture jam: Art pedagogy and creative resistance. *Studies in Art Education, 45*(4), 313–327.

Delgado, R. (1989). Storytelling for oppositionists and others: A plea for narrative. *Michigan Law Review, 87*(8), 2411–2441.

Delgado Bernal, D. (1997). *Chicana school resistance and grassroots leadership: Providing an alternative history of the 1968 East Los Angeles blowouts* (Unpublished doctoral dissertation). University of California, Los Angeles, CA.

Delgado Bernal, D. (1998). Using a Chicana feminist epistemology in educational research. *Harvard Educational Review, 68*(4), 555–582.

Delgado Bernal, D. (2001). Learning and living pedagogies of the home: Mestiza consciousness of Chicana students. *International Journal of Qualitative Studies in Education, 14*(3), 623–639.

Delgado Bernal, D. (2002). Critical race theory, Latino critical theory, and critical raced-gendered epistemologies: Recognizing students of color as holders and creators of knowledge. *Qualitative Inquiry, 8*(1), 105–126.

Delgado Bernal, D., Burciaga, R., & Flores Carmona, J. (2012). Chicana/Latina testimonios: Methodologies, pedagogies, and political urgency. *Equity & Excellence in Education, 45*(3), 392–410.

Duncan-Andrade, J. (2006). Utilizing cariño in the development of research methodologies. In J. Kincheloe, P. Anderson, K. Rose, D. Griffith, & K. Hayes (Eds.), *Urban education: An encyclopedia* (pp. 451–486). Westport, CT: Greenwood.

Duncan-Andrade, J. (2009). Note to educators: Hope required when growing roses in concrete. *Harvard Educational Review, 79*(2), 181–194.

Duncan-Andrade, J. M. (2010). *What a coach can teach a teacher.* New York, NY: Peter Lang.

Duncan-Andrade, J., & Morell, E. (2008). *The art of critical pedagogy: Possibilities for moving from theory to practice in urban schools.* New York, NY: Peter Lang.

Freire, P. (1970). *Pedagogy of the oppressed* (1st ed.). New York, NY: Continuum.

Freire, P. (1993). *Pedagogy of the oppressed* (2nd ed.). New York, NY: Continuum.

Garcia, L.-G. (2012). Making cultura count inside and out of the classroom: Public art & critical pedagogy in south central Los Angeles. *Journal of Curriculum and Pedagogy, 9*(2), 104–114.

Garcia, L.-G. (2015). Empowering students through creative resistance: Art-based critical pedagogy in the immigrant experience. *Diálogo, an Interdisciplinary Studies Journal, Center for Latino Research at De Paul University, 18*(2), 139–149.

Garcia, L.-G. (2017a). *La Lotería, art education and creative resistance: A funds of knowledge approach to art education in working-class schools.* ProQuest Dissertations and Theses.

Garcia, L.-G. (2017b). La Loteria and creative resistance: A funds of knowledge approach to art education. In J. M. Kiyama & C. Rios-Aguilar (Eds.), *Funds of knowledge in higher education: Honoring students' cultural experiences and resources as strengths.* New York, NY: Taylor and Francis.

González, N., & Moll, L. (2002). Cruzando el puente: Building bridges to funds of knowledge. *Journal of Educational Policy, 16*(4), 623–641.

González, N., Moll, L. C., & Amanti, C. (2005). *Funds of knowledge: Theorizing practices in households, communities, and classrooms.* Mahwah, NJ: Erlbaum.

Hicks-Peterson, T. (2009). Engaged scholarship: Reflections and research on the pedagogy of social change. *Teaching in Higher Education, 14*(5), 541–552. https://doi.org/10.1080/13562510903186741

Huerta, A., & Rios-Aguilar, C. (2018). Treat a cop like they are god: Exploring the relevance and utility of funds of gang knowledge among Latino male students. *Urban Education.* https://doi.org/10.1177/0042085918794766

Hughes, A., Hughes, A., & Williams, T. (Producers), & Hughes, A., & Hughes, A. (Directors). (1997) *Menace II society* [Film]. United States: New Line Home Video.

Kiyama, J. M., & Rios-Aguilar, C. (2017). *Funds of knowledge in higher education: Honoring students' cultural experiences and resources as strengths.* New York, NY: Taylor and Francis.

Lessher, J., Ayer, D., Sinclair, N., & Jackson, M. (Producers), & Ayer, D. (Director). (2012). *End of Watch* [Film]. United States: Open Road Films.

Malagon, M. C., Huber, L. P., & Velez, V. N. (2009). Our experiences, our methods: Using grounded theory to inform a critical race theory methodology. *Seattle Journal for Social Justice, 8*(1), Article 10.

McLaren, P. (1994). *Life in schools: An introduction to critical pedagogy in the foundations of education.* New York, NY: Longman.

Moll, L. C., Amanti, C., Neff, D., & González, N. (1992). Funds of knowledge for teaching: Using a qualitative approach to connect homes and classrooms. *Theory Into Practice, 31*(2), 132–141.

Moll, L. C., & Greenberg, J. B. (1990). Creating zones of possibilities: Combining social contexts for instruction. In L. C. Moll (Ed.), *Vygotsky and education:*

Instructional implications and applications of sociohistorical psychology (pp. 319–348). Cambridge, England: Cambridge University Press.

Morrell, E. (2013). *Critical media pedagogy: Teaching for achievement in city schools.* New York, NY: Teachers College Press.

Pérez-Huber, L., & Solorzano, D. G. (2015). Racial microaggression as a tool for critical race research. *Race Ethnicity and Education, 18*(3), 297–320.

Pizarro, M. (1998). "Chicana/o Power!" Epistemology and methodology for social justice and empowerment in Chicana/o communities. *International Journal of Qualitative Studies in Education, 11*(1), 57.

Rios-Aguilar, C., & Kiyama, J. M. (2012). Funds of knowledge: A proposed approach to study Latina/o students' transition to college. *Journal of Latinos and Education, 11*(1), 2–16.

Rios-Aguilar, C., Kiyama, J., Gravitt, M., & Moll, L. (2011). Funds of knowledge for the poor and forms of capital for the rich? A capital approach to examining funds of knowledge. *Theory and Research in Education, 9*(2), 163–184.

Singleton, J. (Director) & Nicolaides, S. (Producer). (1991). *Boyz n the Hood* [Film]. United States: Columbia Pictures.

Shakur, T. (1999). *The rose that grew from concrete.* New York, NY: Pocket Books.

Solorzano, D. G. (1989). Teaching and social change: Reflections on a Freirean approach in a college classroom. *Teaching Sociology, 17*(2), 218–225.

Solorzano, D. G. (1997). Images and words that wound: Critical race theory, racial stereotyping, and teacher education. *Teacher Education Quarterly, 24*(3), 5–19.

Solorzano, D. G. (1998). Critical race theory, race and gender microaggressions, and the experience of Chicana and Chicano scholars. *International Journal of Qualitative Studiesin Education, 11*(1), 121–136.

Solorzano, D. G., & Delgado Bernal, D. (2001). Examining transformational resistance through a critical race and LatCrit theory framework: Chicana and Chicano students in an urban context. *Urban Education, 36*(3), 308–342.

Solorzano, D. G., & Yosso, T. J. (2001). Critical race and LatCrit theory and method: Counter-story-telling. *International Journal of Qualitative Students in Education, 14*(4), 471–495.

Yokley, S. H. (1999). Embracing a critical pedagogy in art education. *Art Education, 52*(5), 18–24.

Yosso, T. J. (2005). Whose culture has capital? A critical race theory discussion of community cultural wealth. *Race, Ethnicity, and Education, 8(1)*, 69–91.

Yosso, T., Smith, W., Ceja, M., & Solorzano, D. (2009). Critical race theory, racial microaggressions, and campus racial climate for Latina/o undergraduates. *Harvard Educational Review, 79*(4), 659–690.

CHAPTER 4

CRITICAL REFLECTIONS ON TENSIONS IN AUTHENTIC YOUTH–ADULT PARTNERSHIPS

Juan C. Medina
The University of Wisconsin, Madison

Bianca J. Baldridge
The University of Wisconsin, Madison

Tanya Wiggins
Pace University

Community-based youth organizations (CBYOs) are an essential feature of out-of-school time (OST) and have been critical spaces for youth development. Research has shown that CBYOs are philosophically and pedagogically diverse—"a complete mix: identifiable yet extraordinarily heterogeneous; vibrant yet fragile; a protected space for play and enriching experiences" (Halpern, 2000, p. 186). Community-based youth organizations engage young people in a variety of opportunities, including academic enrichment, recreation, cultural development, and sociopolitical

At Our Best, pages 61–79

development (Baldridge, Beck, Medina, & Reeves, 2017; Eccles & Gootman, 2002; Fusco, 2012; Hirsch, Deutsch, & Dubois, 2011). Communities of color have long-established programs and organizations to support youth and serve as a buffer against a racially hostile society and inadequate schooling (Baldridge, 2014; Ginwright & James, 2002). Further, within communities of color, CBYOs often focus on empowerment and resistance in response to the lived realities of participants; these organizations have been effective in developing youth holistically while promoting equitable academic and career preparation (Ginwright & James, 2002; Riggs, Bohnert, Guzman, & Davidson, 2010).

While there are many documented benefits for youth involved in community-based programs, youth–adult partnerships and connections are a celebrated element of these programs, which have created intergenerational ties based on authentic caring relationships, while cultivating high expectations and opportunities for youth to both belong and disrupt inequalities they may face (Baldridge, et al., 2017; Brion-Meisels, Fei, & Vasudevan, 2017; Eccles & Gootman, 2002; Ginwright, 2007; Hirsch, et al., 2011; Valenzuela, 1999). Community-based youth organizations can be loosely-coupled or distinct from traditional school spaces, which affords them greater flexibility to incorporate youth voices, reflect youth interests in programming, and promote authentic youth–adult partnerships. Yet, much like school, CBYOs are shaped by the sociopolitical context within which they exist, and this context can lead them to reproduce inequalities and harm already experienced in school and within society (Baldridge, et al., 2017).

Within communities of color, CBYOs have shown success in promoting social justice youth development (Ginwright & Cammarota, 2007) and preparing participants to challenge systemic inequalities in their schools and communities (Ginwright, 2007; Kwon, 2013; Nygreen, Kwon, & Sanchez, 2006). However, current federal grants, state and municipal funding, and philanthropic foundations play a significant role in sustaining community-based programming for youth, and although well-intentioned, these institutions have always and continue to be informed by paternalistic and deficit views of low-income youth of color. These aforementioned institutions have set a precedent by funding programs that frame youth in deficit ways and narrowly focus on academics or behavioral containment, referring to attempts to control/monitor youth of color based upon deficit narratives that position them as simultaneously vulnerable and dangerous (Baldridge, 2014; Kantor & Lowe, 2006; Kwon, 2013). In turn, the growth of interest and investment in CBYOs (Dryfoos, 1999; Smith, 2003; USDOE, 2014; Zhang & Byrd, 2006) has produced a landscape of community-based youth work shaped by market-based practices stemming from neoliberal logics, which thrives on deficit and cultural pathological explanations about youth of color and expectations for who they are and who they should become (Baldridge, 2019). This political context, which is also tied to the current educational policy context, has forced social justice-oriented CBYOs to function more like schools that are rigidly controlled and continuously offer limited programming (Baldridge, 2019). This trend reduces the capacity of CBYOs to provide a holistic education and flexible structure, essentially limiting development and opportunities for youth to engage authentically with adults.

Education is a socially collaborative process that requires youth be treated as knowledge holders and active participants in learning (Vygotsky, 1983). From this point of view, schools and other educational spaces should focus on developing youth holistically while treating them as agents with voice, knowledge, and experience. However, in the current context of neoliberal ideology, schools continually fail to do so and perpetuate a subtractive environment (Valenzuela, 1999) that frame youth in deficit and paternalistic ways. Whereas CBYOs are often celebrated for cultivating authentic youth–adult partnerships, the political context shaping community-based youth work—including racist and deficit-based views about youth of color, the struggle for power in youth–adult relationships, and funding pressures—threaten these relationships.

The opportunity to form authentic youth–adult partnerships in CBYOs, and the inherent tensions that exist in forming them, are of central concern to this chapter. Taking a critical-reflective approach, this chapter examines the inherent tensions in creating authentic connections between youth and adults within social justice-oriented CBYOs. As researchers and practitioners within CBYOs, we present three central tensions that pose obstacles to establishing authentic youth–adult partnerships while simultaneously producing harm within CBYOs. First, we examine the framing of youth as a category to interrogate the construction of youth–adult partnerships in community-programs. Second, we discuss the ways deficit framing and White fragility disrupt authentic youth–adult partnerships. Last, we explore how funding stressors and demands also weaken the possibility for youth–adult relationships. In addition to examining these tensions, the authors consider potential opportunities to disrupt or mitigate tensions in establishing authentic youth–adult partnerships.

This chapter is informed by our collective experiences as researcher-practitioners within community-based organizations where we each have developed wonderful relationships with youth. However, this chapter does not romanticize the potential of CYBOs or assume there are "turn-key" solutions to address all tensions. Rather, the following chapter recognizes that CBYOs are embedded within society and can reproduce inequalities and harm even within the most critical of spaces.

CONSTRUCTIONS OF YOUTH AND THE STRUGGLE
FOR CONTROL IN YOUTH–ADULT PARTNERSHIPS

Youth work in the context of CBYOs is lauded for the ways in which young people are engaged, guided, and nurtured by adults. Despite the widespread finding that authentic youth–adult partnerships in community-based organizations foster critical social capital that leads youth to make better informed choices and engage in social activism (Baldridge et al., 2017; Ginwright, 2007; Kirshner, 2015; Kwon, 2013)—deeply embedded into youth–adult relationships is an underlying struggle for power and control that is predicated on ideas and logics about the socially defined category of "youth."

Youth as a Social Construction

Throughout educational theory, research, and practice, an abundance of energy is spent interrogating how inequities in education inform the experiences, life outcomes, and opportunities of youth. The social identity markers of race, class, gender, sexuality, and ability are used to capture the distinct processes of inequality. Yet, the ways in which the concept of "youth" (itself a socially constructed category) contributes to the reproduction of inequality in schools and other educational spaces are rarely examined with as much depth and nuance as they deserve. Narratives about "youth" structure our thinking, relationships, and engagement with youth in educational spaces. Therefore, examining the construction of youth as a socially constructed category is critical in our efforts to understand how youth–adult partnerships are formed and sustained.

"Youth" as a concept is a fluid, socially constructed, context *and* culturally contingent category (Griffin, 1993). How we classify youth has shifted and continues to shift over time and space (Griffin, 1993; Soung, 2011). Age designations, for example, have been used to classify the adolescent years. However, these age designations are often arbitrary and are used for specific political and state agendas (e.g., drinking age, military participation, driving age). As a socially constructed category, youth are always juxtaposed to adulthood and are constructed as "other" (Soung, 2011). Adults designate the standards, boundaries, and conditions by which youth develop in ways that reinforce their construction as "other" (Lesko, 1996; Soung, 2011). In the context of schooling, this construction of the adult as an all-knowing authority renders youth as empty vessels waiting to be filled (Freire, 1970). Schooling itself reproduces top-down authoritarian conditions that silence and restrict youth voices and expressions in classroom spaces (Baldridge, Hill, & Davis, 2011; Patel, 2016). Community-based youth organizations—a central site of learning for many youth—have been celebrated for the ways youth can be free of policies and sanctions on their expressions and modes of being (Baldridge, et al., 2017). Many community-based spaces have the capacity and flexibility to allow youth to exist free of the draconian restrictions found in school spaces. Yet, even in these progressive spaces, the construct of "youth" is, itself, upheld and used to organize the work.

Research has highlighted the many ways that youth have been engaged in partnership alongside adults for educational change and social activism (Kirshner, 2015; Rogers, Mediratta, & Shah, 2012). Although youth–adult partnerships are celebrated widely among researchers and practitioners in community-based youth work and OST, these partnerships are often still operating within societal understandings that perpetuate hierarchical, deficit-oriented constructions of youth. For example, social capital building is typically viewed as an important and valued outcome of positive youth–adult relationships in the context of youth work (Baldridge, et al., 2017; Ginwright, 2007; Hirsch, et al., 2011). Even as this outcome of positive youth–adult partnerships is celebrated, adults are typically positioned as the role model and the standard of adulthood in the process of youth *becoming* an adult (Griffin, 1993; Lesko, 1996). Additionally, the construction of youth and adult as static, hierarchical categories also surfaces within community-based youth work. The tensions that surface from these constructs are rooted in historical and contemporary theorizations and framing of youth. Tropes about youth being "out-of-control" or the notion that every generation of adolescents are "the worst" are perpetuated through popular discourse and culture, through film and other forms of media. Imagining youth in these ways sets them up for containment, control, or "taming" by adults (Lesko, 1996)—especially within the context of community-based youth work—where OST programs are ideologically positioned and structurally pressured to be spaces of containment and control for youth of color (Baldridge, 2019; Kwon, 2013).

Conceptions of Youth in Social Justice-Oriented Community-Based Youth Work

In the context of youth work—where the purpose(s) are to guide, nurture, mentor, and care for young people across a range of settings (Fusco, 2012; Pittman & Fleming, 1991)—paternalism almost naturally occurs. Yet the lines between mentorship/guidance and paternalism/control are often blurred because of dominant logics ingrained into the public's imagination of youth, including ideas about who they are, who they should become, and what they are capable of doing (Baldridge, 2018). No matter how difficult it is to disrupt these dominant logics (set by adults), interrogating and disrupting these power dynamics in order to have authentic and mutually beneficial partnerships between youth and adults is imperative.

Within educational spaces, beliefs about adults as all-knowing teachers and youth as unaware students passively waiting to be taught dominate the field (Noguera & Canella, 2006). Perhaps best articulated by Paulo Freire's (1970) analysis of student–teacher relationships, whereby education "becomes an act of depositing, in which the students are the depositories and the teacher is the depositor" (p. 72), the "banking-model" captures perfectly the dynamic in which youth themselves are viewed as depositories. Freire calls the student–teacher relationship a contradictory arrangement; the solution, he posits, is to consider that both are *simultaneously* both teachers and students. Accepting the premise that teachers and students are both students and teachers at the same time creates a dynamic within educational spaces where students/youth are recognized for the knowledge they possess and for what they can teach others. Critical pedagogues who operate from a Freirean framework reject banking models of education and incorporate the type of problem-posing frameworks described by Garcia in Chapter 3 of this book. These adults engage students in critical thinking about social and political problems and, in concert with youth, work to create social change (Ginwright, 2007; Ginwright & James, 2002). At the core of this perspective is a willingness to give up and relinquish control. In a society where the very construction of youth and adolescence is predicated on adult control of their bodies and minds, tensions surface within the educational spaces youth occupy as the battle over control arises in youth–adult partnerships.

Critical pedagogues and critical ethnographers have engaged young people in the creation of research that directly shapes students lived realities in their schools and neighborhoods through various forms of participatory research methods (Fox et al., 2010; Patel, 2012). For many youth workers and critical researchers engaged in this kind of work, it can feel rewarding to guide youth through complex social and political problems and chart a pathway for their understanding, growth, and social action. Even in the midst of these goals, youth workers engaged in social justice-oriented organizations can also succumb to limiting beliefs associated with widespread narratives about youth as a category. As such, because of these dominant logics about youth as a category, the line between paternalism and care, or control and guidance, can become less defined in youth–adult partnerships. Paternalistic rhetoric of control over minoritized youth is also shaped by the dominance of racialized neoliberal and market-based logics that can create tension within youth–adult partnerships (Baldridge, 2017, 2019; Kwon, 2013). Failing to name and address structural conditions that shape the lives of youth participants, for example, in order to reach "bottom-lines", or imposed narrow measures of success threaten relationships between adult youth workers and young people (Anderson & Larson, 2009; Baldridge, 2014; de St. Croix, 2018). Even more, paternalistic discourses frame minoritized youth as "at risk" and "broken," which positions OST programs as their savior in order to appeal to philanthropists (Baldridge, 2014; Brown, 2015).

Given the current sociopolitical context of education reform, dominated by neoliberal market-based forces, discourses of control and paternalism have become more common and distinctly racialized. More specifically, Black and Latinx youth are positioned as in need of "fixing," in educational spaces and in the context of youth–adult partnerships (Baldridge, 2014). Research on mentoring, role modeling, and resilience for Black youth, for example, often positions them as culturally deficient and in need of saving by other Black people who have "made it" (Baldridge, 2017; Brooms, Franklin, Clark, & Smith, 2018; Clay, 2019). This dynamic reifies cultural and individual explanations for academic achievement thereby obscuring structural oppression that informs the academic and social lives of youth of color. As such, the current climate of education policy and reform, which often shapes community-based youth work, threatens the creation of authentic, mutually beneficial, and sustaining youth–adult partnerships.

Negotiating and Relinquishing Control in Youth–Adult Partnerships

From role modeling, to academic and career guidance, to playing the role of confidant as an adult that is not a parent or a traditional teacher, research has shown that youth workers hold a significant place in the lives of young people (Baldridge, et al.a, 2017; Ginwright, 2009; Watson, 2012). All too often, the relationship between adult and youth is top-down, one-sided, and not seen as mutually beneficial, largely rooted in social constructions of these categories. The construction of adult and youth as categories places youth–adult partnerships in an unsteady relationship where the struggle for power and control is constant (Lesko, 1996). This struggle undergirds youth–adult partnerships even if it lies beneath the surface. Given our many years as youth workers in diverse community-based organizations, we suggest that an important strategy for disrupting these power dynamics is for community-based leaders and youth workers to (a) critically reflect on the ways power functions within and through youth–adult relationships, (b) establish a community of practice that deliberately shifts the power of decision making to young people, and (c) provide opportunities for youth-driven programming as part of the community of practice.

Each of this chapter's authors has worked in community-based settings that have established rules and policies (typically generated by leadership/

board of directors) for youth that mirror what they experience in schools. For example, standards and expectations for clothing and speech shape some OST spaces. In these spaces, the struggle for control over how youth exist and how they may want to express themselves can cause tensions, thereby rendering the community-space as yet another place where youth are controlled by adults. If CBYOs can be sites where youth can come to just "be," those leading community organizations should consider removing policies that mirror what youth experience in schools.

Research has shown that young people consistently choose to participate in community-based spaces because they are *not* like school (Baldridge, Hill, & Davis, 2011; Woodland, 2016). As such, it is incumbent on community-based leaders and youth workers to eliminate policies and practices that perpetuate the cultural shedding and violence youth of color endure in schools (Baldridge, 2019). In order for this to occur, youth workers and community-based leaders must critically reflect on the ways they carry and enact power in their relationships with youth in the context of their organizations. Through our practice and our research, we have witnessed organizations develop and sustain strong communities of practice (Wenger, McDermott, & Snyder, 2002)—a systematically shared cultural process through routines established and sustained throughout an organization. Community-based youth organizations that are deliberate and intentional in disrupting hierarchical relationships of power between youth and adults place young people at the center of all decisions made and provide opportunities for youth to drive all or portions of the program. Most importantly, community-based leaders and youth workers who are deliberate and intentional about their *praxis*—who think deeply about their desire and need for control over youths' behavior and decisions—are in a better position to relinquish control.

DEFICIT FRAMES OF YOUTH OF COLOR AND THE FRAGILITY OF YOUTH WORKERS

Frequently, CBYOs struggle to address deficit-based views, and stereotypes, of youth and communities of color that youth workers carry. Deficit-based views inform youth workers imaginations, interactions, and practices with youth of color. The following section will examine the ways in which youth workers' belief in deficit-based stereotypes, namely that student have "low" educational abilities and/or that they "do not value" education, create tensions in the formation of partnerships with youth.

Deficit-based beliefs of youth of color have a long history in education, having been perpetuated and upheld through seemingly "impartial" individualizing practices such as intelligence (IQ) and standardized tests, tracking, Eurocentric curriculum, and the very structure of schools (Apple, 2006; Baldridge, 2014; Reese, 2013). The origin of deficit-based stereotypes has shifted over time from viewing students as inherently deficient due to either biological (genetic), racial, or cultural inferiority (Valencia, 2012). As a result of these deficit-based frameworks, youth of color, and the communities from which they come, are viewed from a position of "lack" (Baldridge, 2017). In recent years, popular media and the current U.S. presidential administration have portrayed and discussed communities of color as deviant populations that are inherently "less" than their White counterparts. Regardless of the explanation given, the promulgation of deficit-based narratives of students has resulted in the adoption of these beliefs into the popular (nationwide) psyche in conscious and unconscious ways. Thus, prior to ever setting foot within a CBYO, youth workers carry preconceived ideas of who youth are, what they are capable of, and what they "need" to be "saved." These preconceived ideas inform youth worker mindsets and shape their practices towards youth.

Tensions Arising From Deficit-Based Stereotypes of Youth of Color

For some adults who decide to work at CBYOs, deficit-based stereotypes of youth of color form the basis of their motivation to engage in youth work. These youth workers, often White adults, are motivated to serve youth "in need" because they believe youth come from "poor," "crime-ridden," and "low-educated" communities/families where education is of secondary importance (Baldridge, 2014). For these deficit-lensed youth workers, their desire to work with youth of color is driven by a "savior mentality," or the belief that they, as the adult, know what is best for youth to succeed (paternalism) and must actively "save" them. When adults view youth as "in need of saving" tensions inherently arise in forming authentic partnerships because youth are infantilized or treated as children who cannot think or do anything for themselves. Thus, when working directly with youth of color, White "savior" adults tend to talk down to them, try to control their every action, and ignore their capacity to make decisions. Youth of color who are treated in this way frequently refuse to work with or form a relationship with adults they believe infantilize them.

A second tension that arises, particularly with White youth workers who buy into stereotypes of youth of color, is the existence of "White fragility...a state in which even a minimum amount of racial stress becomes intolerable, triggering a range of defensive moves...includ[ing] outward displays of anger, *fear* (our emphasis), and guilt" (DiAngelo, 2011, p. 57). Within CBYOs, some White youth workers who are motivated to work with youth "in need" are hesitant to engage youth of color due to an underlying fear of potentially offending youth, being seen as racist if they say or do anything wrong, or simply not knowing *how* to engage youth of color because of cultural differences. Their fear, this White fragility, interrupts the creation of authentic partnerships as youth workers either avoid engaging or fail to hold high expectations of youth of color, leaving the responsibility of supporting, encouraging, and forming relationships with young people to youth workers of color. Authentic partnerships are further prevented because these same adults who are fearful of working with youth of color leave organizations quickly due to the discomfort they feel, though in some cases they may learn to question their previously held beliefs and overcome the White fragility that paralyzes them through structured engagement. The stereotypes that White youth workers carry about both youth and communities of color inform the goals they set for students and shape their practice. These youth workers may not be overtly racist, or aware that their views and motivations are deficit-based, but their actions and practices towards youth of color are aligned with the "single story" they have heard about racialized youth (Adichie, 2016). When deficit-based stereotypes influence the goals and expected outcomes of interactions with youth of color, the potential to form authentic partnerships is interrupted because youth and youth workers approach the partnerships with different expectations, leading to the tensions described above.

Creating Humanizing Practices as Resistance

Where tensions exist, there are opportunities to disrupt or mitigate them. Within CBYOs, the largest opportunity to interrupt tensions is having an organization-wide, asset-based culture. An organization that works toward an asset-based, or humanizing, culture views the community and youth they serve as possessing strengths and being capable of high achievement (Baldridge, 2014). Further, such an organization implements practices that promote positive views of the community and youth, while creating partnerships that equalize relationships with all participants. Community-based youth organizations dedicated to promoting a humanizing culture—that emphasizes and acknowledges the humanity, strengths, and full lives of young people—implement asset-based practices at two levels, organization wide and site-specific, to reframe youth workers' potential deficit-based views of youth of color while encouraging all staff to utilize humanizing practices.

Potential practices that can be implemented at the organizational level include presenting strength profiles of the community and creating a "new employee" orientation that focuses on humanizing practices. Organizations can benefit from offering an asset-rich orientation because they can introduce youth workers to the community by illuminating strengths, and challenging any preconceived, deficit assumptions that may inform their thinking. Further, by avoiding superficial "needs assessments" and presenting humanizing processes, CBYOs can avoid perpetuating a single story about the communities they work with, while modeling expected strategies. This would entail moving away from survey tools that document what is lacking in the community, or the perceived "needs," towards tools that showcase community strengths, individuals, community resources, and potential partners. Though a seemingly simple change, by highlighting community strengths, or "assets," the organization would actively resist deficit framing of the communities and youth they work with while challenging any preconceived ideas youth workers might carry with them.

Similarly, site-specific humanizing practices that CBYOs can implement to mitigate tensions arising from the stereotypes youth workers carry include: apprenticing new youth workers under strong mentors (Kirshner, 2006), encouraging new youth workers to find common ground with youth, and making youth workers critically reflect upon their own practices on a weekly basis. Having new youth workers shadow "model" youth workers who utilize humanizing practices is effective in reducing anxiety and fear of engaging with youth from different cultures. It also allows new youth workers to observe the strategies utilized in engaging youth, finding common ground, and building relationships with youth of color. Similarly, asking youth workers to critically reflect upon their practices on a weekly basis, and discuss them with a supervisor, helps them recognize successful interactions, identify areas of improvements, and avoid approaching their work with a "savior" mentality. Continued commitment to these practices makes it possible to disrupt tensions stemming from deficit-based stereotypes.

Although the opportunities described above can be successful at mitigating tensions created by the racial stereotypes that youth workers carry, one should be careful not to assume that their implementation alone would avoid the tensions described herein. The aforementioned organizational and site-level practices, including strength profiles of the community, asset-based orientations, apprenticing new youth workers, and daily reflections, are made possible by the specific context of the CBYO, as well as the commitment of administrators and frontline staff to view youth from a humanizing lens. Having an asset-based culture can create the context where additional opportunities can be implemented, however, as will be seen, a humanizing culture can be disrupted by the nature of funding an organization pursues.

COMMUNITY-BASED YOUTH ORGANIZATION FUNDING
AND YOUTH–ADULT PARTNERSHIPS

Precarity and deep uncertainty in funding is a major stressor for CBYOs. Funding obstacles, including the struggle to maintain financial support and the strings often attached to government and foundation grants, can create challenges within organizational practices and pose a threat to youth–adult partnerships. In this section, we highlight examples from two organizations—*Our Kids, Our City* and *Road to Success* (both pseudonyms)—with funding obstacles and describe the impact on youth–adult connections as a result.

Potential Risks of Funding Choices

Less than 5 years old, finding and securing funds for working with youth in their extremely underserved community was always a priority for Our Kids, Ours City. Development for this organization consisted of one person, who focused on identifying and applying to all grants relevant to supporting youth. These efforts were quite successful, as the individual secured several significant private and public grants, doubling the budget and reaching million-dollar levels in record time. On the surface, the work done by Our Kids, Our City reads as a success story. The funds secured were above average in relation to organizations similar in size and time of existence. This was a point of pride for the organization, as it meant they would not only endure, but would also be able to expand their services. In a 3-year period, Our Kids, Our City expanded from serving 150 youth and families to over 800.

Beyond the surface, however, success in funding came with administrative and programmatic tensions, and excluded youth from having a voice in the direction of programming. New funding, in some cases, required the development of programs or initiatives that aligned more with the stipulations of funders than with the organization's mission and vision. Despite this tension, staff were required to incorporate elements imposed by funders into programming. For full time programming staff, the additional requirements increased work hours and stress, accelerated burnout, and limited time for program planning and assessment. Part-time, frontline staff were also impacted, as the changes required additional hours for them as well, which their schedules could not always support. This led to inconsistency in scheduling that also potentially impacted their ability to build strong partnerships with youth.

Administratively, funding often came with additional responsibilities in the form of increased data collection and reporting. Streamlining reporting was often challenging, as some funders requested specific information that others did not, or required reporting via proprietary interfaces. The need to sustain funding presented yet another challenge, as the development department, now consisting of a director and an intern, worked to find and secure even more funding by applying for any grant applicable to programs serving youth. Within applications, the actual work of the organization was framed either to emphasize a particular element, or to suggest new initiatives that needed funding to be implemented. In reality, the proposed initiatives often originated from the request for proposal (RFP) to which the organization was responding. For example, applying for a 21st Century Community Learning Centers grant, a government grant program providing funds for organizations offering academic enrichment during OST (USDOE, 2014), often meant emphasizing academic components of the program and proposing extensions of these components in ways that spoke directly to the kinds of programming the grant would fund. Grants such as this tied funding to academic outcomes for youth, increasing pressure on the organization to align more with traditional educational settings in approach. Throughout this process, youth were seldom, if ever, involved in developing or informing new initiatives.

In contrast, Road to Success was a long-standing youth organization that utilized a different funding approach. The development team consisted of a director and assistant, who focused on appealing to private funding and individual donors. Private funding came in the form of foundations that saw a "fit" between the organization and previously funded programs. Funding of this nature often categorizes programs funded by a single or select criteria, which often pigeon-holes organizations into: offering specific services, servicing a prescribed segment of the population (often defined via deficit-based perceptions), or limiting the funds that can be secured altogether. Similarly, this level of funding can also challenge organizations' fidelity to their missions and visions, and engagement of youth through the imposition of explicit and implied conditions on fiscal support communicated by funders. These conditions are often steeped in paternalistic and/or deficit-based assumptions about the youth being served.

For example, a private donor to Road to Success offered to give upwards of $25,000, but had one "request" before doing so. As a huge supporter of the arts, the donor wanted the organization to establish a drama workshop series for participants. The prospect of such a generous donation moved leadership to honor the request. The workshop was announced to program youth, and a facilitator was hired for the series. Program directors worked to sign young people up, even targeting specific youth whose interests connected to the workshop in some way. On the first day of the workshop, few if any youth attended. Staff were charged with seeking out more youth and ensuring their attendance. Yet, attendance was minimal for the duration of the workshop.

This example represents not only the pressures applied by funders, but the potential risks of prioritizing the demands of funding over the needs and wishes of youth participants. Participating youth were never provided a voice in shaping the opportunity in a way that would interest them. Instead, they were told what to do and when, and "voted with their feet" as a result by simply choosing not to attend. Approaching work with youth in this way jeopardized the established relationships with participants, leaving youth to question their desire to continue with consistent participation.

Funding Decisions and Arising Tensions Within Youth–Adult Partnerships

Although these two organizations took disparate approaches to funding, the nature of funding created the shared challenge of reconciling organizational systems with the youth development work to which they were committed (Larson & Walker, 2010). For Our Kids, Our City, the push for funding created additional responsibilities for staff and shifts in program delivery to accommodate the rapid expansion of services to more youth. While more youth were served, resources (human and physical) were stretched to their limits to do so, and program quality may have been compromised as a result. Increased administrative responsibilities decreased the amount of time available to build relationships with participants. Further, the approach used in finding funding pushed the organization toward the burden of being accountable to funders, rather than to the youth served. Funding regulations and reporting requirements do not always align with the needs and day-to-day realities of youth (Fusco, Lawrence, Matloff-Nieves, & Ramos, 2013; de St. Croix, 2018). This essentially pushes youth voices out of the space of partnership, while also potentially endangering consistent youth participation.

At Road to Success, the need to sustain a relationship with a donor took precedence over youth development principles and practices being implemented. Prioritizing the request of the funder created a tension, or what may even be seen as a disregard for youth participants' lives outside of the organization (Larson & Walker, 2010). Demanding more of youth's time, or taking a "high dosage" approach to the work, can be interpreted as paternalistic (being in the program and doing what the adults say is what's best) and deficit-based (youth don't have family, other responsibilities, or other opportunities deserving of their time). These competing priorities left staff in the challenging position of managing the requests and expectations of leadership with the feedback received from, and relationships built with, young people in the program. Experiences like these leave both staff and youth feeling disempowered and undervalued, effectively interrupting the formation of youth–adult partnerships.

Funding not only challenges the development of youth–adult partnerships from a programming perspective, but also from a human capital perspective. The uncertainty of funding, and the often-limited pay scales with which organizations work can result in a high turnover cycle for staff (Matloff-Nieves et al., 2018). Added pressures created by on-time funding and responsibilities, along with constantly negotiating between the priorities of funders and youth, can increase turnover rates even more through staff burnout. The temporal nature of funding—and therefore staffing—jeopardizes the capacity of organizations and youth to build consistent, meaningful partnerships.

While the nature of funding for CBYOs may be beyond their control, the approaches used by organizations to secure funding are where opportunities to address funding-related tensions can be managed. Identifying funding opportunities more closely aligned to the work and mission of the organizations is one such approach. Recognizing youth–adult partnership as an active programming element of CBYOs is another approach, which can be positioned in funding narratives as integral to the work of staff, allowing for the funding of training and other resources that could address tensions in other areas.

CONCLUSIONS

Throughout this chapter, we have argued that CBYOs do not exist in a vacuum. Like schools, CBYOs are informed by the sociopolitical context in which they exist. Within this current context, CBYOs and the processes by which they are funded are linked to, and shaped by, market-based education reforms, neoliberal logics rooted in privatization, individualism, and competition which impacts organizational culture and practices (Baldridge, 2019). These sociopolitical pressures have the power to influence the organizational culture and the practices of youth workers, which can ultimately reorient, weaken, or change youth–adult partnerships in community-based organizations.

The above tensions do not have to dictate the future landscape and success of CBYOs. Despite the influence of political context, funding patterns, and broader hegemonic narratives about youth of color, community-based leaders and youth workers can and should be subversive in the ways they disrupt these tensions. As has been argued, adults working in community-based organizations can resist the aforementioned tensions by being intentional and critically reflective on the power they possess in youth–adult partnerships. Opportunities for critical reflection among adult allies and youth must begin to move towards praxis, where they are able to build a community of practice within their program that takes seriously and utilizes the voices, experiences, and talents of youth to contribute to meaningful youth–adult partnerships. In so doing, adults can create a community of practice where power dynamics are examined and deliberately shifted to youth whenever possible, while moving towards a humanizing culture. This requires adults to re-examine the ideas they hold about who youth are and who they should become.

As we engage in youth work within OST programs, it is important to remember that we must not romanticize the potential of CBYOs or assume the opportunities discussed in this chapter are a "turn-key" solution to solve all tensions. Rather, we must keep in mind that CBYOs are embedded within society and can reproduce inequalities and harm even within the most critical of spaces. Our task, as researchers, practitioners, youth workers, and adults dedicated to working with youth, is to illuminate common tensions that may arise and the various ways they shape youth–adult partnerships.

ACKNOWLEDGMENTS

We would like to acknowledge the youth we've had the privilege to work with, learn from, and who remain an inspiration for the work we do.

REFERENCES

Adichie, C. (2016). Transcript of *The danger of a single story* (TED talk). Retrieved from https://www.ted.com/talks/chimamanda_adichie_the_danger_of_a_single_story/transcript?language=en

Anderson, N., & Larson, C. (2009). "Sinking, like quicksand": Expanding educational opportunity for young men of color. *Educational Administration Quarterly, 45,* 71–114.

Apple, M. W. (2006). *Educating the "right" way: Markets, standards, God, and inequality.* New York, NY: Routledge.

Baldridge, B. (2014). Relocating the deficit: Reimagining Black youth in neoliberal times. *American Educational Research Journal, 51*(3), 440–472.

Baldridge, B. J. (2017). "It's like this Myth of the Supernegro": Resisting narratives of damage and struggle in the neoliberal educational policy context. *Race Ethnicity and Education, 20*(6), 781–795.

Baldridge, B. (2018). On educational advocacy and cultural work: Situating community-based youth work[ers] in broader educational discourse. *Teachers College Record, 120*(2).

Baldridge, B. J. (2019). *Reclaiming community: Race and the uncertain future of youth work.* Stanford, CA: Stanford University Press.

Baldridge, B., Beck, N., Medina, J., & Reeves, M., (2017). Toward a new understanding of community-based education: The role of community-based educational spaces in disrupting inequality for minoritized youth. *Review of Research in Education, 41*(1), 381–402.

Baldridge, B., Hill, M. L., & Davis, J. E. (2011). New possibilities: (re)Engaging Black male youth within community-based educational spaces. *Race, Ethnicity and Education, 14*(1), 121–136.

Brion-Meisels, G., Fei, J., & Vasudevan, D. (2017). Building positive relationships with adolescents in educational contexts: Principles and practices for educators in school & community settings. M. A. Warren & S. I. Donaldson (Eds.), *Toward a positive psychology of relationships: New directions in theory and research* (pp. 145–178). Santa Barbara, CA: ABC-CLIO.

Brooms, D. R., Franklin, W., Clark, J. S., & Smith, M. (2018). 'It's more than just mentoring': Critical mentoring Black and Latino males from college to the community. *Race Ethnicity and Education,* 1–19.

Brown, A. (2015). *A good investment? Philanthropy and the marketing of race in an urban public school.* Minneapolis: University of Minnesota Press.

Clay, K. (2019). "Despite the odds": Unpacking the politics of Black resilience neoliberalism. *American Educational Research Journal, 56*(1), 75–110.

de St. Croix, T. (2018). Youth work, performativity and the new youth impact agenda: Getting paid for numbers. *Journal of Education Policy, 33*(3), 414–438.

DiAngelo, R. (2011). White fragility. *International Journal of Critical Pedagogy, 3*(3), 54–70.

Dryfoos, J. G. (1999). The role of the school in children's out-of-school time. *Future of Children, 9*(2), 117–134.

Eccles, J., & Gootman, J. (2002). *Community programs to promote youth development.* Washington, DC: National Academies Press.

Fox, M., Mediratta, K., Ruglis, J., Stoudt, B., Shah, S., & Fine, M. (2010). Critical youth engagement: Participatory action research and organizing. *Handbook of Research on Civic Engagement in Youth,* 621–649.

Freire, P. (1970). *Pedagogy of the oppressed.* New York, NY: Herder and Herder.

Fusco, D. (Ed.). (2012). Framing trends, posing questions. D. Fusco (Ed.), *Advancing youth work: Current trends, critical questions.* New York, NY: Routledge.

Fusco, D., Lawrence, A., Matloff-Nieves, S., & Ramos, E. (2013). The accordion effect: Is quality in afterschool getting the squeeze? *Journal of Youth Development, 8.* Retrieved from https://www.academia.edu/1319423/Turning_training_into_results_The_new_youth_program_quality_ assessment?auto=download

Ginwright, S. (2007). Black youth activism and the role of critical social capital in Black community organizations. *American Behavioral Scientist, 51*(3), 403–418.

Ginwright, S. (2009). *Black youth rising: Activism and radical healing in urban America.* NewYork, NY: Teachers College Press.

Ginwright, S., & Cammarota, J. (2007). Youth activism in the urban community: Learning critical civic praxis within community organizations. *International Journal of Qualitative Studies in Education, 20*(6), 693–710.

Ginwright, S., & James, T. (2002, Winter). From assets to agents of change: Social justice, organizing, and youth development. *New Directions for Youth Development, 96,* 27–46.

Griffin, C. (1993). *Representations of youth.* Cambridge, England: Polity Press.

Halpern, R. (2000). The promise of after-school programs for low-income children. *Early Childhood Research Quarterly, 15*(2), 185–214.

Hirsch, B. J., Deutsch, N. L., & Dubois, D. (2011). *After-school centers and youth development: Case studies of success and failure.* Cambridge, England: Cambridge University Press.

Kantor, H., & Lowe, R. (2006). From new deal to no deal: No child left behind and the devolution of responsibility for equal opportunity. *Harvard Educational Review, 76*(4), 474–502, 726.

Kwon, S. A. (2013). *Uncivil youth: Race, activism, and affirmative governmentality.* Durham, NC: Duke University Press.

Kirshner, B. (2006). Apprenticeship learning in youth activism. In S. Ginwright, J. Cammarota, & P. Noguera (Eds.), *Beyond resistance* (pp. 37–58). New York, NY: Routledge.

Kirshner, B. (2015). *Youth activism in an era of education inequality.* New York, NY: New York University Press.

Larson, R. W., & Walker, K. C. (2010). Dilemmas of practice: Challenges to program quality encountered by youth program leaders. *American Journal of Community Psychology, 45*(3/4), 338–349. https://doi.org/10.1007/s10464-010-9307-z

Lesko, N. (1996). Denaturalizing adolescence: The politics of contemporary representations. *Youth & Society, 28*(2), 139–161.

Matloff-Nieves, S., Wiggins, T., Fuqua, J., Ragonese, M., Pullano, S., & Brender, G. (2018). Returning to responsive youth work in New York City. In P. Alldred, F. Cullen, K. Edwards, & D. Fusco (Eds.), *The SAGE handbook of youth work practice* (pp. 554–567). Los Angeles, CA: SAGE.

Noguera, P., & Cannella, C. M. (2006). Youth agency, resistance, and civic activism: The public commitment to social justice. In S. Ginwright, J. Cammarota, & P. Noguera, *Beyond resistance* (pp. 333–347). New York, NY: Routledge.

Nygreen, K., Kwon, S. A., & Sanchez, P. (2006). Urban youth building community: Social change and participatory research in schools, homes and community-based organizations. In B. N. Checkoway & L. M. Gutierrez (Eds.), *Youth participation and community change* (pp. 107–123). New York, NY: Haworth Press.

Patel, L. (2012). Contact zones, problem posing and critical consciousness. *Pedagogies: An International Journal, 7*(4), 333–346.

Patel, L. (2016). Pedagogies of resistance and survivance: Learning as marronage, equity & excellence in education. *Equity and Excellence in Education, 49*(4), 397–401.

Pittman, K., & Fleming, W. (1991). *A new vision: promoting youth development.* Washington, DC: Academy for Education Development.

Reese, W. (2013). *Testing wars in the public schools: A forgotten history.* Cambridge, MA: Harvard University Press.

Riggs, N., Bohnert, A., Guzman, M., & Davidson, D. (2010). Examining the potential of community based after school programs for Latino youth. *American Journal of Community Psychology, 45*(3/4), 417–429.

Rogers, J., Mediratta, K., & Shah, S. (2012). Building power, learning democracy: Youth organizing as a site of civic development. *Review of Research in Education, 36*(1), 43–66.

Smith, S. (2003). Government and nonprofits in the modern age. *Society, 40*(40), 35–45.

Soung, P. (2011). Social and biological constructions of youth: Implications for juvenile justice and racial equity. *Northwestern Journal of Law and Social Policy, 6*(2011), 428–444.

U.S. Department of Education. (2014). *21st Century Community Learning Centers.* Retrieved from https://www2.ed.gov/programs/21stcclc/index.html

Valencia, R. R. (2012). *The evolution of deficit thinking: Educational thought and practice.* London, England: Routledge.

Valenzuela, A. (1999). *Subtractive schooling: U.S.–Mexican youth and the politics of caring.* Albany: State University of New York Press.

Vygotsky, L. S. (1983). *Collected works, Vol. 3: Problems in the development of mind.* Moscow, Russia: Pedagogika.

Watson, V. (2012). *Learning to liberate: Community-based solutions to the crisis in urban education.* New York, NY: Routledge.

Wenger, E., McDermott, R., & Snyder, W. (2002). *Cultivating communities of practice: A guide to managing knowledge.* Boston, MA: Harvard Business Press.

Woodland, M. H. (2016). After-school programs: A resource for young Black males and other urban youth. *Urban Education, 51*(7), 770–796.

Zhang, J. J., & Byrd, C. E., (2006). Successful after-school programs: The 21st century community learning centers. *Journal of Physical Education, Recreation, & Dance, 77*(8), 3–6, 12.

SECTION II

ON RELATIONAL PRACTICES

LET THE SHOW BEGIN

Kelsey Tonacatl-Cuatzo

I heard the whispers.
I heard the murmurs.
Yet, I did nothing.
The formation of the crowd, I did not heed.
For simply,
I did not need to.
I saw the father figure who raised me into this character,
And focused me on what I was taught, and what I would do.
I stepped forward,
And let the show begin.

In this poem, I describe an adult who taught me how to prepare for a theatre show and my role in it. He taught me how to learn my lines and how theatre is an amazing art that allows one to be someone else and step in someone else's shoes. This adult has had a deep impact on me despite knowing me for less than a year. I have learned a lot from him and appreciate his patience with the youth when others would have brushed them aside.

Bio: Kelsey is a Mexican-American scholar who has a passion for art, including literature, theatre, and poetry. Outside of class, Kelsey participates in the Theatre Club, Poetry Club, Horizons, BuildOn, and Fencing.

Per Kelsey: I enjoy learning in an interactive manner. I identify as part of the LGBT+ community and hold my culture and identity dear to me. My relationships with adults are distant in most cases, but the adult I wrote about in this poem is dear to me and I trust in confiding to them my problems and interests.

CHAPTER 5

REWIND

Ten Years of a Youth–Adult Partnership

Marcellina Angelo
Maine Youth Action Network

Deborah Bicknell
Maine Youth Action Network

This submission was written by Marcellina (Marcy) Angelo and Deborah (Deb) Bicknell, who have worked together over the last 10 years as a part of the Maine Youth Action Network (MYAN). Deb was instrumental in the formation and running of MYAN during the first decade of its formation and implementation. Maine Youth Action Network was then, and is now, a network of powerful youth and partnering adults, with programming that is prevention-based and youth-centric. Maine Youth Action Network offers trainings, supports youth on boards, provides technical assistance, and holds an annual summit, all of which support youth who are creating social change. Marcy was involved with MYAN throughout her high school years and served on the MYAN leadership team for 1 year. Marcy and Deb still work together in the Greater Portland Maine area, doing youth and adult trainings on facilitation, dialogue, and partnership. The following are reflections on their time working together.

Deb: It's hard to believe this many years have passed; strange, this time thing. We are no longer youth and adult in the ways we were when we met. I think back on all the years of partnership at MYAN and in other places, in Maine and all around the world, on what went well and what could have been different. I wonder what you think about it now, a decade later. How do you think about what you wanted, who you were then and who you are now and how those years impacted your life? Let's talk about it. We have a story—you and I— let's tell it. So, Marcy what do you first remember about when we met?

Marcy: I met you and Beth in an interview and I remember recognizing you, but not quite clearly. You knew my dad, and you asked me about my dad and my sister Lilly. You made a joke and we started laughing. That is something from the beginning that we always had in common, a sense of humor.

I was used to people knowing my family, seeing my last name, knowing my siblings; but meeting you felt like it was the first time that someone really was interested in getting to know me. I was not used to anyone wanting to know me, Marcellina. I was used to people saying, "Oh you are an Angelo." It seems minor, but it was really something different. Because of my family and who we were in the community, people would have a certain sense of our mission and vision as a family, but it felt like you had an instinctive sense that I had something unique to offer.

Deb: That's true! I knew your sister and dad, but I didn't really know you, not until that day.

Marcy: What did you remember about when we first met?

Deb: I remember that you made me laugh, so I remember that too, the humor part. I also remember feeling a pretty strong connection from the very start. I had been working with youth for quite a while at that point, and when we had youth interns there were a lot of interviews to sit through. I remember more of the feeling, that it was not so much how you did in the interview process, but more your presence, your strength. I also remember that you were good with words—you were then and you are now— but it was more of a feeling you get when you know someone even if you don't know them, you know what I mean?

Marcy: Yeah. We had an instant connection, it felt a little bit like it was just you and me in the interview because we both just started talking. I wonder what Beth was thinking?

Deb: Okay, looking back, what do you remember about the beginning of working at MYAN? What was different, if anything? What did you think?

Marcy: You were all White, but in Maine that is not really that different. And I guess that I had never worked in an office before. The MYAN office had a lot of people and thank god Aisha was there. I figured her name was Aisha so she might at least be a little bit Black. And she was another young person, so that was helpful. I mean, as a young person, you look around, and you look at older people, and you think that they all have it figured out. For me, in that moment, all I cared about was getting to my field hockey championship and building my college application package. I was not concerned with building relationships with White people who I would probably not know after the fact. You know put on your White-people-looking-good-on-the-outside-and-say-all-the-right-things-face and get it done. I thought honestly that MYAN was going to be bullshit; I mean if I am honest, I thought we were not really going to be doing anything that mattered, you know just some stuff behind the scenes. But then, you took us seriously, and you really expected that we were going to do something. That is really when I learned about youth–adult partnerships. Working at MYAN, people seemed to genuinely care.

I also remember that you asked to see my resume, and I told you I didn't have one. That was not something anyone had taught us; I thought that resumes were what you did in college. I can remember that you made me sit down and make a resume. I think I rolled my eyes like ten times, but you made me do it; then you told me that we were going to add everything that I did to the resume. Now people are like, how is your resume so great? How do you make one? Now that I'm older I realize how important it is, the importance of basic skills. When you are young, especially when you are a young person of color, people don't take you seriously.

Deb: Yah, I remember the extensive eye-rolling. You were also so good at that. [*Laughter*] Skills like being able to write a résumé are so important, they are building blocks to one kind of access and success I think, I wonder how else was MYAN different than what you were used to?

Marcy: If you are growing up in the Whitest state in the country and you have been here since you were a kid, you know that you are constantly going to be the only Black person in the

room. I knew the job at MYAN was going to be predominately with White people, however it felt different to have a
White person who said, like you did, that all the discrimination and prejudice that I felt throughout my life was real.
I remember you showed me this wheel that talked about
privilege—I had never seen my experience validated, especially from a White person. At the time, I felt like you were
giving me a card that said, "Everyone knows this, and it's
real." That partnership, that trust we built with each other,
was monumental.

Interning for you, also helped to trigger something in
me as a writer; I felt like I could finally be free as far as how
I wanted to write. I was always scared because of how I was
raised. I was always afraid that my writing sounded White.
It wasn't my fault, it's just how it is; but I was always terrified
of my voice as a writer. The more I felt empowered because
of what I was experiencing with you at MYAN, the more I
found my voice. Now I can say that I sound intellectual, I
sound smart, and that is not sounding White.

Deb: I never knew that Marcy, about the writing I mean and
sounding White. It is crazy to think how much growing I
have done (and still need to do) as a White person. I was
still really early on in my own process back in the MYAN days
I think. Okay, so going back to the topic of how you were
raised, and how you grew up, can you tell me a bit about
what you learned about youth and adult relationships from
your family and your culture?

Marcy: I am from South Sudan, a very non-western culture. My
culture is rich, and it is pretty clear that young people are
not the same as adults, that we are taught to respect adults
no matter what. For example, we are not supposed to look at
them in the eye; it is so weird when you come here to then
be expected to keep eye contact with adults. I come from
an activist family, my dad always taught us that because you
have a voice, you have a responsibility to use it. Even now, I
am still learning to take a seat at the table. You know people
talk about having a seat at the table; I still get nervous about
that. When I started at MYAN, I felt really insecure about
speaking up, because it was ingrained in me that young
people should never talk back or voice their opinions, that
as a young person you are just meant to listen to your elders.
Our culture at MYAN went against everything that I was
raised to do. Even after all these years, it can still be difficult

for me to speak against an elder, to look someone in the eye. It sounds easy, but when you are born in this type of culture, it is like asking someone to do something so strange.

Marcy: Okay, I have a question for you: What did you see in me anyway, I mean, why did you decide to hire me? What do you remember about how I was back then?

Deb: At first, what I felt with you is what I feel with all young people, all people I guess, honestly, which is that I see possibility, the bigness of who someone is. It's a bit weird, I guess; this way of seeing can be a blessing or a curse. I remember noticing how smart you were, that you had talent with words and with writing, that you had a quick tongue. I saw you of course, young, female-bodied, Black, also as you said, I saw you as an Angelo. I could tell you were perceptive by how you listened and what you picked up on. I knew right away that there was not much that was going to get by you, and mostly I knew I could not fake anything, or lie—that you had a radar for the truth, and you were not afraid to call it out. Just to clarify, I don't mean that I wanted to lie; what I mean is more about inauthenticity. That sometimes I feel like it is easy to get tired, to just "dial it in" if you are sick or overwhelmed or frustrated. I was not going to be able to do that with you. And honestly, this is a big part of what I love about youth–adult partnership work—young people know when you are faking it, they know when you are okay and not okay and often they will tell you. I guess at the end of the day I knew with you, one way or the other, it was always going to be real . . . and I liked that. I liked it a lot.

Marcy: Was it also because I was a super fashionista that you hired me?

Deb: [*Laughter*] That was probably part of it! It was clear I needed help with that.

So, I want to go back to the messages that you got about youth and adults as a child. Can you talk about how our relationship was different from the types of youth–adult relationships that you were used to, if it was?

Marcy: Well, for one, you are not South Sudanese. I mean you are White, but I feel like I knew you, sometimes you come across people who you feel you just know—there were so many parts of you that resonated for me. Beyond that, you gave me a platform, you let me have power, you let me have freedom to do what I wanted to do. The only other person who had done that for me in my life was my dad. I think you *saw* me; it was weird, but I feel like you really did, and you still do.

What I loved about our relationship the most was that you always asked me, "What do you want me to do?" You never questioned my dreams, you just asked what you could do to help me. Sometimes the weight of one's vision is so heavy, you need someone to help carry it. I always did have a big vision, especially at that age; I had all these big dreams. When you are a young person and an adult trusts your vision so much, when you have an adult who is willing to carry part of that weight, it is amazing. Every single day it was about building a bridge. Every day you showed me that you were reliable, that you were not taking advantage of me, that I was not just a number. This helped build a bridge between us, it built the relationship.

Deb: I like that image of people having dreams that they need help carrying. As an adult, sometimes the hardest part is not getting in the way of someone's dreams, really being able to support them without making them into yours or trying to change them in some way. I think that is key.

I can remember being young and having people tell me that I needed to be more realistic. But our dreams ought to be one's own size; you know what I mean? I have a lot of young people share wild-sized projects and dreams, and I think I learned to say yes and then to ask questions. To say yes, first to the dream and the dreaming and the dreamer, so that the person knows that I see them. I mean it is a vulnerable and bold thing to dream. I think we all ought to be a little more careful with each other's dreams. I had to learn this way of being, though, because I came from a background where people said, "You are never going to be able to do that," and so I would find myself asking detailed questions and problem-solving from the jump with youth. There is nothing more annoying than that. The first time I saw a dream deflated by my questions or opinions, I re-thought how I wanted to do it. There is nothing more powerful than someone believing in you.

Can you share a bit about what you think happened in our relationship that was useful in terms of your own leadership, your own development?

Marcy: Our work relationships made me think about youth and adult partnerships in a different light. I mean, I had not really thought about this before. Before I thought all youth and adult partnerships meant that youth did all the work and the adults stood out front to get the credit. The supervisor gets the credit, even if you created it. You always told me to document what I did. Honestly, I thought at the time you were just being anal; but you were being true and honest with me. It's hard as a young person to trust an adult, to trust that they have your best interest at heart. As young people, we want instant gratification and we want to see the work pay off. I needed to see something that worked. Trust and consistency were key.

Also, I remember this one time you talked to me. You were driving me to the airport, and I had done some stuff that my dad didn't like. I was going to my cousins for the weekend to get away and think about what was going on in my life. You looked right at me and said that I needed to think about whether I was going to use my power for good or for evil. I didn't like it at the time, but I remembered it. My dad had said something similar, so I thought if two people were saying something, maybe I ought to pay attention. I remember that thought, and I think that sort of helped me to start taking responsibility for my own use of power.

Deb: [*Laughter*] I have had to ask myself that same question at times. [*Laughter*] It is hard to really realize how powerful we all are, how much impact we can and do have. I remember that. You have shared a lot about what you loved and what was unique or important about our relationship. What about our relationship was hard? What do you wish I had understood or known at the time?

Marcy: When I was that age, I wish you could have seen how difficult it was to be one of three Black people in my school, and how much that impacted everything. I was not open about being a Black person in Maine; I wish you could have seen and known how much that affected me. I am a natural joking person, I make jokes about race, but it deeply affected me and how I felt . . . how I felt being Black and being in school. I felt ugly most of the time, insecure because I was Black—and being one of the darkest skinned students. I wish not just you, but other people also, had seen how uncomfortable I was in my own Blackness. I did not have time in the morning to do my hair; I didn't feel pretty enough.

Deb: I thought a fair bit about race back then, but of course I wasn't thinking about it as deeply as you were. I knew that as a White woman I really could not understand your experience.

I knew that I needed to honor our difference, to respect it. But that was before I had done the real, internal work on my own racial identity, I felt like I would trip over myself in ways or I would feel self-conscious or like I needed to do or say the right thing or nothing at all. I started to realize that I had a lot to learn, both as an adult and as a White person, and I could feel that you were teaching me as much as I was teaching you. You always gave me the gift of honesty. You always gave me the gift of honesty, you shared what is real and true and you trusted me to be able to listen. I love that about you. And, over the course of our relationship, I think I've learned to let myself *be* me a bit more.

Marcy: Yah, I could tell you had done some work about race, but I could tell that you could not totally handle all the complexities of my identity. Okay, so was there anything that was hard for you about me and how I was? Anything you wish I didn't do?

Deb: At times, I felt like you took shortcuts, and sometimes I felt frustrated or challenged by your choices. I could see that you had big dreams, and also that in ways you were afraid. I just knew that my job was not to meet you in that doubt, but instead to push a bit (though not too much) and to promise not to settle for mediocrity; that is the worst thing that adults can do—expect young people to just get by.

I think my relationship with your dad was also part of it. I knew your dad, I knew he had a big life, that he was a powerful man and that he was a global citizen, that he had risked and sacrificed a lot. At times, I wanted you to push harder for him and for your mom, for all they had been through. That is one thing that is hard in youth–adult partnerships, it can be easy to start putting your narrative on top of a young person's, your own sense of a young person's situation, what their dreams and goals ought to be. That is not our job, though; our job is to create the conditions for youth to explore and know themselves. Sometimes, it was hard to watch you try and navigate between the world of a Sudanese daughter and that of an American young person coming of age. It is such a complicated experience. There were times I had to tell myself, "This is hard and there is nothing you can do about it."

Now that you are a bit older and you are working with young people, what is your perspective on what youth and adults most need for working well together?

Marcy: What needs to happen is more communication—it is literally the key. As a young person, your strongest (sometimes your only) tool is your voice. You cannot advocate for other people if you cannot advocate for yourself. Working within multiracial communities now, I try and be what I wanted and needed back then. I want to be an adult who talks to them, who listens to them. Youth need to know that they are in a safe place; they need to know that you respect them. Once they feel that they are respected, you will be surprised, they will open up. Respect goes both ways—it requires an even playing field. Youth can feel it when adults are genuinely asking about them and their experience.

Some of the young people I have worked with will see me and say "Marcy!" They remember me, but they don't remember me for what I did, they remember how real I was with them. The capacity for young people to evolve, that evolution of character is really incredible. If we don't take advantage, it is a waste of an opportunity. Adults who are working with young people need to ask themselves, "How committed am I to the evolution of a young person? How committed am I to being in this young person's life?" If you want to work with young people—you need consistency, trust, respect—it works both ways. You have to teach and to learn . . . and you cannot be afraid to call young people out on their shit, either.

Deb: Like when you used to tell your parents that you were with me, but you were really off with your friends?

Marcy: [*Laughter*] Like that, but I knew you were going to call me on it. You called me out on it, but I needed that. You were like, "You want to be an adult? I am going to treat you like an adult, and you are accountable for your actions."

Deb: I just knew that I was not going to lower the bar. Respect is showing you that I know you are better than that. Holding you accountable, not in a punitive way, just in being real, I guess.

Marcy: Yah, if you had lowered the bar, I would never have accepted that; I would have started questioning you and your integrity. I would have questioned whether you really cared about me. We went through the steps of building a relationship. You knew I was smart, but we still went through the steps of building a relationship. I always knew that you would love me regardless . . . but that was about trust and consistency and, like I said, calling me on my shit.

Where did you learn to be like that?

Deb: From my parents, I think, and grandparents. They all had really high standards and even though that was stressful in a lot of ways, it also taught me a lot. I had strict parents, sort of like yours; I think this is another reason why you and I could relate. As I took on the role of a youth worker, I thought a lot about what I had wanted as a young person. I wanted someone to really talk to me, not like I remembered as a kid, with people thinking I was less smart because I was 10 years old. I felt like I could see and understand things way beyond what adults gave me credit for... I always wanted to remember that feeling and treat everyone, no matter their age, like an equal, like they had something to say—because they do! I definitely carry my parents' high expectations when working with youth—high expectations and high support. I think that you cannot do *for* young people, you have to do *with*—even if lots of times it feels easier to do *for*. It takes a lot of patience and self-discipline to be able to sit with frustration or your own expectation and/or disappointment. Partnership with young people can be hard when it triggers your own stuff.

Marcy: Did you ever feel like you wanted to do things for me?

Deb: [*Laughter*] Did I? I still do sometimes. But I learned that it is not what it is about. That is not what anyone really needs, because we are all stronger than we think. No one learns when you don't push them a bit... but it has to be with love and care and real listening. It is hard though. Watching other people's learning unfold can be really painful. At the same time, though, when there are accomplishments, you can really see the light go on.

Marcy: That is sort of like when you would say to me, "It's your choice," right?

Deb: Right. I guess that is just part of growing up—this becoming of yourself. It is funny, it is talked about in literature as "coming of age" and you hear people talk about growing up as if it is an event. But really, it is a biological, cognitive, and psychological *set of events* that help you grow, little by little. It is ongoing.

Adolescence is a particular time of pulling away from what is known, experimentation, and integration. It is a time when you need to be making your own choices, with support and safety. This is the time to stretch into what you think and believe, not just what you grew up being told. I could see with you, and I can see with a lot of young people who come from super strong cultural backgrounds, that this is hard in a very particular way. How do you become yourself, but also respect the norms of your culture and context? How do you be a leader and all these things your parents want you to be, but also discover who you are, what you feel and what you believe amidst it all? I love youth for this edge-walking. It is a time for finding your voice, like you said, telling the truth, whether people like it or not.

Marcy: So, what do you think is the hardest thing about working with youth?

Deb: In general, or with you?

Marcy: Both.

Deb: I think, in general, it is balancing the desire to demonstrate genuine care with the constraints of our given roles. I cared about you a lot; we had a natural connection from the start, and this has been true with lots of the youth I have worked with over the years. It is important, though, for adults to be really clear about what role we are playing in any given situation and to try and stay appropriate to that role. Being transparent creates the conditions for trust. In our case, this meant that I had a different standard for what I would share with you about me and my life when you were a teen then I do now. The relationship we had then was one that involved a difference in power. Being aware of my own power and being thoughtful about it—finding ways to share it, but not pretending imbalances of power did not exist. This can be tricky, because it can feel like a young person, especially one you really click with, is your friend, but that is not what the role demands.

Marcy: What about with me, specifically?

Deb: Well, I am not Black right? I am not from South Sudan. There are so many ways in which we are not the same. Then there are these things that we have in common: We are both middle children, we are both writers and slayers, we both have great hair. [*Laughter*] Anyway, it is important, especially in youth–adult relationships, but I think in all relationships, to be comfortable being yourself. This means not "over-linking" yourself. It means being able to see and be okay with same and different. For me, this means that even though we have some similar experiences in our families, and that I can relate in many ways, we also come from different lineages, different continents, different races, and I have to be really comfortable with both the depth of our connection and the ability to see and know our differences.

It is important to observe and to understand how to connect. Without real connection and relationship, you are just in a job or a role. When I started working a lot with young people from an immigrant and refugee background for example, I realized that there was a lot of fear from the parents, understandably so . . . I started making it a habit to go and meet the parents so they could see me, ask questions (often through others translating). I found that really changed things. I could start to build relationships which were grounded in a larger relationship and sense of trust. I had not been doing that before with young people from Maine, and I think I realized that different young people have different needs. Knowing when to step forward and reach toward and knowing when to back off a bit and not over push, this is the dance of youth and adult partnership.

Marcy: What do you love about working with youth? You must, I mean you have been doing it a long time.

Deb: I love how young people are less afraid than adults. Young people sometimes try and be cool—there are ways that they start to not want to be weird or standout; but with a little push, a bit of open space and invitation to do something meaningful or creative, young people rise to the occasion. They are like these crazy beautiful flowers or plants or something that are ready to bloom and just need the right conditions. The thing is, each person has their own conditional needs, so as an adult you have to listen and connect and find the right way to contribute to the conditions that allow that innate strength to emerge.

Marcy: That description is so you—flowers and shit . . . and it's true.

Deb: And related to you. I guess if I am honest, things changed your senior year when your brother was killed. We were still in that youth–adult mentorship role, but something deepened or changed.

Marcy: Yah, we definitely crossed into a different kind of relationship when James was killed. I texted you, and I think immediately you came an hour later. That changed things for me, because that was a time in my life in which I instinctively knew that there would be a lot of transitions. I needed consistency, and you brought me that type of consistency. Also, you were not one of those people who wanted to hug me. I knew you could see that I had grown up in an instant—went from a child to an adult in that moment. Everything was out of control. You let me have that moment. You were the one person who was not stressing me about school, and you told me that you would come and get me. That was the reassurance of knowing that someone could see me, that I could lean on someone. There are very few people who will be there when you are falling, really falling, you are about to hit the cement...All I knew was that I was falling, and it felt like a pitless, bottomless hole with no one to catch me. But then, you were there. And you shared your experience with me—and I knew that this was not the end, that there was someone else out there that knew what it felt like, the deepest feelings of grief.

Our relationship shifted then from you being a mentor to you being a part of my life. That moment changed it for me. You really saw me; you saw the little girl, the part of me that was clawing to breathe. You saw her, and you helped me, step by step. I don't think I would have graduated without you. All that rage. I felt like I walked around with a sign that said, "my brother was murdered." You were the only person who said, "Marcy, you need to do this. You need to graduate." Sometimes you just have to do things, or you will miss out; I got that from you. I have never been more glad.

Deb: Yes, I knew that you had changed, that there was no going back, no childhood now...and still, still I could see that you needed to be seen and listened to, that you had a lot to say, maybe even more now. I had gone through something similar, I had some frame of reference and I knew that I could be a force for holding steady some of your dreams, your bigger life. You know how I always say, "Take the long view Marcy"? I think in that moment I was trying to hold the long view for you.

Marcy: I think you were. Because we both had built this foundation of trust, I was able to let you in when I needed you the most. That is the definition of a genuine youth and adult partnership that has been able to last more than a decade.

Deb: Okay, there is more to talk about but I am getting hungry. I wish I had some of your Sudanese donuts in front of me right now. I love those. You think we better wrap it up? You want to say anything else?

Marcy: Yah, sounds good. You know what Maya Angelou said Deb, "When someone shows you who you are, believe them." You have shown me who you really are, and I have shown you. It has changed both of us for the better don't you think? I do.

A DELICATE DANCE

Sylvia Boguniecki

The whistling of the atmosphere coincides with the
Presence of the flourishing petals
Of the flower garden ahead; containing the memory of
Your firm form against the malleable field that, with
Light, illuminates the everlasting imprint of your soul.

Bringing the fallen leaves with the swirling force with
Me, following the delicate dance of your creation.
Nothing, not even the rips in the earth's crust, will limit the
symphony,
But if dictations of motion be twisted,
Comfort still prevails with the essence of your soothing touch.

Guides with maps of labyrinths and waterfalls may slow
My system of spontaneity to an unstoppable fall; bringing this
Life of mine to a questionable destination, but your words call out to
my heart,
Towards the possibility of syncing up once more, leaving
Worthiness to forever stay in my thoughts, to lead me out of these
caged walls.

With the new generation experiencing changes that are hard to
    comprehend, the
Wisdom of the adults—those whom we call "old" and "not with the
    time," who
We're quick to avert our attention from, but could quickly form
    strong bonds with us, keeping us
Safe and comforted by altering the paths we walk on, to make them
    easier to handle.

Bio: Sylvia Boguniecki is a young artist of age 17 who attends the Baccalaureate School for Global Education. Sylvia is a part of multiple volunteering programs like the Greenpoint Hunger Program, GSA at the Brooklyn Museum, and the Children's Smile Foundation. Additionally, they tutor young students, sharing their academic knowledge and their passion for the arts. Working weekly, they try to find new ways to help others in whatever way they can.

Per Sylvia: The arts have always been close to my heart, allowing me to inform others about complex emotions human beings can feel that can't simply be spoken out loud. Expressing myself through dance, creative writing, and painting, I try to raise awareness about the importance of personal connections within society. My hope is to motivate others to stand up with one another, to create a powerful movement for the benefit of all of generations without discrimination.

CHAPTER 6

"TO PICK UP A PEN INSTEAD OF A GUN"

Rewriting Richmond Through RAW Talent

Donté Clark
RAW Talent

Molly Raynor
Neutral Zone

Donté

There is no middle class where I come from. Either you're from the gutter and you live amongst the rats, sharing government cheese, or you live in the mountains, sipping Moscato and enjoying satellite TV.

I come from the bottom city, where neighborhoods are divided up by train tracks and Richmond bodies fall on both sides, boosting the homicide rates that rise each year. There are no flashy lights, skyscraper buildings, or bustling downtown areas. There are just black gates and concrete complexes that we call the projects, which house most of the African-American and Latino communities. Police in our neighborhood ride four to a car, sometimes three or four cars deep. We're taught at a young age to carry a gun, and never hesitate to shoot. You take your chances of being arrested or you're high-speeding, hoping to get away. Everyday decisions can cost you your life or your freedom.

To deal with the struggles in the hood, my people smoke crack or get lifted from marijuana. We drown ourselves in alcohol or in a cloud of cigarettes, as if Chevron chemicals aren't enough. I've had friends who dropped out of school because they didn't believe in wasting their time in a classroom. "Can't eat no books" is the expression. People don't understand why we hurt each other or why we live the way we do. To me it's simple. This is learned behavior, inflicted upon my people long ago, and we are struggling to break this cycle.

At 16, I was sucked into this lifestyle and felt the effects firsthand. I had run out of hope of ever finishing high school and going off to college. As far as I was concerned, school wasn't for me. I can still hear my sister telling me to think about my future: "If there are no goals, then there's no dream to live." She didn't know that I wanted to become a street legend—and that growing up in these streets, I was already living that dream. To us on the bottom, becoming a street legend was as close as we thought we could get to making it—to living the good life Kanye preached about. The corner was where I thought I belonged. With brothers on trial for murder charges, with close friends and family being killed all around me, I didn't expect to live past the next day. I thought that if God had a plan for me, he'd allow me to see 18.

But at 17, after years of watching my loved ones harden behind metal bars in prison or burn from the fire of metal barrels, I began second-guessing my role in the streets. I no longer saw hustling as profitable long term. I had to get out but college wasn't the way, sports were out of the question, and I wasn't going to settle for flipping burgers or waiting tables. All I could do was write, and I figured that writing could be my way out. I practiced writing and performing my words aloud each day, building my identity through the pen. I knew that I would develop a sound to capture everyone's hearts, and that I would speak until the world felt me.

Molly

I grew up in Ann Arbor, Michigan—a majority White college town with university money and segregated pockets of low-income housing. I love my hometown, but there are aspects of it with which I struggle. It's hard for marginalized youth to find a sense of belonging in a city that prides itself on being liberal but that routinely profiles and polices youth of color.

At 14, I was a privileged, middle-class White girl—insecure and uncertain about who I was. I remember walking the hallways of my public school, so packed with people that I couldn't step in the direction I chose. To turn against the flow of traffic was to get trampled. To go against the status quo was to be ostracized, othered. Fitting in meant being quiet. It meant looking the other way when girls were groped without consent, biting my tongue when my Black classmates were punished more severely than my White classmates. But there was a nagging sense of social responsibility in my gut: I could feel my need to stand up for myself and others clashing against my desire to conform. Beneath my fear, I could feel brave words writhing under my tongue, planning their escape.

At the end of that year, I met Jeff Kass, a teacher at my high school who had just started a weekly poetry workshop at Neutral Zone, an after-school teen center in Ann Arbor.[1] I attended my first workshop nervously—I didn't think I was a poet. But Jeff saw potential in me that I couldn't yet see. He built up my self-esteem as a writer; he encouraged me to think critically and have more courage. The moment I entered the spoken word community, my life changed. When I stepped onstage, I became a fiercer version of myself. My fears fell away and I felt a sense of conviction in my voice that wasn't there before. I felt heard.

I made the Ann Arbor slam team at 15, which enabled me to go on a trip to San Francisco for Brave New Voices, a teen poetry festival with youth from all over the world. I met poets from the Bay Area, the Hopi Nation, India, Bosnia, and beyond. I heard teens talking about poverty, war, rape culture, police brutality, and other forms of violence they experienced daily. I came home politicized: more conscious of my privilege and complicity in others' suffering; more committed to unlearning my biases and working to be not just an ally, but an accomplice. Through poetry, I found a safe space to address my own marginalized identities as well. Hearing brave artists share their stories allowed me to explore my queerness and heal from my sexual trauma.

Inspired by that experience, I immersed myself in Neutral Zone, where I was empowered to dream big and step into leadership through the organization's youth-driven model. I was invited to become a teen facilitator, helping to plan and run several weekly programs around diversity, inclusion, and intersectional feminism. I continued to develop my craft and shadow Jeff, assisting him in facilitating poetry workshops. Poetry and activism became intertwined for me: Writing led me to learn about the injustices of the world, and those ongoing lessons fueled my writing.

I continued to explore this intersection through my undergraduate years at the University of Michigan. I created my own major, "Critical Pedagogy and Activism Through the Arts," inspired by Paulo Freire's (1970) *Pedagogy of the Oppressed*. After college, I moved to the Bay Area, where I landed a job at Making Waves Educational Program, a college prep program in Richmond, California. While I valued my time with the students in the program, I was frustrated by the limitations of the traditional academic curriculum. Seeking a different way to connect with my students, I asked my boss if I could start a poetry workshop. She agreed and connected me with Donté Clark, a student she thought could also use a creative outlet.

Donté

I have been writing raps since I was 11 years old. In the fifth grade, I was recruited to join Making Waves. There, I had dozens of teachers and guidance counselors who pushed me to reach for a better life. They provided me with a space to develop as a young man, and to find my passion to write.

Inspired by Tupac Shakur and his ability to be honest about his emotions and inner demons, I began to write more and more poetry. Poetry infused my rap format and delivery; corner stores and trap houses echoed through my writing. On the page, I was allowed to process the trauma and pour out the tears I held back. I was vulnerable. Poetry became everything to me. If not for Making Waves, I would've dropped out of school and fallen to the streets. Instead, I was opening up and allowing the peace to settle in. I wanted my writing to be the blueprint for the rebuilding of Richmond. The streets were in my rear view.

Wanting to advance as a poet, I sought additional support and knowledge from a mentor. This is when I met Molly Raynor, who had just started working at Making Waves. I was 17 years old, in my senior year in high school. A friend told me about the writing empowerment workshop he had with Molly, and how much he thought I would benefit from working with her. He offered to introduce us and I agreed. First time I saw Molly, she looked like one of the younger students in the program. I wasn't sure if I was going to take her seriously. I thought: *A short White lady from Michigan? Of course she writes poetry; all White people do.* Judging by her looks, I thought Molly couldn't possibly understand where I was coming from with my writing or where I could take it. Still, I was willing to try something new, just for the experience.

Molly and I met every Thursday for an hour. I usually blow off workshops and teachers if I'm not feeling it, but with Molly, there was something about the vibe that kept me coming back. Molly had a way of making you feel welcomed and appreciated for being yourself. I felt that she was genuinely interested in what I had to say, and I liked that she showed me ways to enhance my delivery. Molly provided me a space to try something new, and she was encouraging with every step I took.

Molly

When my boss agreed to let me start a workshop with Donté, she shared that he was a talented writer, but that he showed no interest in pursuing college. She worried he would end up following in his brothers' footsteps. From his reputation in the program, I was expecting resistant behavior and flaky attendance. On the contrary, Donté showed up consistently and was always respectful. I didn't know him well enough to create workshops around his particular interests, so I started with simple lesson plans: We would analyze a poem or song, and then he would write his own piece off a prompt inspired by the reading. Once I got to know his interests, strengths, and areas for improvement, I was able to cater to them through my curriculum.

Donté was the most brilliant and centered young person I had ever met. He thought deeply, observed those around him carefully, and was intentional about every word he wrote and spoke. But he also struggled with uncertainty, standing at the crossroads between who people expected him to be and who he knew he could be. The stakes were high. When the year came to a close, I wanted to keep working with Donté on his writing. I could also see that he had a lot to teach me about his community. The ugly, and more importantly, the beautiful. The teens in the program, particularly the young men, looked up to him because of how he carried himself and the street cred behind his name. I could see his potential to pull in younger students and be the kind of mentor they needed but rarely had. Someone who could relate to them. I asked my boss if we could bring Donté on as paid intern to teach additional poetry workshops, and she agreed.

Donté

During my years as a student at Making Waves, I had come to believe that there was a life out there for me to live, and that I had a way to obtain it: poetry. Still, when my high school career was coming to an end, I had no idea what was ahead for me. Molly knew my uncertainties, and she asked if I would be willing to come back to help her continue workshops for other students in Making Waves.

At first, I was apprehensive. I didn't believe my writing was strong enough, nor did I think that I was anyone's teacher. These were not the shoes I ever dreamed of walking in. But I couldn't turn down the offer, because I cared so much about the idea of having a safe place for young people like me to go to and vent their frustrations—to process trauma and heal. I stayed because Molly believed in me so much that she thought I could be a teacher. Other people thought I was a good writer but no one believed that I would be capable of being a teacher. Without credentials and fresh out of high school, I wanted to believe that she was right. This was my way towards my dream.

I came back as a volunteer to help build on what Molly and I had started. The next semester, I was added to the payroll and given students of my own. Before we knew it, Molly and I were onto something big. We were both driven to make this dream a reality. The young people in Richmond were hungry for a creative outlet and the opportunity to be heard.

Molly

Over the next few years, the writing workshops that Donté and I co-founded evolved into a full-fledged program: Richmond Artists With Talent (RAW Talent) became the creative arts department of Making Waves. We developed a theory of change with our vision, values, and mission statement: to provide a safe space for creative expression and self-exploration that [would] increase young peoples' self-esteem, their identities as artists, their connection to their histories, and their belief in the power of their own voices to transform themselves and their communities.

Donté

Every day I came into work at RAW Talent with new ideas and a burst of energy. I was ready to meet the needs of these young teens who were looking for someone to talk to, someone who cared enough to listen.

I joined RAW Talent when I was in the 8th grade

RAW Talent is the family I never had

Before I joined, I was never a poet

I thought that poetry was a confusing language and a waste of time but after the murder of my father my RAW Talent family helped me channel my feelings to the page and before I knew it a Poet was born from within me

RAW Talent has been there for me every step of the way, challenging my writing skills and helping me break down the walls of hurt

When things are hard, and I feel my back is against the wall, RAW Talent has showed me that not only will they not turn their back on me, but neither will a pen and paper

Something crazy about me is that if it was not for the murder of my father, I would have never found the artist that has been living inside of me

Throughout my tragedy I have found my blessing and that is writing

My father will always be alive through my work and I thank god for helping me find sunlight through my black cloud

—Jamaya Walker, RAW Talent Alum
& Founder of the Non-Profit "Daddyless Daughters"

Our program offerings grew more varied and advanced. In addition to spoken word poetry, we offered workshops in jewelry design, photography, visual art, music production, theater, and dance. We started making an annual anthology of the students' poetry and a CD of their spoken word. Each year, we would go on field trips, put on shows for the public, host town hall discussions with Richmond youth, and take the most committed students on a weekend writing retreat in Marin. At the end of each year, we brought on previous students as teachers-in-training. With more interns, we were able to recruit more young people to join RAW Talent.

Like me, my fellow teachers at RAW were talented artists and critical thinkers, but had not excelled in school. Like me, they had almost succumbed to the pull of the streets before they found themselves through creative expression. This is one of the reasons that RAW Talent became so appealing to youth in Richmond—they saw themselves reflected in the staff. They saw a group of people who had gone through the same struggle, but who ultimately chose to pursue their craft and give back to their community.

Molly

As RAW Talent grew, we became more intentional about our values. We wanted to avoid the patronizing approach that I'd witnessed in many college prep programs that target low-income youth—programs that embrace a bootstrap mentality, tell young people that college is the only way to succeed, and teach them to assimilate to White, mainstream standards of higher education.

I've also witnessed a tendency in some youth nonprofits to exploit their most marginalized teen participants in order to appear "diverse." I've been to nonprofit fundraisers where youth participants are asked to get up in front of a mostly White, middle-class audience and speak about how the program saved them from their traumatic past. When I've followed up with these youth, I've often learned that the teen speakers do not actually hold legitimate leadership roles within these nonprofits, and that some feel pressured by their mentors to speak about triggering experiences in order to pull on the heartstrings of funders and secure more donations.

The most successful model of youth development work I've witnessed occurs when youth are given true decision-making power within the organization. Neutral Zone, the organization I worked with in Ann Arbor, is one example of this model. At Neutral Zone, half of the board is comprised of teens, and almost every program is run by teen facilitators in partnership with adult program coordinators. When I was a teenager participating in programs of Neutral Zone, I felt seen, heard, and supported. This experience showed me the kind of leadership I wanted to cultivate and celebrate in young people in Richmond.

When Donté and I co-founded RAW Talent, it was critical to me that he was treated as a true equal and not a token "face" of our program without actual power. Donté was given opportunities for creative control (e.g., designing his own curriculum), and we made bigger programmatic decisions together. This required constant communication to make sure we stayed on the same page. Donté also came with me to every meeting with funders. After years of collaboration, we built a shared vision and a deep trust in one another's ability to represent RAW Talent to others when we weren't able to be together.

Donté

Molly mentioned earlier how best practices are youth-driven, not youth-led. The idea is for adults to give young folks guidance, and train them in how to lead.

When I began working with young people, I had no training. I was 18 and in a leadership position. I walked and talked the way Richmond raised us; that's what made me authentic and relatable to the youth. I didn't understand then, but that's what Molly meant when she thought I could be a teacher: I am their reflection. My experience gave me the edge to be a partner. I knew how to take the ideas Molly had and implement them in a way that catered to our community. What's more youth-driven than that?

The fact that Molly believed I was capable, and that young people were showing up to my workshops, meant that I had to be present. I told myself, "If I can make the young people feel heard, loved, and supported, their investment and enthusiasm about me and the program will be my deliverables." I listened to them vent their frustrations, checked in with them regularly, made sure they felt heard and supported to make their best decisions. When the administration at Making Waves couldn't reach the young people, they turned to us. They couldn't deny the connection that RAW Talent built with youth, and our contributions to their development.

Molly

I remember hearing my teachers in high school say "leave your drama at the door" when my peers and I talked about our personal lives. When we say that to our students, we are really saying "leave your trauma at the door," which means asking them not to bring their whole selves into the classroom. We're asking them to forget the fact that they haven't eaten that day, that their friend was just shot, that their boyfriend hit them this morning. We're not only ignoring their pain, but also missing critical opportunities to connect with our students, to affirm them, and to understand what brings them joy, happiness, and success.

In the same way that students are asked to leave their drama at the door, educators are, too. Teachers are trained not to share about their personal lives. But by making ourselves blank slates, we don't allow our students to see our humanity—our flaws, our fears, our growth. So, in RAW Talent we asked both youth and adults to bring their whole selves into the space. While we were careful not to overshare (e.g., talk about our sex lives or gossip about co-workers), when issues arose that we could relate to, we'd use that moment as an opening to share our past experiences. We hoped to give our students guidance through modeling a strength-based approach, sharing how we had turned life's obstacles into opportunities for growth.

We took this holistic approach to conflict as well. In contrast to the disciplinary practices that most of our students faced in over-policed Richmond public schools with zero tolerance policies, RAW Talent didn't kick students out; we worked with them to get to the root of the issue. Our staff went through trainings at the RYSE Center[2] with indigenous healers who taught us how to utilize restorative justice practices, such as holding homicide healing circles after losing young people to gun violence. They explained, "the medicine is in the circle"—that if you sent the talking piece around enough times, the conflict would usually be resolved. In RAW Talent, if two members were getting into a fight, Donté would sometimes stop a workshop or rehearsal halfway through and hold a healing circle with the entire group. We wouldn't leave until they collectively worked it out. This forced everyone to be accountable for their actions and engage in each other's healing. Instead of bringing them out only when conflicts or tragedies arose, we used circles routinely to check in and wrap up workshops.

Donté

Looking back, the teachers who inspired me were the ones who allowed space for me to be my full self. Mr. Morgan would listen and wait for me to rap through the math problems until I found the answer. He was my Math Empowerment teacher at Making Waves. He encouraged me to do whatever I needed to do to be present and learn. Once, I asked Mr. Morgan why I had to call teachers by their last name and they could call me by my first name. He said it was a sign of respect. I told him that respect goes both ways, and if you want respect, you have to earn it by giving respect. From then on, Mr. Morgan called me Mr. Clark.

I appreciated when adults came to ask me for my name and introduced themselves before telling me to pull my pants up, turn down my music, or bring my voice volume down. This level of respect comes from intimate relationships. When love is present, we all function as our best selves. I felt that Stacy D and Mrs. Mejia—my after-school providers—cared for me like a big sister or mother would. Sometimes giving me rides home, coming to my school to check in with my teachers, feeding me if I hadn't eaten lunch that day. Because I knew that they cared for me, I felt inclined to do better, not just for the sake of school but for my life outside of that. Whatever route I chose to take, I didn't want to disappoint them.

At RAW Talent, we intentionally treated each other like family. I knew my students' parents. We had fish fries at their houses to celebrate our book releases. Some of us came from big families and some of us, given previous experiences of neglect, yearned to belong to a warm community. At RAW Talent, we made sure everyone was included. We made sure young folks were fed.

Molly

Donté and I shared a commitment to respecting the dignity, humanity, and autonomy of the young people we worked with. We practiced love as a radical teaching tool. Love in action, not just in theory (hooks, 2000). This often looked like taking young people's calls when they were in crisis, or driving them home so they weren't walking alone in the dark. If we expected them to keep coming back, we had to go the extra mile to show them they were cared for. We had to show them we weren't just asking them to write about their trauma, but we were working to address that trauma. Since we weren't mental health professionals, this also meant recognizing when an issue arose that we couldn't handle and referring them to the appropriate resources. While we wanted to provide quality programming, we ultimately believed that supporting our students' skill development was secondary to fostering their emotional well-being.

Donté

When I led workshops at RAW Talent, before anything else, I'd ask each young person who came into my classroom how they were feeling at that moment. If they had trouble at home with money, parents, or homelessness, it would be hard for them to avoid voicing what was on their minds. I just had to be patient enough to allow the words to form. I was coming from an environment similar to the young people I taught, so they already knew I could relate to their struggles. Still, although there was a level of comfort, I had to earn their trust.

One student, Dimarea, would tell me about people wanting to harm him. I remember being on him about participating in one of our first RAW Talent performances. The show was about to start and he wasn't there. He called me and told me he was on his way but someone caught him slipping at the train tracks and posed like they were going to shoot him. It wasn't clear to me what happened next or how he managed to escape unharmed, but he ended up walking away, very upset. He wanted to respond according to this anger. I told him that it was more important for him to come to the show than to go home and sit with this anger. I went against Making Waves policy and walked up the street to meet him at the train tracks where the altercation happened.

Dimarea needed to know that he wasn't alone. I had to prove to Dimarea that I was willing to risk my life if I was asking him to risk his. This made him trust me, and listen to me over others who hadn't shown their concern. He knew I wasn't just talking. I was willing. He walked back with me to the show, and it became the only show where Dimarea performed with RAW Talent.

Molly

While I think the success of our program was rooted in that family bond we created, I also know that we burnt ourselves out by being there for our young people 24/7, and by not practicing more self-care. I learned over time—and I'm still learning—that while teens are seeking supportive mentors, they also need structure and boundaries. Being a "safe adult" means finding that balance.

Donté was 18 and I was 23 when we started RAW Talent. We were learning as we went, so although we made magic with what we had, it was just that: magic. I had my college jargon and teen leadership experiences, but we didn't have true language for why we did what we did. We were just following our hearts and instincts. Over time, we learned from what went well and where we still needed to grow. We became more intentional and strategic. Eventually, we started getting asked to present at conferences. After years of learning through doing with no formal training, it was incredible to realize that we had wisdom and best practices to share.

But our faith was shaken when one of our founding members, Dimarea, was shot and killed in 2013—lost to the very gun violence we were working to eradicate. My staff—all young men close to Dimarea—questioned if there was a purpose to our work, and if it was possible to stop the violence in their community. Ultimately, we used the loss to fuel our fire and continue pushing. DeAndre Evans, one of Dimarea's best friends who had joined our RAW staff, had the idea to start a workshop in Dimarea's memory, where Dimarea's loved ones could come process their grief through creative writing.

Dimarea's mom, sister, and girlfriend joined our teens for a weekly writing workshop called "Phoenix Rysing."

Donté

Dimarea's death was one of the most challenging periods of my life. A young man who looked up to me as a brother, and who I looked at as my young brother, was killed. We argued over the years about his involvement in the streets. We both knew what this lifestyle brings. In our own ways, we were both trying to escape. He told me in one of our arguments that if anything were to happen to him, I shouldn't retaliate; I should keep RAW Talent my priority. I told him I would have to retaliate, because he's my brother. What he said next changed my life: "Then everything we're talking about is a waste of time. If you want me out the streets, you can't jump back in if something happens to me, that makes everything you're telling me now pointless. You gotta practice what you preach."

Dimarea was right. The day he was killed, this conversation played over and over in my head. I wanted to kill everyone who had something to do with it. *But if I drop this pen for the gun, then who gon' raise the children?* I repurposed my mission. I resolved to go harder each day, knowing that lives depend on it. I got through this time by writing and performing. Pouring all of my pain onto the stage, bringing Dimarea's name to memory.

Molly

In "The Future of Healing: Shifting from Trauma Informed Care to Healing Centered Engagement," Shawn Ginwright (2018) explores the desire of young people to be seen as more than "the worst thing that ever happened to them." He recognizes the important shift from zero tolerance to trauma-informed practices and the recognition of our students' lived realities, but encourages youth workers to refocus on healing:

> A healing centered approach to addressing trauma requires a different question that moves beyond "what happened to you" to "what's right with you" and views those exposed to trauma as agents in the creation of their own well-being rather than victims of traumatic events. Healing centered engagement is akin to the South African term "Ubuntu" meaning that humanness is found through our interdependence, collective engagement, and service to others. Additionally, healing centered engagement offers an asset driven approach aimed at the holistic restoration of young peoples' well-being. The healing centered approach comes from the idea that people are not harmed in a

vacuum, and well-being comes from participating in transforming the root causes of the harm within institutions. (Ginwright, 2018, para. 12)

Here, Ginwright proposes a framework for youth development that moves beyond the traditional individualistic approach to trauma, towards a more radical pedagogy that confronts systemic oppression and encourages collective healing. The teens we served in Richmond were living at the intersection of so many forms of violence—historical, environmental, communal, and interpersonal. We didn't shy away from these issues, but rather addressed them head-on through dialogue, curriculum, and public performances. We wanted our students to see the bigger picture and understand their positionality, so they could push for systemic change instead of accepting injustice, utilizing their art as a tool for social transformation.

While youth shared that the social justice-themed workshops and shows we produced felt empowering, we also realized that every poetry event we put on was heavy. We worried our students were re-traumatizing themselves and the audience with their pieces. We started integrating self-care practices and mental health awareness (e.g., trigger warnings, deep breathing, and guided meditations). We encouraged students to rewrite their trauma narratives and reclaim themselves—supporting them to see themselves as survivors, as authors of their own lives. This shift towards healing-centered engagement was reflected in the art we created: While our first few shows focused solely on the ways youth were impacted by poverty and the prison industrial complex, our later productions were much more complex and celebratory, exploring the powerful history of Richmond and encouraging community-building and self-love.

Donté

Finding joy in moments of struggle was the best part of being in RAW Talent. Our best self-care practice was laughter. Laughing at each other in a way that makes you feel part of a family, not isolated. I believe this made us feel closer, more human than teacher or student.

Acknowledging our turbulent past gave us context for the present. Moving forward, we questioned ourselves and pushed ourselves to reimagine what the future might be. Not 5 years from now, but tomorrow. Tomorrow makes the present moment more urgent. We taught about healthier food choices, brought different foods to our workshops, encouraged more water intake. We also kept self-care books on our desks and lent them out to RAW members whenever they wanted.

Molly

In 2014, the Making Waves after-school program closed and RAW Talent merged with the RYSE Center, becoming their current Performing Arts Program. In 2017, I found out Jeff Kass, my former poetry mentor, was retiring from the Neutral Zone, so I moved back to Ann Arbor to take over the Literary Arts Program that gave me a voice as a teen. Donté and I decided it was time to pursue new paths, and we left the program in the hands of several amazing staff at the RYSE Center, including Ciera-Jevae Gordon and Nyabingha Zianni McDowell—two of our past students who are now powerful community leaders in Richmond.

Often, when journalists and outsiders of our program tell the story of RAW Talent, they narrow it into an easily digestible White savior narrative, labeling Donté and our students as "at risk" and using a slew of other terms that pathologize them with deficit-based language. They'd have you believe that Donté needed me, when in reality I needed him. Having watched Jeff Kass build a poetry program from the ground up in Ann Arbor, I had a blueprint for how to create such a program. But Donté had his finger on the pulse of Richmond youth; he had the creative vision and he understood his community's needs in ways I could never know as an outsider.

Adults—White, middle-class educators in particular—need to reckon with our privilege. Instead of assuming what our students need, based on stereotypes, we have to actively listen and learn about their lived realities, cultures, dreams, and passions. We have to truly believe that the youth we work with have knowledge that we don't, and that their knowledge is necessary to our collective liberation. Then we must center their wisdom in our organizational mission, vision, values, infrastructure, and programming. This is how we work in authentic partnership with young people.

Donté

Recently I went back to North Richmond to visit some family, and found myself standing on the same corner where I spent so many days when I was young. That corner where so many ghosts remained screeching from the cracks of concrete, where the living dead roam. The place I'd known as my home had been turned into a war zone, and all of the men I looked up to as a teen had been either murdered or incarcerated. Had I continued following in their footsteps, I would be gone too.

Thinking back on those days, it hit me that I am now a legend to many. But instead of making money through drug-dealing, I am making music and poetry. I am making a living through my teaching and my art. I have become a new symbol of success in Richmond, and I try to use my path as an example for the youth I work with, to break them out of their belief that violence is the only way to express their anger, and hustling is the only way to get what we rightfully deserve. I wanted more than what these corners could offer me, and I know that there are other young people who want more, too.

Places like RAW Talent allow young people to discover their voices, write their realities, and be who they dream to be. These programs are homes for the abandoned hearts, shelters for those who feel unprotected. In the last 10 years, Richmond has changed. If more people get involved and invest in our youth, I believe we can transform our city into a more peaceful, positive, and creative community where young people feel safe enough to walk down the street, where they choose to pick up a pen instead of a gun.

NOTES

1. As described on its website (https://www.neutral-zone.org), Neutral Zone is "a diverse, youth-driven teen center dedicated to promoting personal growth through artistic expression, community leadership and the exchange of ideas" (para. 2).
2. According to its website (https://rysecenter.org/), RYSE is a teen center in Richmond, California that "creates safe spaces grounded in social justice for young people to love, learn, educate, heal, and transform lives and communities" (para. 1).

REFERENCES

Freire, P. (1970). *Pedagogy of the oppressed.* New York, NY: Continuum.

Ginwright, S. (2018, May 31). *The future of healing: Shifting from trauma informed care to healing centered engagement.* Retrieved from https://medium.com/@ginwright/the-future-of-healing-shifting-shifting-from-trauma-informed-care-to-healing-centered-engagement-634f557ce69c

hooks, b. (2000). *All about love: New visions* (1st ed.). New York, NY: William Morrow.

PICTURE OF JENNIFER

Arie Dowe

At Our Best, pages 117–118

The art teacher at my school helped me a lot with this painting. She inspired me to keep making art, and to want to continue to one day be an art teacher. She was a huge part of the process of creating this, and even went out of her way to bring in other artist friends she had. Our relationship is important because I—as a youth—need someone to look up to, to better myself and to one day do the same for others.

Bio: Arie Dowe enjoys the arts, theater, painting, and drawing. Arie takes art classes on Saturdays and spends a lot of time imagining future, past, and alternative lives.

RICANS WITH PRIDE

Arianna Ayala

At Our Best, pages 119–120

One day my mother talked to me about the Taíno blood in me. I had no clue what Taíno was. I asked my family and researched. I was fascinated with the culture, so I tried everything I could to best interpret it in my artwork. This started in school, but I decided to make it a personal project.

In my figure drawing class, I began to play with designs that came from Puerto Rico, which is where my dad and the majority of my family is from. My teacher noticed that this was different from my past artwork, seeing that I was being more personal, so she pushed me to experiment more with symbolism that resembled both Puerto Rico and Taíno Indians. After school, she would suggest that I take the portraits home and work on it more, to really take the time and see if what I used best represented my culture and myself. I really liked the outcome and it was fun being able to share my culture with other people. I am very thankful to that teacher for her support and giving me the confidence. I call the series "Ricans with Pride."

Bio: Arianna Ayala attended the Educational Center for the Arts—ACES in New Haven, Connecticut. She is now entering her first year at Lesley University's College of Art and Design.

CHAPTER 7

CARE/FUL KINSHIP

An Intergenerational Reflection on the Risks and Possibilities of Youth Work

Amanda Torres
Anna West

This chapter is co-written by Amanda Torres and Anna West, longtime collaborators in the field of grassroots youth arts organizing and education. In this chapter, we reflect on how reciprocal intergenerational relationships form inside of youth development contexts. Through the example of our relationship, we show how intergenerational relationships can be vital, transformative shelters, both deeply powerful and also precarious. We explore how intergenerational relationships can be sites of positive transformation, but are also potential places of exploitation, particularly when youth workers fail to reflect on their own power and engage in their own healing. This dynamic is complicated because the structures of youth organizations are deeply under resourced, and therefore unable to prioritize staff wellness. Ultimately, we discuss how—without necessary reflection—mirrored partnerships between youth and adults can lead to the exploitation of both youth and youth workers.

At Our Best, pages 121–135
Copyright © 2020 by Information Age Publishing
All rights of reproduction in any form reserved.

We begin this chapter by sharing our personal and shared histories, explaining how our lives intertwined through the years and our process of reflecting on our experiences. In Section II, we evoke the symbol of the mirror to discuss the way intergenerational relationships change over time and contribute to the process of shaping oneself alongside others. We then describe the ethics of this work in Section III, considering how these relationships can simultaneously surface trauma and healing for both youth and adults. Subsequently, in Section IV, we discuss how the intergenerational mirror is not merely about a series of individual relationships, it is also about the mirrored relationships between structures and selves. Ultimately, we argue that mirrored intergenerational relationships are the building blocks of youth organizations; therefore, these organizations are ineffective and potentially harmful if healthy and reciprocal intergenerational relationships are not prioritized.

MAPPING OUR STORY

Since 1999, when Anna was 23 and Amanda was 13, we have worked together, first as mentor and mentee, and now as peers. Our relationship is grounded in two decades of conversations, which have crisscrossed through the terrains of youth organizing, the ethics of mentorship, and gender dynamics within youth spoken word and arts organizing communities. These conversations, have centered on how to create compassionate, justice-oriented spaces for young people to make the selves and worlds they truly desire.

Amanda was 13 years old when she entered Young Chicago Authors (YCA), a youth arts community that would change the direction of her life. By age 17, her life was in an uncertain place; she had dropped out of high school and was living on her own without the support of family, and struggling to keep afloat. Anna was in her mid-20s, just married with a newborn son, and the director of YCA at the time, where she taught and mentored Amanda in various contexts. Anna invited Amanda to live with her to ease Amanda's struggle of making rent, provide some structure and accountability towards getting a GED, and to help Anna with childcare. Over the course of 3 years, Amanda attained her GED and founded the first youth advisory council at YCA. Through YCA, Anna and Amanda became close collaborators. In 2005, Anna left Chicago to move back to her hometown of Baton Rouge, Louisiana, where she co-founded what would later become Forward Arts, a youth arts nonprofit. Meanwhile, Amanda continued teaching and organizing in Chicago and got her associates degree in education.

In 2010, they both moved to Boston and back in with one another; Anna was getting her masters in arts education, and Amanda was exploring new professional opportunities. They continued to co-parent: both Anna's son as well as a burgeoning youth arts and social justice organization, MassLEAP. Anna left Boston after finishing her degree, and Amanda stayed to build MassLEAP into a youth nonprofit organization alongside a number of collaborators while she also worked as a teaching artist and organizer within multiple communities and academic institutions. Back in Baton Rouge, Anna got her PhD in English education and, with numerous collaborators, built Humanities Amped, a program aimed at transforming public schools into collaborative learning spaces that generate grassroots action towards social justice. Over the years, the two have stayed close friends and collaborators who have always found some way, big or small, to keep the conversation that began two decades ago going between them. This chapter is a continuation of that conversation.

In October 2018, we met to create a timeline of our relationship, reflecting on the key events and conversations that have shaped it. We felt it was important to use a participatory method, emphasizing how knowledge is constructed through lived experience that has been reflected upon.[1] We retold stories of our friendship to excavate personal tensions and growth that we have experienced over the past 20 years. Using our stories, we identified and analyzed themes we thought might resonate with others in the field of youth organizing. With those themes in mind, we began to write emails to one another over the next few months. Throughout this chapter, we share excerpts from our correspondences, along with our analysis of key themes that have shaped our reflections on intergenerational relationships.

INTERGENERATIONAL MIRRORING

We offer the symbol of a mirror as a way to represent how intergenerational relationships in youth development contexts take shape across time. Michel Foucault (1967/1984) explains:

> In the mirror, I see myself there where I am not, in an unreal, virtual space that opens up behind the surface; I am over there, there where I am not, a sort of shadow that gives my own visibility to myself, that enables me to see myself there where I am absent: such is the utopia of the mirror. (p. 72)

We view Foucault's utopic mirror as a way of understanding the presence of a reflected self. This reflection is not actually oneself, but rather, a projection; a space to imagine possible other ways of being. Foucault describes seeing oneself "over there, in a place where I am not;" we understand this as an imaginative leap to recover a lost self, or a possible future self. Though Foucault would not have used the word "desire," we understand this mirror as a reflection of desire, containing a knowledge that other, more desirable possibilities are obtainable.

Below, we share excerpts from our correspondence that narrate where we come from and how our lives became, and continue to be, reflected in one another's. We illustrate how we first constructed our sense of self in the reflection of our parents, and then how we chose to create a reflective space with each other.

> **Anna:** I was raised at the table where the grown folks sat peeling back endless layers of questions, just as we do now. They beat their hands on the table and said that everything must change. I remember the love that emanated inside of that reaching; it was a fire that warmed my own youth immensely. I am the child of all that, and in many ways we were both beneficiaries of some madly generous adults who sustained themselves somehow as they nurtured us when we were young. And yet, I also remember the long darknesses, the way my mother, a school teacher, would moan, "Lord, if I knew how to do any other work but this, I would do it," the bone exhaustion and periods of depression, the way she rose at 4 a.m. to study Paulo Freire and Dorothy Day because she was starving to be fed in the ways that she was feeding others. Through all of this, I remember thinking, "I never want that to be my life. Anything but that." And yet, it was the only life I could seem to make. Without trying, I made it again and again.
>
> **Amanda:** You grew up around the table. I grew up alone in my room, trying to know my parents through their absence. Both first and third generation Mexican immigrants who worked hard and late into the evening for our life. I was taught to be respectful of adults and engage in conversation but also not to take up space, to disappear into the background. I was raised to be self-sufficient, which meant that most of the time I was alone, and that was fine with me. I had so much space for dreaming when I was younger. Laying on the roof and staring up at the clouds for hours, imagining new worlds that could exist just beyond the sky, while the sounds of my neighborhood spilled upwards and my parents worked past dark. I am the child of books, of authors and their imaginations. I am a child of my mother's depression and her fearless imagining of a freer, wilder life for herself. The first time I felt seen was in a poetry circle at YCA. And I am a child of the mentors, the friends I found through

slam, the healing I found through poetry, the confidence I found through teaching, and the personhood I found through organizing. I am a daughter of so many, and it is important to name them all.

Anna: It's a funny thing how this works, how belonging to the same lineage means we hold each other's origins. When you describe this simple truth, "You grew up around the table," it is the most succinct biography of my own life I've ever read. And as I read your descriptions of the lonely house, the dream-world you found in books and looking up at clouds, your mother folded into the darkness of work she hated, and the stolen freedoms of singing alongside your father on the I-94 interstate, I'm like, damn, I hold these memories, they are sewn into my ribcage too, because I have inherited them from you. I remember the first time we began to really look to one another and see more than the roles we played as youth and mentor. We were at the national youth poetry slam festival, wide awake on the last day of the tournament, and we talked late into the night. Abuzz with the circle of what could be, staring up at the ceiling as we talked, the questions widened and widened as we explained our way across that space. I remember the recognition of who you truly were, a girl like me, afraid and full of doubts, but in whose reflection I could see some new angles of my own past and future self.

Amanda: Anna, I think, perhaps, I am the daughter of you. And you of me. It's a really special thing. You speak of seeing a little of yourself in me that first all-nighter in LA, and the same could be true for me. Except, I wouldn't say that I saw myself in you, I would say that I was in such incredible need. That I was searching for some kind of trustworthy adult as a way into or beyond myself. I was looking to be loved, and it felt like kinship between us. It was a mirror, yes, but like the Mirror of Erised in *Harry Potter and the Sorcerer's Stone* (Rowling, 1998). A mirror that showed me what I could be, it felt like possibility.

In the above correspondence, we describe how the origins of our relationship involved a mutual recognition in which we each saw the possibilities of recovered and future selves in one another. This recognition is at the heart of a mirroring relationship, which forms a basis for building kinship with one another.

Eve Tuck (2010), in an imagined argument with Gilles Deleuze, who himself argued with Foucault about the nature of desire, asserts that desire is agentive and wise. Tuck writes that desire "accumulates wisdom, picking up flashes of self-understanding and world-understanding along the way of a life" (p. 645). Tuck also understands desire as an expertise or wisdom that is produced by, and produces, intergenerational inheritances. She explains:

> This wisdom is assembled not just across a lifetime, but across generations, so that my desire is linked, rhizomatically, to my past and my future. It is in the way I can tell my grandmother's stories with as much fullness as I tell my own, a practice among many first peoples. (pp. 645–646)

Like Tuck's conception of her grandmother's stories as her own, our deep and long-standing relationship means that we inherit one another's life histories. Tuck's argument about desire as inheritance can be reapplied within a youth development context, asserting that kinship can be formed through chosen communities, thus queering the notion that memory is only passed through heteronormative family structures. Because we have chosen each other as kin, our histories are more than pieces of information that we possess about one another, indeed, they are a form of wisdom that profoundly shape our sense of who we are and who we might become.

Our personal histories and future desires are intertwined with those of the organizations in which we have both worked and helped to build. Within these organizations, mirrored individual histories and desires exceed the personal and take on a public dimension, forming a rhizomatic network in which many people may link histories and desires with one another. Because many young people come into youth organizations seeking supportive, caring networks, these organizations, and the relationships within them, can be sanctuaries in which it is possible to process trauma, learn, advocate for, and build another world.

THE ETHICS OF REFLECTION

Anna: When I look back to those early years at YCA, I can see more clearly now how I was operating from wounds I carried with me, unhealed, or just beginning to heal. It came to light two times in that period that young people at YCA had been assaulted by adults who were working at the organization. Even more stories surfaced in the years to come. As someone who was assaulted as a young person by an adult I knew and trusted, these violences landed heavily on my heart. I was totally unsatisfied by the official organizational response, even though I was part of forming that response. The culture of silence about rape felt like a physical presence in my body; I carried it deep within me, and did not know how to speak without finding myself caught further in a net of shame and silence. I began to understand that my experience alone did not make me someone who could facilitate healing, that I also had to come to recognize and unlearn the oppression I had internalized. I don't know if I would have ever had the courage to begin speaking about and healing my own wounds if I didn't see the larger, repeating narrative in the lives of young people whom I felt a responsibility to, young people like you, whom I wanted to be seen by as capable and whole.

Amanda: Anna, you and I both know that the kind of intimacy that occurs within relationships between young people and adults is an incredible, delicate, and dangerous thing. We have both witnessed how adults can be made sick by power, power they inflict on those more vulnerable than themselves—those like me when I was young and hungry for care, love, and kinship. As someone who was assaulted by a former mentor, I have devoted much of my life to creating loving, challenging, and safer spaces for young people. And yet, I think physical and emotional predatory behavior becomes even more possible within grassroots youth arts organizations where young people show up looking to be seen, respected, and in relationships with adult artists. In these spaces, we see young people as full, capable human beings; but young people are not adults, though they may be tasked with more responsibility than anyone should be. If adults ignore these differences in power, that's when abuse happens. Anna, we have talked exhaustively about this over the years, this link between the healing we have each had to do and the healing we want to see in the people and spaces we care about. How do the spaces we create mirror our own unprocessed traumas? How do we create more equitable relationships between youth and adults without pretending that adults don't have more power and influence?

As Amanda explains above, people working within grassroots youth organizations can too easily mistake the notion that young people are powerful and agentive with the notion that young people are the same as adults. This ignores the power and privileges that our society confers to adults, which, when overlooked, can lead to harm, including physical and emotional abuse. The power implicit in intergenerational relationships is not removed in a mirrored relationship, it is amplified. As a young person, you are far more vulnerable to the influence of an adult in whom you recognize a possible version of yourself, and as an adult, you are more likely to project your own unprocessed wounds onto a young person you see as a reflection of your younger self.

Anna further complicates this idea by considering some of the risks involved in the mirrored intergenerational relationship in which the mentor, who is ethically called to create a compassionate and reasonably safe space for the mentee, is acting out of an impulse to recover their own lost safety. This impulse is risky because without the awareness, resources, and stability needed to create our own reasonably safe spaces as mentors, we risk inviting youth into increasingly precarious, even harmful, relationships. Without critical reflection and a sense of boundaries to guide us, mirroring holds the possibility of passing on trauma that remains unchanged. Youth workers who think of themselves as "whole" and want to be seen that way by others must be willing to engage with their own wounds, even when it is deeply unsettling. Self-work is ongoing work for those of us in the profession of facilitating self-work with others.

In their discussion of public dialogues about race, Zeus Leonardo and Ronald K. Porter (2010) ask us to rethink the notion of safety by arguing that liberatory transformation always requires risk. They explain, "If it is a safe condition [that we seek], then it is the safety of being able to take risks, of putting oneself at risk" (p. 141). Ideally, an intergenerational mirror creates a sanctuary where people are "safe enough" with one another to be unsettled. The conditions of this safety require an acknowledgement by adults of the responsibility that comes from the power differentials within intergenerational relationships, an awareness of adults as people who are also works in progress. The intergenerational mirror is not a safe space insomuch as safety suggests complacency and negates a desire for change. Rather, as Leonardo and Porter suggest, the mirror requires a rigorous commitment to being unsettled in order to grow. Mentors who want to create reasonably safe spaces for young people must be willing to put themselves at risk by engaging in self-work. For organizations, this means doing the unsettling labor of reflecting honestly on the impact of abuse, and deepening our understanding of how our work is situated within a larger culture that perpetuates silence and abuses of power. Without this critical reflection at both individual and organizational levels, youth organizations do the opposite of what they intend to do, and as a result, young people are harmed.

In the following exchange, we show the importance of reciprocity to healthy mirrored intergenerational relationships.

Amanda: I was young, unrooted, and struggling to survive on my own when I came to live in your house to help take care of your son. And I know you worried that it was dangerous to bring me into a house already full with too many bodies and too little space as you barely held up the role of mother of a newborn, director of an organization just getting on its feet, and wife in a struggling marriage. But I wouldn't ever give up the memories of waking up every morning to Anton's small, fat hands on my face, bouncing around my room in his diaper. Loving him, having a small say in how he was raised, being responsible to him, gave me a focus I did not have before. He was so small, so tender-headed and doughy. How could I be less than my best self in his presence? He demanded me to love myself enough to love him. Anna, you inherited a large and inviting heart from your parents, and you used that heart to call me into a family so much softer than mine—even with its rough edges and hard times. I think this mother-like responsibility gave me the confidence and drive I needed to be a shaper of my own life and begin taking leadership within YCA at a time when it was hard to believe in myself.

Anna: I remember during that period driving myself to the hospital in the middle of the night thinking that I was having a heart attack. It took me years to understand that I was having a panic attack. I was in over my head at work, in a marriage that asked too much of me, a new mother in my mid-20s. But I thought I had to have it all together, and so I hid my own vulnerability even from myself. Now, looking back, I can see clearly how hard those years were, and how having you there helped me to see what I might have hidden from even longer—that I needed to learn how to protect myself, or I would never be able to protect the ones I love. You could see how much I was struggling in those times, and you were gentle with me. I remember your gaze on me, not judging, but wanting me to be safe. I internalized that gaze. In that way, it was good for me to love you, little sister, like I wanted to love myself.

The above dialogue demonstrates how our care, Anna for Amanda, and Amanda for Anna's son, created conditions through which our own need for wellness and healing were made visible through the other. The responsibility we felt for the safety and wellness of someone we understood as more vulnerable than ourselves, a younger person, called us into action, into a more ethical relationship with ourselves and who we could become. The process of transforming oneself and one's conditions does not happen in a silo. Self-work happens in relationship to others —often, because of others. An intergenerational mirror is an extremely rich form of relationship in which to do self-work because of the perceived vulnerability of the other and because of the ties of kinship in which care for the other is linked to care for oneself. In this way, the act of sheltering is mirrored reciprocally between youth and adults.

In a healthy youth organization, mirroring is not merely about individual relationships, but also expands through networks of relationships in which care for one another is cultivated and supported. Our relationship is just one example of how intergenerational mirroring can be a positive, motivating force in individual lives and within the collective work of larger communities. However, this is not without significant struggle. We discuss these struggles, and the structural dynamics of youth organizations that shape them, at length in the following section.

REFLECTING AND RESISTING OPPRESSIVE STRUCTURES

Amanda: Science fiction writer and luminary Octavia Butler (1995) writes, "Positive obsession is about not being able to stop just because you're afraid and full of doubts. Positive obsession is dangerous. It's about not being able to stop at all" (p. 133). My entire life in Boston was Mass LEAP, every connection, every street corner was connected to the work of youth organizing. The last 2 years working at Mass LEAP, I became so tired and disengaged. I thought it was a long overdue burnout and began looking for an exit plan. Last year, I went to the doctor for the first time in my adult life. I have lived without health insurance for as long as I can remember. This could be seen as irresponsibility... which it might be. It could also be the result of a lack of knowledge, resources (for both me and the adults in my life) and a positive obsession that didn't require me to care for myself in the ways it required me to care for others. After going to the doctors, I was diagnosed with a chronic illness.

In my worst moments, I am afraid that the work I have spent the entirety of my life doing, I won't be able to continue doing because of my health. Sometimes, I am angry at my body because it won't do the things I need it to do or that need to be done. Other times, I am angry at this work that asks more of me than I can give. I am constantly advocating in the spaces I build and work in—the organizations, the collectives, the interpersonal relationships—for more accessibility. But what does accessibility look like in a field that asks you to stay for a 5-hour planning meeting? Or can only meet in the evenings if you require childcare? Or to work without a living wage? Or healthcare? This is the world we live in. We exist under the same oppressive systems that the young people we serve do. And so how would it be possible for us to provide safety for them if it is not a safe place for us?

Anna: Youth work can be all consuming, so can organizing and teaching in schools and grassroots youth organizations. I've spent my working life navigating and surviving these systems. Sometimes I think that standing in this work, being this work, even, is the most exhilarating life I could ever have. Other times, like today, a Sunday, when I wish I were a leaf floating down a stream, it feels cruel to have brokered nothing more than a tightrope, no real safety net below for me or the ones I love. I look up now in middle age and understand my choices differently—the fact that my decades of work in grassroots youth nonprofits now means having no retirement, no savings, my own school debt looming large even as Anton heads to college in a little more than a year. Like many people, I was raised to believe that being educated and working hard would create some foundation on which I could one day slow down, as my body and spirit desire, but I know now that they do not. The love and community created through this work is real, but so is the exhaustion. As I grow older, I worry more and more about the toll it takes on my family, on my aging body, on my ability to find reasonable boundaries so that I can sustain myself. I love this work. I know it is life changing, for me and so many people, and still I am afraid that I won't be able to stay alive within it.

Our dialogue in this section reflects the exhaustion, burnout, and lack of care for self that is particularly high among youth workers who labor within grassroots, justice-oriented organizations. Within a capitalist economy that fundamentally does not value youth work, youth workers are in an impossible bind in which being effective too often requires working without proper resources: a living wage, health insurance, sufficient staffing, and professional development, to name a few. How do we change conditions for youth workers in order to prevent passing on unsustainable ways of being in this work from one generation to the next?

Poet and disability justice theorist, Kay Ulanday Barret (2018), discusses:

We are told above all: to produce. We are taught the American way of work hard enough and eventually, glory. We are taught as poets that writing is a labor of constant output, of competition, corporatized or circulated with the goals of able-bodied exceptionalism deeply out of touch with the realistic systemic impacts of oppression ... (n.p.)

Barrett explains how the American myth of hard work tells us that we are only as good as what we produce. This mythology upholds oppressive, ableist norms. This oppression is internalized by youth workers and institutionalized by youth organizations within which advocating and caring for oneself can too easily be seen as "unproductive," whereas advocating and caring for others is legitimized as "productive." This complicates our assertion that ethical, reflective intergenerational relationships, rooted in care for the other, lead to healthy, beneficial outcomes for both youth workers and youth, because being committed to relationships that are not valued by the prevailing system can put both youth and youth workers at risk of being harmed or burning out.

The challenge of wellness for youth workers is compounded by the fact that youth work itself is considered "unproductive" under the prevailing logics of neoliberalism.[2] From this point of view, spaces for intergenerational care and learning are deemed a luxury; therefore, youth work (this is especially true for youth *arts* organizations) is considered "unproductive" labor.[3] The resulting lack of investment in youth organizations, especially those that challenge neoliberal assumptions, put an unbelievable pressure on people who choose to organize, mentor, teach, and somehow attempt to make a living in a chronically underfunded field, which routinely asks more of the people engaged in the work than they can possibly provide. The unsustainability of youth work is a systemic form of exploitation.

Though community care existed long before the field of youth work, many recognize youth services in the United States as having its origins in the settlement house movement started by Jane Addams and Ellen Star, who were both wealthy White women (Kwon, 2013). And to this day, we argue that the field continues to be structured as if everyone were a wealthy White woman for whom basic needs like healthcare, a living wage, supporting a family, and retirement are not pressing concerns. Able-bodied youth workers in their 20s, like Anna was when she began to mentor Amanda in this work, unintentionally normalize and model working conditions that are unsustainable for people who are not holding some forms of privilege. We have begun to understand this exploitation as a condition that is, in some senses, inherited from one generation of youth worker to the next.

Ongoing exploitation creates a sense of scarcity for people working in the field of youth work. One outcome of scarcity is that a competitive dynamic can emerge, disrupting the sense of sanctuary and solidarity present within mirrored intergenerational relationships. Our professional and personal relationship have been so closely intertwined that we have needed to step back and take stock many times to ask who we are now in comparison to who we were before. Now that we are in our early 30s and 40s, our 10-year age difference does not mean as much as it once did, though earlier in our lives, this age difference meant that tensions surfaced regularly. We have had to constantly negotiate the gaps in our power, experience, racial identities, and positionalities. There have been numerous moments while co-teaching or organizing together when our instincts were opposing, but we needed to make choices together anyway. In these moments, we struggled with each other in ways that often made the work harder and less productive. Eventually, through many vulnerable conversations and over time, we learned to stick it out and be more intentional about sharing power, avoiding competition, and celebrating what the other brings to the table.

While neither of us enjoys yielding to the other, we recognize that the struggle for power and recognition is not just about our individual personalities, but rather it is a byproduct of working in a field that demands more of us than we can possibly provide. Understanding that these tensions are the products of larger systems helps us to redirect conflict that would be turned inward, or towards one another, at the larger structures that frame our work. Instead of standing against one another, we stand beside one another in solidarity, reflecting the gaze of unjust systems back onto themselves (Fine, 2008, p. 226). This reflective space is a sanctuary that helps us to grapple with a question that remains important in our current work: *How do we speak in more honest and open ways about the costs of this work, resist internalizing the invisibility of our "unproductive" labor, and assert the essential worth of intergenerational care?* The difficulty of this question is its own form of positive obsession that we trace and retrace so that we may experience a continued mirrored and mirroring wellness, even as our bodies age, even as we face disability, even as our gendered and raced labor remains just below visibility within the circuits of empire.

CONCLUSION: FINDING REFUGE

In this chapter, we argue that mirrored intergenerational relationships are at the heart of youth work, invoking networks of kinship and transformative wellness for both youth workers and youth alike. We explore the risks of youth work when dynamics of power are overlooked and when youth organizations fail to engage in ethical reflection that is both personal and structural in nature. We confront systemic injustices that leave the field of youth work vastly under-resourced and perpetuate a cycle of exploitation.

Finally, we explore how critical reflection creates a refuge in which youth organizations can grapple with these structures.

Our letter exchanges speak to both the vulnerabilities and the sanctuaries that are invoked within youth work and call upon our connectedness as an indispensable resource. The grassroots youth poetry and educational organizations that we have spent our lives building insist, in unison with Audre Lorde (1984), that "poetry is not a luxury" (p. 37), and that networks of intergenerational care are essential to our survival. The intergenerational relationships to which we belong have created homes for us, essential sanctuaries that are sources of both strength and connection that extend far beyond ourselves and into the structures that we participate in making. The struggle to create more just and sustainable conditions will not be over anytime soon, but neither will the sense of love and kinship that grow from it.

NOTES

1. Participatory methods pose a "radical epistemological challenge to the traditions of social science, most critically on the topic of where knowledge resides" (Fine, 2008, p. 215). In other words, participatory methods presume critical knowledge to be located not solely among few legitimized "experts," but rather, among people whose experiential knowledges too often remain unauthorized by formal gatekeeping institutions and modes of knowing.
2. Neoliberalism, a term coined by David Harvey (2004) argues that all forms of public value are converted into private wealth through the capitalist marketplace.
3. This nonproductivity is further reinforced by associating youth work, like other forms of intergenerational care, with feminized labor, thus rendering it largely invisible.

REFERENCES

Butler, O. (1995) Positive obsession. In *Bloodchild and other stories.* (pp. 125–135). New York, NY: Seven Stories Press.

Fine, M. (2008) An epilogue, of sorts. In J. Cammarota & M. Fine (Eds.), *Revolutionizing education: Youth participatory action research in motion.* (pp. 213–234). New York, NY: Routledge.

Foucault, M. (1984) Of other spaces: Utopias and heterotopias (J. Miskowiec, Trans.). *Architecture, Mouvement, Continuité, 5,* 69–83. (Original work published 1967)

Kwon, S. A. (2013). *Uncivil youth: Race, activism, and affirmative governmentality.* Durham, NC: Duke University Press.

Harvey, D. (2004). The 'new' imperialism: Accumulation by dispossession. *Socialist Register, 40,* 63–87.

Leonardo, Z., & Porter, R. K. (2010). Pedagogy of fear: Toward a Fanonian theory of "safety" in race dialogue. *Race, Ethnicity And Education, 13*(2), 139–157.

Lorde, A. (1984). *Sister outsider: Essays and speeches.* Trumansburg, NY: Crossing Press.

Rowling, J. K. (1998). *Harry Potter and the sorcerer's stone.* New York, NY: Random House.

Tuck, E. (2010). Breaking up with Deleuze: Desire and valuing the irreconcilable. *International Journal of Qualitative Studies in Education, 23*(5), 635–650.

Ulanday Barrett, K. (2018). *Poetry as offering: To practice in poetry & live in the body-mind.* Retrieved from https://www.vidaweb.org/poetry-as-offering-to-practice-in-poetry-live-in-the-body-mind/

SECTION III

ON ORGANIZATIONAL PRACTICES

CHAPTER 8

PROFILES, KEY MOMENTS, AND A CONTINUUM OF YOUTH-LED PARTICIPATION

An Inclusive Model of Youth Development Work

Pegah Rahmanian
Rhode Island College

Youth in Action (YIA) is housed in an old New England four-story home on the Southside of Providence. The building has no shortage of narrow hallways, each of which opens to a large, cozy room, painted in warm colors and filled with couches. The hallways are lined with photos from two decades of programming, creating the feel of a memory portal; it is always a conversation starter when guests visit. There are very few doors at YIA, and fittingly, the ones that do exist are either made of glass or don't fully close. What this lends itself to for all 75 youth, 3 full-time staff, and 2–3 interns is a shared experience. We playfully tease one another about things being a "*we* problem"—that one person's actions are all of ours. *If you make a scene,*

At Our Best, pages 139–155
Copyright © 2020 by Information Age Publishing

I'mma make a scene. While there are no secrets at YIA, there are private moments—times when folks grapple with religion, sexuality, death, and challenging family dynamics. Those moments are sacred, even when the doors don't close fully; they are respected and protected by the YIA family.

At YIA, there is always music playing, loudly, weaving in and out of conversations and laughter, welcoming anyone to join in whether or not they can hold a beat. The music follows us wherever we go, an homage to the 1980s boombox and hip-hop culture in urban communities. At any given moment, there is a display of love and joy: a hug, big-belly laughter, tears of a long day followed by a feast of snacks, pop-up dance parties. Youth in Action is a constant amp-up. When programming ends, youth spill out onto the porch and sidewalk. On the side of the building is a mural designed and painted by YIA youth and staff: two youth helping each other lay bricks that create the foundation of a tree (see Figure 8.1). Underneath the tree are the words "Youth Lay the Foundation. Providence Grows."

Figure 8.1 Mural at Youth in Action building, Providence, Rhode Island.

Founded in 1997, in the wake of a major infrastructural and cultural re-vitalization in Providence, YIA was among the local pioneers of "youth-led" work. The organization became a flagship for centralized youth organizing efforts, responding to the most urgent and critical needs of the community. "Nothing About Us, Without Us, Is for Us,"[1] was our primary call of action in the early days.

Over the years, YIA has been curated to create the kind of youth–adult relationships that honor the wisdom of intergenerational work. We always operated with the understanding that to work in a silo would alienate our young people and be counterproductive to systemic change. We value vul-nerability and transparency, lean into discomfort and taboo, work to dis-rupt conventional notions of love and replace them with radical ones. All of our work aims to reiterate our central values of collaboration, cooperation, and a collective power.

In youth program design work, rarely are new models developed within communities of color. Instead, communities of color are the recipients of models that tend to have a clinical approach rather than a creative one. I have worked in some of the most vibrant communities—Chicago, New Orleans, Oakland, and now Providence—and always in pockets of poverty, often with communities of color. I have always been a brown queer wom-an, a daughter of immigrants, doing this work; my colleagues have always been folks of color, oftentimes from the neighborhoods we have served. And yet, I have struggled to articulate the importance of this in the spaces provided—in the grants that ask what populations we serve, the statistics that require us to list the odds we're beating, or the stories that pull at your heart strings. This story of *who* we work with is intrinsically important to the work; it defines it. And yet, too often work in marginalized communi-ties is regarded with a caveat, "This is great for a program that works with that population." The caveat undermines the quality of the work as simply, "great." In all of the work that we do, we weave this notion of "best selves" into the narrative. We ask each individual, youth and adult, to be the best versions of themselves, and, in so doing, our youth and adults demand the same from the organization itself.

In this chapter, I will talk about how YIA builds youth voice and notions of best selves through a scalar model that works from the individual outward to the ideological. The heart of this model creates a space where youth and adults can be vulnerable and brave, alongside one another. Youth in Action is seeking to redefine what youth-led leadership looks like through a model that aims to develop their skills and sense of self by engaging in different forms of leadership through participation.

CONTEXT: OUR APPROACH

Youth in Action is a youth development organization that specifically supports young people in Rhode Island's frontline communities. We define frontline communities as those suffering from a disproportionate share of social, economic, and environmental burdens. Our youth come from predominantly immigrant families, communities of color, and working-class backgrounds and are often confronted with the message that they are inherently inadequate, either because they are dealing with more challenge or because they have fewer resources than others. This message comes in the form of scarcely resourced schools, mass incarceration, over criminalization, and geographically-isolated poverty. With a lens on social justice and the intent to undo internalized, institutional, and ideological oppression, YIA offers a different message to our youth: *It is not our youth that are inadequate, rather it is structural imbalances of power that limit their opportunities.* Our aim is to demonstrate that systemic social change is possible, and that youth *are* and *will* be the agents of this change. By building power, leadership, and action among youth in frontline communities, we believe a more equitable and safer world is possible.

Youth in Action is one of many "youth development" or "youth leadership" organizations in Providence; this concentration of like-minded organizations has forced YIA to define its identity and role in the local youth development landscape. Doing this has required a youth–adult collective defining what youth development means, generally speaking, and then articulating how that understanding is reflected in our mission and work. Youth in Action is committed to being a place where youth share their stories, practice leadership, and create change in their communities: that is, we *share, lead, change.* For YIA, youth development means nurturing a brave space that is curated to provide practice and reflection for young people, such that they may safely explore cognitive and social/emotional milestones in their development. These milestones include their ability to: reason, think more abstractly and hypothetically, make decisions, develop a set of ethics, offer and experience peer acceptance, develop a sense of self, articulate emotion, and explore their social and sexual selves. If young people can *share* in this experience together, we believe they can better *lead* their lives, and ultimately *change* their circumstances. This is important given that our youth are often told through the multiple institutions they interact with that they have limited agency over their lives.

Although many programs seek to foster positive youth development[2] among youth of color and those growing up in poverty, rarely do these programs create the space and support for people to examine the structural causes behind the mental and physical pain they have experienced. Often, we save these difficult conversations for college-aged students, but we need to be starting earlier. Even less often do youth have the opportunity to begin to heal and to develop and lead efforts for community empowerment. The *space* to examine, heal, and mobilize around internalized racism is the hardest to define and cultivate, because it is uncomfortable, and it is messy. It deals in human emotion and it requires and demands a bravery to lean into the places and conversations from which we all shy. Instead, YIA holds these discussions as journeys for which we have been waiting. At YIA, we build and reflect on our understanding of positive youth development to create critical consciousness, agency, and power among our young people.

Our collaborative and cooperative values guide both our programmatic outcomes and our external partnerships across the New England region. For example, these values motivated our multi-year, collaborative work on the Youth 4 Change (Y4C) Alliance,[3] which helped to launch a youth movement and elevate young people as critical thinkers and decision makers. The alliance created new ways for organizations, youth, and adults to collaboratively spearhead projects and campaigns. It strove to create a community where young people were acknowledged and elevated as powerful leaders for change. It imagined a critical mass of youth leaders transforming policies and systems, our collective actions changing a culture of complacency and fear to one of progress, hope, and action. In solidarity, young people brought about positive, concrete, and sustainable change through direct action, organizing, advocacy, governance, and other forms of civic participation. The culmination of that work was a Youth Bill of Rights, which was ultimately signed by local politicians and stakeholders.

All of YIA's work begins and ends with the question: *Who are you?* This question asks youth to locate themselves in a society where they are often marginalized. Through this exploration, they better understand the possibility of change and the power of connection, whether on an individual, collective, or global level. The answer to this question "Who are you?" becomes a tool for change; it facilitates the building of ethical codes that shape the ways youth engage with the world around them; and it provides a starting point from which they can move toward their goals. So often as a society we focus on where we want our youth to end up, we talk about goals and destinations; but if we don't take the time to name where we are starting, then those goals can feel like abstract destinations without clear pathways. When you work with young people, you begin to understand that youth often express themselves using languages of anger or sadness. Although they can be unpredictable, these emotions are treasures; it is in these emotions that we find new pieces of our identity.

In recent years, YIA has developed and honed a programmatic structure that facilitates conversation, participation, healing, and collective power in community, as described below. Core to this framework is the scaffolding of participation and inquiry, the integration of critical consciousness, and a commitment to collective action. This framing of the work extends into all areas of organizational culture, including strategic thinking, fundraising, crisis management, programming, and relationship building. Positive youth development is not limited to the work an organization does with the young people; it is a framework that informs the approach to all other actions. Youth developers have many roles at YIA—administrative assistants, grant writers, youth workers, finance brokers—but we share a common approach. To be a youth developer means to be playful, to lean into the uncomfortable, to take risks, challenge the status quo, and to value relationships and connections. Positive youth development is more than a set of skills, it is a set of ethics. For example, when we fundraise at YIA, we do so with the same set of ethics that we facilitate programming: We are creative, we think outside the box, we are genuinely curious, and we invite others to join us in the work. By integrating the ideologies that guide our programming into the operations of our organization, our message is consistent and clear; it pushes adults and youth alike, to examine the causes behind the confusion of growing up, particularly as related to poverty and structural racism.

The Youth-in-Action Model

The YIA model is based on a 4-year process that ideally follows youth from their first year of high school through their senior year. The model and curriculum is designed with different types of learning in mind: service learning, project-based learning, adventure learning, scaffolded learning, and inquiry-based learning. The trajectory through YIA begins with recruitment, which takes place starting in the middle of April and stretches to the beginning of June. A young person may hear about YIA in many ways: through a friend, a family member, another program, the Providence After School Alliance, or a YIA staff member's presentation in their classroom. Every year we receive over 100 applications and accept about 60. Youth are asked to answer three questions: (a) "Who are you?"; (b) "What other activities are you involved in?"; and (c) "What is one challenge you've had to face, and how did you move through it?" The questions are designed to give us three pieces of information: How *willing* are youth to find their voice? Is this a program they will be able to commit to fully and completely? And, most importantly, do they have the capacity to be vulnerable and reflective? We are looking less at their writing ability and more for that kernel of vulnerability and truth-telling that emerges even in the most fragmented essay. After multiple days of reviewing applications and considering both the individuals and the group dynamic, YIA staff select 60 youth to join the newest cohort of YIA. Youth development is often a retention game that starts from the onset, and our retention rates reflect the intention in our application strategy:

- Retention rates for YIA programming week to week: 97%
- Retention rates for YIA programming over the course of a year: 95%
- Retention rates for YIA programming over the course of 4 years: 92%

In order to receive 100 applications, we make sure to hand out at least 1200 applications. From that starting point, we apply the half rule: Half of those 1,200 applications will end up in the trash, half of the remaining will go home, but never get filled out. That leaves us with 300 potential applications. Of those 300 applications, only half will actually get submitted. In selecting applications, we again accept more than we need knowing that some will have lost interest. On average, of the 60 youth accepted into the program, 40 show up to the mandatory parent/guardian meeting, and then of those that show, only 30 will actually attend the orientation. After the orientation, we assume that at least five will drop off with the start of school. From that original 60, we are left with 25 youth and we know that with the start of school and the talk of the YIA orientation we will get applications from about 7 youth interested in joining. This means that every year we start a new cohort of about 30–35; these youth have made a significant commitment to the application process and, as a result, have a higher rate of completing their 4-year journey through YIA. In this application process, you never know which youth you may have overlooked, and which you've accepted that end up stepping away from YIA, so you decipher a baseline through applications, set an expectation of commitment through the parent orientation, and gauge a level of engagement in the orientation to ensure some consistency and stability for the cohort of youth.

The Start of the Journey: Orientation

Once the application process is complete, youth begin a 4-year journey that starts with a grant-funded, 2-week orientation in the late summer, a few weeks before school starts. The first of the 2 weeks is a practice in wilderness, a YIA rite of passage in the White Mountains of New Hampshire. In partnership with the AMC's Youth Opportunities Program,[4] YIA sets off into the mountains equipped with enough camping gear for 40 people—a mix of youth, staff, and volunteers. The group sets up camp, complete with tents, tarps, and a makeshift kitchen area. Our youth, most of who have never been beyond their own backyard, put the camp together almost entirely themselves and spend the next week using pit toilets, walking a quarter of a mile to fill the water jugs, and preparing all of their own food. We play team building games, summit a 3,100 foot mountain, orienteer, and every night around the fire, our youth begin to offer their voices and their stories to the family we're creating together.

This trip is unique to YIA and is critical to the type of youth leadership development that happens back in Providence. It's a practice in trust, in vulnerability, in risk-taking, and most certainly in being uncomfortable. The experiences and bonds that are created over the course of that week in the mountains are transformative for youth and adults alike. There is a magic that happens in shared and cultivated discomfort. The hike to a nearby summit offers youth the idea of possibility, and the experience of challenge. The management of the campsite translates into shared ownership of space—the idea that we're creating space together and holding that space in respect. Team building, often dismissed as trivial, becomes the portal to imagination and playfulness and serves as an opportunity for the youth to creatively fill the uninterrupted time. For the orienteering activity, youth are split into smaller groups, and unattended in the woods, they are asked to find their way back with only a compass and a set of directions. This provides a true and authentic sense of independence and capability. The orienteering portion of the trip is toward the end and takes place only after a trust has been created with the adults and among each other. Though students are meant to rely on one another and are told adults aren't accompanying them, there is an inherent trust that the adults would not ask youth to take such a risk without ensuring a safe parameter. Finally, the fire circle at night is a reminder that whenever as a group we circle together, no matter where we are, there is a fire at the center of us, holding our secrets and cleansing our hurt, celebrating our achievements, and giving life to our stories.

When the group returns from the woods, there is a culture established that is contagious. The second week of the orientation is held at YIA, where we can transpose the experience in the mountains into the building, while still holding the momentum and joy from outside. During that week, youth translate camp management into community agreements, map skills into scavenger hunts across the city, and build pop-up dance parties. The "hike" turns into projects that have to be completed, and the "fire" morphs into conversations about identity. The YIA orientation is the secret sauce to our work: Filled with ritual and tradition, it is a piece of the work that we come back to again and again. In their fourth year at YIA, a small handful of youth return to the trip as mentors, reliving the experience from a different vantage point, supporting the newest youth in their journey.

UNDERSTANDING, SUPPORTING, AND TRACKING POSITIVE YOUTH DEVELOPMENT AT YOUTH IN ACTION

When adults talk about "youth-led" work, we often disregard the adult role, placing the burden of success on young people. Youth in Action doesn't believe that to make youth voices visible you have to make the adult role invisible. Instead, we offer the notion of "best selves," suggesting that transformational relationships between adults and youth open up possibility (Cohen, 2017). We do this through differentiating our unique curriculum in ways that honor and strengthen young peoples' identities and define pathways. By personalizing our program for students based on several different dimensions, we enable them to practice life and leadership skills, and innovate to lead community-change. The success of YIA's model is characterized by, and assumes, the kind of staff that are deeply in tune and connected to each young person. Staff who can pay close attention to their social emotional well-being, clearly identifying and naming the programmatic "key moments" that are necessary for each young person's growth, and fulfilling their role in the rearing and inspiring of each young person with conviction. The success is also embedded in each young person's deliberate choice to return to the program every week, their capacity for vulnerability, and their willingness to value reflection and growth. In tandem, adults and youth each contribute critical pieces to make the model, and the pedagogy that informs it, comes alive.

The program model uses several different metrics that help us to assess youth needs and growth across different domains and dimensions. Staff begin by considering each young person's readiness to *participate in the different levels of leadership*, which forms their *youth profile*. Next, we use *key moments* to push youth out of their comfort zones and help them to experiment with new approaches. Finally, we measure growth over time across a set of *outcomes* that were determined collectively by YIA youth and adults.

THE STAGES OF PARTICIPATION

With the start of school also begins the second leg of the journey for youth at YIA. This work is designed around multiple forms of youth participation that include: adult-led, youth–adult partnership, and youth-led. Broadly, the trajectory scaffolds participation so that students are growing their skills in order to do work that is predominately youth-led. But, it isn't necessarily a straight line. That is, they are doing all forms of participation from the moment they come through the door, so that they are practicing leadership all the time. Imagine each type of participation as a continuum, expanding and contracting, giving growth the permission to move fluidly, and dismissing the idea of absolute. It is also possible that while a young person may be in a particular participation-dominated experience, they are still receiving opportunities to practice the other participations. For instance, if a youth is in adult-led programming, they are still expected to step into youth-led practices that have been adjusted to adult-led participation. In this way, we

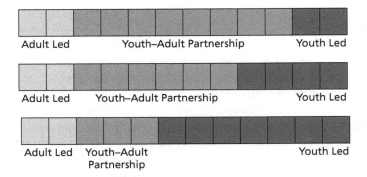

Figure 8.2 Different modes of moving through the participation trajectory.

set our youth up to succeed and continue to succeed as they move along the trajectory (see Figure 8.2).

The first year builds upon the work started during the wilderness orientation. All new students participate in what we call *Core*. Core is adult-led and, as indicated above, serves as a foundation for youth to build a strong sense of self tied to a broader set of identities. The adult-led work is limited and highly structured. This is for two reasons: The first is that the structure encourages weekly commitment to the organization and the second is that it fosters purpose. Its content is designed to encourage youth to experiment with different types of leadership through participation. Core meets as a cohort once a week for 3 hours. Staff facilitate workshops that begin with an exploration of self and then move to deeper and harder conversations about internalized racism and identity politics. We utilize forms of communication including storytelling, interviewing, mapping, and public exhibitions. While everyone who joins YIA has to participate in Core, it is designed to be accommodating to different levels of leadership, allowing some youth to take a more active role and others the space and time to find their individual voices. We find that some youth move very quickly along the trajectory from adult-to-youth led, while others move at a steady pace, and some remain in one type of participation until the final months at YIA and then suddenly jump forward, growing into the deepest kinds of engagement quickly.

The second and third years of youth work at YIA, are designed around youth–adult partnerships called *Immersion*. Immersion is grounded in the practice of collaboration. This experience is often the least structured because the partnership means that no one person is taking ownership, so both the youth and the adult are contending with what it means to collaborate. Youth–adult partnering is one of the more challenging passages of growth, because of the oscillating dynamics of agency and collaboration.

Both of these experiences aim to foster a sense of the personhood of the youth while also contending with broader social issues. While Core aims to address internalized racism and oppression, Immersion works to understand institutional oppression. Learning to authentically partner youth and adults around movement building also means being willing to endure the challenges that arise when facing institutions that one cannot change alone. The work that our adults and youth take on in Immersion tend toward opportunities through community partnerships on issues of outdoor equity, faith as resistance, education liberation, language justice, and health advocacy.

The last year of leadership growth, called *Collective*, celebrates the youth's independence and skill as a leader. For us, youth-led does not mean closed sessions where adults are absent, where agendas are entirely designed by youth, or raw and unfiltered soliloquies. For YIA, youth-led means that a young person is comfortable in their own skin (developed through the last 2–3 years). Based on the work they have been doing, these youth are able to take ownership in designing and implementing work. They are comfortable organizing large-scale events that demand a clear sense of vision, they are comfortable carrying culture and setting a tone in their mentorship, they are comfortable facilitating a room full of people, and they do all this with courage, conviction, and vulnerability.

YOUTH PROFILES

Early on in Core, staff begin to build a youth profile for each youth. These are informed by the kind of questions the young person asks as they begin to explore who they are and how they fit into the world around them. Staff also take into account the way in which the youth participates in the leadership activities, and how comfortable they feel when given more autonomous roles. For instance, a youth who is Profile A tends to ask "Yes/No" questions and thrive in an adult-led space. A youth who is Profile B tends to ask "how" questions and works best in a youth-adult partnership. Finally, a youth who is Profile C tends to ask "what if" questions and is their best self when they have total ownership of their experience. The aim is to find which profile best suits each youth, and within that profile provide an experience in which the young person is growing and pushing the boundaries for themselves. This is why, even though each year is designed to provide the youth with a growing sense of ownership, it isn't necessarily a straightforward model. Some youth need more time, others take off like a rocket. The profiles help us be attuned to the needs of different youth, no matter what that year looks like (e.g., Core or Immersion). Each profile has a series of key moments that help trigger their growth, which I will go into further in the next section.

Three profiles alone don't capture the growth some of our youth experience transitioning from one profile to another during their time at YIA. For this reason, in practice, we have developed closer to seven profiles and use the three primary ones as anchors. The profiles are not simply skill sets that determine a young person's strengths, they are blueprints for entire ways of engaging with the world. Each profile takes into consideration challenge points, strengths, pathways, needs, self-actualized moments, relationships needed with adults, communication styles, responsiveness to structure or repercussions, and how they relate to their peers and to their family. Profiles not only support our young people to focus their development and allow the organization to be more effective in the kind of experiences we're providing, but they also make it possible to serve 75 youth and make each of them feel seen and understood. Operationally, the profiles function as seven executions of 75 personality types. Below is an example of a profile written by staff, and informed by the close observation of a young person at YIA, over the course of 4 years. This profile works for a youth that asks "how" and "what if" questions, oscillating between youth–adult partnerships and youth-led spaces. It should be noted that there are two or three sub profiles that fall under this category, each showing a different side or dimension of the anchor profile.

> Logistically and practically geared, needs some structure to succeed. Considers all information in order to make a decision. They are inquisitive. They frequently misunderstand others or are misunderstood themselves and find support in their adult allies to help translate, though as they mature in this profile they learn to do this for themselves more naturally. "That's what I said" is a common phrase they say. There is sometimes a disconnect between language and thoughts. Loves to be silly and is a performer, is witty and clever because they are very observant, but honors time and place for silliness. It is important for them to come across as cool, calm, and collected. They are not reactive, instead they are very calculating and thoughtful. Unexpected situations can derail them in a moment. When a situation arises, space and time are valued before a response is given. They are hard on themselves, but value feedback framed in an asset-based way. Perfectionism/detail-oriented. Intentional and successful with communication when given a project, especially mentoring. Loyal to the work, achievement, and self-growth. Works within a system and values rules, holds very strong ethical codes. Doesn't hold grudges. Fear of unknown, likes control, is self-critical (good about knowing what they need or want). Framing is absolutely necessary. Has self-set high expectations and may have a background of feeling invisible or not affirmed. Fear of being criticized, but asks for critical feedback.

The profiles provide a broad stroke and insight into our young people, making it possible to establish a solid foundation and relationship early on. However, the profiles alone don't facilitate a young person's growth in participation. The information a profile can provide paired with the appropriate experiences and opportunities, or key moments, accelerate the process of growth.

KEY MOMENTS

To guide youth through their journey and across the continuum of participation and leadership, there are a series of programmatic *key moments* that trigger the development of their best selves. Key moments are points of engagement that deepen a young person's experience. They are moments that we actively facilitate so that growth may take place. There are five types of key moments: *transactional, decision-based, encounters, reflections,* and *crisis or adventure* (see Table 8.1).

There are some key moments that are intentionally repetitive throughout a young person's time at YIA, in order to support their development. Other key moments appear at the right time and place, and still others we know will happen but have little control over when (especially crisis moments). While a young person may experience all five types of key moments, there might be some that are more powerful given the type of profile they have. For instance, young people that fall under Profile C (most inspired by asking "what if" questions in youth-led spaces), may completely transform with a crisis/adventure key moment, whereas a decision moment doesn't bear as much power. Young people that are Profile B (most comfortable asking "how" questions in youth–adult partnerships) often feed off of transactional moments, whereas reflection moments don't have the

TABLE 8.1	Types of Key Moments
Transactional Points	Relationship-based moments, e.g., a key conversation, application process, performance review, promotion, or awarding of more responsibility
Decision Points	Situations that require youth to find an alternative way forward, e.g., forced decision-making, choosing a small group, curating exhibits, participation in YIA extracurricular activities, or time commitment priorities
Encounter Points	Meeting new people or learning new ideas that inspire or provide insight, e.g., attending conferences, anything that sparks their imagination, sitting on a panel, or facilitating a workshop
Reflection Points	Processing sessions, e.g., debriefs after activities, performance reviews, junior/senior retreat, or discussions
Crisis/Adventure Points	Extraordinary events that are turning points, sometimes planned and sometimes not, e.g., wilderness retreats, field trips, service learning, or organized actions like a student walkout

same effect. Though it could be argued that through proximal development, young people who are most comfortable asking "Yes/No" questions in adult-led environments may benefit most from being pushed toward co-constructing the answer to "how" questions with their adult counterparts or peers, at YIA we have found that the most depth and growth is achieved when they are given the space to fully explore and actualize the strengths they find in their respective zones or profiles.

OUTCOMES

There are seven outcomes we measure across one final continuum for growth. The markers of growth go from *beginning* to *progressing*, then *proficient*, and finally *exemplary*. These outcomes have been identified by our staff, key stakeholders, our board of directors, and our youth as clear indicators of youth leadership development. They are also aligned to some of the Rhode Island Department of Education's academic standards. The outcomes are the following:

1. critical thinking for power analysis and social stratification;
2. collaboration and movement building for frontline communities;
3. communication for critical self-care, resourcefulness, and agency;
4. intuitive learning;
5. sense of self rooted in wisdom, ethics, and empathy; and
6. contributes to a culture of joy.[5]

At the beginning of their journey at YIA, youth sit down with our program director and determine a baseline for each outcome, placing themselves along a continuum, knowing that they will be tracking their growth over the course of (potentially) 4 years. Once a baseline is determined, and action steps are established for growth in each area, staff and youth meet quarterly to review progress and adjust action steps. The outcomes and the manner with which we measure them serve as both a way to collaboratively document the growth our young people experience, and as a way to incentivize improvement in attendance or a particular skill. Measurement shows mastery but, just as importantly, it shows growth.

Over the years, since the introduction of this particular model to YIA, the staff have evaluated it on an annual basis. We've asked whether we're truly reaching the essence of each youth, if there are too many moving pieces, or not enough moving pieces, we've identified components that aren't working well, and others that seem to have gotten it just right. The model has shifted and developed many times in an effort to meet the needs of our young people and put our staff in roles that give them the most impact. In the last 2 years, the central question for us has been whether we are giving a meaningful experience to each young person that walks through the doors; are they engaged and growing? We found that more than anything else, our young people, regardless of the kind of space they thrived in (adult-led, youth–adult partnership, youth-led), wanted to be seen and understood by the adults at YIA. Overwhelmingly, they wanted to have the kind of relationship that pushed them beyond their comfort zones and into growth. So, we prioritized relationships over structure and growth over trajectory in order to get at it. Our model went from a 4-year, scaffolded model organized around three distinct skills to one that felt very tailored and unique. In lifting up relationships, we invented the profiles so that we might be able to reproduce and simulate relationships more easily, or at the very least, step into them more deeply. Once we created those profiles, a pattern of transformative moments surfaced, which we started coding and naming as key moments. These moments were critical because the further we dug into them, the more we realized they were the moments that defined our young people. The profiles were important for the relationship building, but the key moments triggered growth. We wondered if these moments were happening by chance; having named and identified them, we sought to recreate them in intentional ways, so that we could be sure to offer our youth consistent growth opportunities. Key moments became the most direct way to change access for our young people. And with access, we knew that we could point to clear outcomes. We chose outcomes that felt reflective of the actual work at YIA, and an assessment tool that valued growth and process more fully rather than just a mastery. Weaving these three pieces together was tedious and many times we lost our way in the design process, but in the end, it felt like an honest response to what our youth asked of us. And that felt like the most profound act of youth–adult partnership we could offer.

CONCLUSION

Youth In Action continues to hone and evaluate whether we are offering the best possible version of ourselves. We do so through annual staff retreats, frank conversations with youth and key stakeholders, and tests of our model outside of our building. In 2017, YIA piloted its Core programming in two Providence Public Schools to see what it might look like to scale, but also to serve a group of youth that hadn't self-selected into the program. We wanted to know if our model would still yield the same results, the same kind of relationships and culture. One of the schools housed a large English language learners program, which again tested the model, but this time in terms of accessibility. Could youth even access the material to yield results? Committed to remaining a responsive organization and model, YIA went back to the drawing board, convinced that addressing these challenges would offer insight into program improvement. In a way, YIA is just another young person, moving across the different continuums, asking questions, assuming different profiles in different settings, contending with key moments along the way, and measuring its growth in respect to its best self.

ACKNOWLEDGMENTS

Many thanks to YIA, a place that shaped me as much as it does our young people. Thank you to the people that *are* YIA and indulged me in this life changing journey of program and cultural design, in particular: Court King, Michelle Veras, Cecilia Acosta, Lindsay Tarnoff, and Nicole Verdi. Thank you also to the cohort of youth that endured the design and implementation of this model from start to finish, in particular: Latifat Odetunde, Thaina Merlain, Ashley Gomez, Sydnee Gross, and Missy Ottun. For always working through these ideas and supporting the writing process, Siri Colom.

NOTES

1. James Charlton (2000) wrote a book entitled, "Nothing About Us, Without Us," which discussed disability rights. The phrase became the mantra for many groups to communicate that no policy should be decided by any representative without the full and direct participation of members of the group(s) affected by that policy.
2. Positive Youth Development believes that youth lack access to support and opportunities. The solution is then to provide those supports to the individual to realize their inherent potential. Youth in Action goes a step further by thinking of positive youth development within the empowerment perspective, which identifies our society's power imbalances as the reason youth are denied access to opportunities. The solution then becomes to create opportunities for youth to correct those power imbalances through collective action that transforms community institutions and systems into more caring and supportive environments. This framing is taken from the *Nonprofit Quarterly*, December 21, 2001 "Building Youth Movements for Community Change" by Taj James and Kim McGillicuddy.
3. The Alliance was funded by the Nellie Mae Education Foundation and brought together four cornerstone organizations in Providence over the course of 4 years.
4. Since 1968, AMC's Youth Opportunities Program (YOP) has introduced over 250,000 youth to the outdoors. They do this by providing outdoor leadership training to urban youth workers and teachers across New York, New Jersey, and New England, and by supporting them with the resources they need to independently lead their groups on outdoor adventures. YOP is committed to

making the outdoors accessible to youth who have not traditionally had access to these opportunities. The YOP's training and support model ensures that young people enjoy meaningful outdoor experiences with adults who know them and their unique needs.

5. Somewhat of an unconventional metric to measure, this outcome is one of the more defining and critical pieces of the work at YIA. When initially identifying what the outcomes were, "culture of joy" was not included, but when asked if the outcomes listed painted an authentic picture of YIA or if there was anything missing, unanimously we pointed to laughter, playfulness, and joy as big pieces of the work that made YIA unique. Youth in Action works to restore or in some cases introduce these qualities to our young people's lives.

REFERENCES

Charlton, J. I. (2000). *Nothing about us, without us: Disability oppression and empowerment*. Berkeley: University of California Press.

Cohen, S. (2017). *Transformational relationships for youth success*. Washington DC: Center for Study of Social Policy.

James, T., & McGillicuddy, K. (2001). Building youth movements for community change: Street children's movement in Brazil. *Nonprofit Quarterly, 8*(4), 1–3. Retrieved from https://nonprofitquarterly.org/2001/12/21/building -youth-movements-for-community-change/

THE DIFFERENCES

Tianna Davis

The summer before my freshman year of high school, I took part in a group called Girls Taking Action at the Russell Youth Center in West Cambridge. The group met 4 days a week and had Mondays off. Girls Taking Action brought together approximately 14 girls from different ethnic backgrounds, to discuss the obstacles facing women—particularly women of color. In the program, we would do activities and group discussions about what women should do to stand up for themselves. My teachers recommended me for the program because they saw how engaged I was with learning about racism and sexism. Girls Taking Action supports young women like me to be heard and valued by society.

One day, the organizer of the group—an adult from the Russell Youth Center—thought we should do an activity to demonstrate in a physical way how advantages or disadvantages can propel some women forward and hold other women back. At the end of the activity, the majority of the girls of color were behind the girls who were White. This opened my eyes to how unfairly young women like us are treated, even at such a young age, because of race.

During the program, I also met the woman who runs all the youth centers in Cambridge. She talked about her point of view in life, including how she is a biracial woman. I related to her stories about how kids tended to put her in one race group and not both. It reminded me of the kids who put me in one race category and not the other, not recognizing and valuing each part of me.

All in all, the experience of Girls Taking Action made me feel like I should do something more in the world to open people's eyes about the experiences of women of color. Since participating in the group, I have felt empowered to stand up for women of color who don't or can't stand up for themselves. For example, the other day when I was taking the bus, the driver refused to stop for a passenger who was a woman of color, and made a derogatory comment to her. She just ignored it, but I stood up and said to the driver: "The reason why you skipped her stop is so disrespectful to her and also to me."

I will share what I learned in Girls Taking Action with younger women of color so that they understand that they have a voice too. I have been very involved with learning about racism and sexism since fifth grade. I feel like it is important for young women of color to know that they are not alone in this world, and that people can be disrespectful and that it isn't their fault. I do hope to be in Girls Taking Action again, to share what I learned in the previous year.

Bio: Tianna Davis is a 14-year-old, biracial teenager who loves to read and write. Born and raised in the North Cambridge area in a housing development called Jefferson Park, Tianna now attends Cambridge Rindge and Latin School.

Per Tianna: Where I live, there is a lot drama and sometimes violence. There are some racist people that live in the area and they always talk negatively about people of color. I decided to start doing clubs that stand up for people of color. At my school there is a club called Black Student Union, and we talk about different situations and how we can change them.

CHAPTER 9

BETTER TOGETHER

The Promise, Preconditions, and Precautions of a Youth–Adult Partnership Approach to Collaborative Research

Sarah Zeller-Berkman
The Intergenerational Change Initiative

Mia Legaspi-Cavin
The Intergenerational Change Initiative

Jessica Barreto
The Intergenerational Change Initiative

Jennifer Tang
The Intergenerational Change Initiative

Asha Sandler
The Intergenerational Change Initiative

At Our Best, pages 159–177
Copyright © 2020 by Information Age Publishing
All rights of reproduction in any form reserved.

The walls in room 407 are covered with collages representing maps of the journeys that members of the research collective took en route to joining the Intergenerational Change Initiative (ICI). Some maps have branches that dip sharply, representing a stretch in a juvenile facility. One features a year when depression had a tight grip, another shows an incident between a parent and a police officer that kick-started an ICI member's path of activism. Other maps show years of working in an alternative-to-incarceration program before enrolling in both a youth sudies master's and law program, or a move to the United States to pursue a PhD.

The group gathers in a circle near the maps on the wall for the opening icebreaker. Ben, a youth researcher, begins by having everyone play a few minutes of hacky sack and we laugh at our collective ineptitude. Antonio, another youth researcher, then decides we should get a little deeper and do an exercise modeled at the Free Minds Free People conference we all attended that July. We get into pairs and answer the questions: "Who are you?"; "Who do people think you are?"; "Who do you want to be?" After answering questions with her partner, Jen, an adult researcher, reminds the group that we should jump into the day because there is a ton of coding to do. Monica, a youth researcher, gets the iPads out and signs one out to each person. Marcus, another youth researcher, picks the music that accompanies the coding session. After each group gets their focus group transcript, sheets of codes, a highlighter, and a pen, we begin the tedious process of coding. There is some laughter and banter as members highlight pages and pages of text...

INTRODUCTION

The scene above represents a meeting of our research collective, the ICI, during our Summer Research Institute.[1] The ICI started convening in June of 2017. Our group formed at the behest of a charismatic group of leaders from the New York City (NYC) Administration for Children's Services (ACS) and the NYC Department of Education (DOE), who believed that they needed to learn from young people who had personal experiences in their systems. With public and private funding,[2] an intergenerational group of approximately 15 young people (ages 14 to 22), four youth studies master's students, one doctoral student, and one Youth Studies Academic Director at CUNY School for Professional Studies gathered to develop a research project that delved into the lived experiences of youth who at some point had fallen behind in school, experienced an ACS intervention, entered the juvenile justice systems, or navigated the well-worn paths that youth travel between these agencies. Some of the members of our collective had these experiences, and we were all committed to doing research that could change these systems for the better (see Figure 9.1 for more about our research design and Table 9.1 for our research findings and recommendations).

Research Questions

1. What are the experiences of NYC youth ages 14–21 who have dealt with multiple city agencies in their lives?
2. What are the policy and/or programmatic recommendations that could benefit youth ages 14–21 who are dealing with multiple city agencies in their lives?

Data Collection

- Six focus groups in the New York City boroughs of Bronx, Manhattan, and Brooklyn, with 68 participants ages 14–24.
- Participants included youth on probation, youth who fell behind in school, and individuals who had interactions with ACS.
- Focus group discussions that included word associations, short written personal narratives, as well as problem and solution trees.

Data Analysis

- Developed analytic framework through a collaborative, iterative process.
- Analyzed data using 3 categories, 10 themes, and 46 codes.
- Our analysis surfaced 6 key findings that repeatedly stood out across all 6 focus groups.

Figure 9.1   #ChangeFocusNYC project background.

TABLE 9.1	Key Findings and Recommendations
Key Findings	**Recommendations**
Youth in our study felt that agencies and programs are falling short in meeting their basic needs.	• Prioritize funding that goes directly to young people in the system to help meet their needs. • Equitably resource all NYC public schools. • Ensure that teachers have the resources and means to maintain positive and effective learning environments. • Develop a leadership pathway where young people who have lived through these systems can be trained as youth workers, heal themselves (if needed), and be part of transforming these systems from within.
Sometimes, the way agencies and programs try to help youth actually ends up having the opposite effect.	• Youth and adults should regularly audit how systems interact so that they are complementing, not obstructing, each other (i.e., youth doesn't miss school for meetings with case workers, and agencies don't funnel youth into more punitive systems rather than creating a web of supports). • Addressing bullying without using extractive interventions—use a restorative justice approach where youth and adults co-determine disciplinary action and healing. • Make the accountability system transparent—to everyone including youth—so gaps and barriers can be easily identified and addressed. Establish a mechanism for young people to report failures in the system. Let youth know where reports go and be able to see if there is follow-up and resolution.

(continued)

TABLE 9.1   Key Findings and Recommendations (continued)

Key Findings	Recommendations
Interactions with agencies led youth in our study to feel unheard, stressed, and put down.	• Liaise with NYC youth councils to monitor and improve school climates and cultures by conducting listening and problem-solving sessions across the city. • Use age-appropriate methods to inform youth of the choices they have and what these choices mean. Let them be part of the decision-making process.
Youth wish their services providers were more professional.	• Have trainings informed by youth experiences and have youth and adults partner as co-trainers.
Youth want more personalized support and a sense of connection with people working in city agencies.	• Conduct youth–adult co-led trainings on developing supportive and caring relationships during professional development days when youth can work without being pulled out of class (figure out how young people working in these partnerships can be credited or paid). • Prioritizing funding to hire more qualified staff and decrease their workload so they can personalize their interactions. • Reduce the overuse of testing and move towards more personalized education.
Youth want programming that meets their needs to help them achieve their goals.	• Systematize a way for young people who have aged out of the system to reflect on their experience, make recommendations, and monitor and improve the agency's work. • Offer programs and support early in a child's development (i.e., a child doesn't have to be on probation to find a program that offers mentoring, internships, tutoring, and caring/trusting relationships with adults).

Although our research collective was mainly focused on disseminating our findings during this period of time (please see a brief summary in the text boxes), this chapter is about our *process* of intergenerational collaboration. For this piece, five members of our research team (three adults and two young people), all of whom were interested in delving deeply into the relationships between youth and adults in our collective, decided to write collaboratively. We examined data that our group collected via daily reflections, examining mentions of the relationship between youth and adults. We analyzed an outside researcher's interviews with four youth and three adult members. Lastly, we each wrote our own reflections about our experiences in ICI and the nature of our youth–adult partnerships. These data sets inform and illustrate the promising practices, tensions, and possibilities that we lift up in this chapter. Our chapter begins with a brief articulation of our approach to youth–adult (Y–A) partnerships, outlines a series of strategies based on our experience, teases out the tensions and challenges we encountered, and ends by imagining the possibilities and promise of this approach.

INTERGENERATIONAL CHANGE INITIATIVE'S APPROACH TO YOUTH–ADULT PARTNERSHIPS

Youth-adult partnership is a process. It is a framework young people and adults can use to shift traditional power dynamics. It is a process that evolves through relationship development. Trust, structure, and group cohesion build out the partnership so that young people and adults alike share power. (Adult ICI Member, 2018)

The look, feel, and flavor of the Y–A partnerships in our research collective was greatly influenced by the fact that the ICI firmly situates itself in a critical participatory action research lineage (Torre, Fine, Stoudt, & Fox, 2012). Critical participatory action research (CPAR) is an epistemology that engages research design, methods, analysis and products through a lens of democratic participation (Torre et al., 2012). Regardless of whether one is working with adults or youth, a CPAR approach invites members to collaborate at the more "participatory" end of the spectrum, be transparent about issues of power, and celebrate what differently positioned researchers bring to the knowledge-building process. Torre (2014) articulates how CPAR interweaves critical social science, feminist theory, queer theory, indigenous theory, and liberatory practice in order to interrupt injustice, democratize knowledge creation, and build community capacities.[3] In the context of a critical participatory research process, Y–A partnerships embody democratic principles, as well as an analysis of power within and outside of the research setting.

Our research collective intentionally used an intergenerational partnership approach, rather than a youth-led model. We believe that the value-add to this approach is that both youth and adults are transformed by working in egalitarian partnerships, and that the products of these collaborations are better with the combined expertise, assets, creativity, and social cachet of both groups. While being cognizant of power differentials, we think it would be condescending to withdraw or silence the knowledge or skills that the adult co-researchers bring to the table. Engaging in deep, mutual, intergenerational partnerships reflects a respect for both groups as equally important in the struggle for a more just world.

PRINCIPLES AND PRACTICES THAT SUPPORT INTERGENERATIONAL CHANGE INITIATIVE'S YOUTH–ADULT PARTNERSHIP APPROACH

In 2011, one of our team members, Sarah Zeller-Berkman, conducted a research study with youth and adult activists that outlined the following conditions of engagement that facilitate productive Y–A partnerships: power-sharing, transparency, explicit common goals, caring relationships, and reflective practices. As we examined our data on the Y–A partnerships in our research collective, many of the promising practices that we surfaced fit well into Zeller-Berkman's (2011) framework.[4] Here, we define a "productive" Y–A partnership as one that has impact on multiple levels—individual and community, as well as institutional or societal.

POWER-SHARING

Following in a Critical Participatory Action Research (CPAR) tradition (Torre, 2014), our project involved those most impacted by youth-serving city agencies—namely young people who at some point in their lives interacted with the ACS, the juvenile justice system, or experienced some element of pushout in school—in *all* phases of the research process. The research process involved designing the research study; developing focus group protocols, problem/solution trees, and word walls; collecting and analyzing qualitative data; creating research products (a research brief, website, postcards with our findings, animated videos, applications for conferences, social media postings, etc.); budgeting; and presenting about the project at conferences and meetings with city officials. In addition to working on research activities collectively, we shared responsibility for the facilitation of the group. This approach takes concerted effort and substantial time, but we are convinced that our research is better because of the joint efforts of all of our team members. Sharing responsibility helped to deepen our connections, shift our power dynamics, and ensure that each member developed a sense of efficacy and accountability in our collective. Below are some of the ways we did this:

Shared Tool Kit

The commitment to equal contributions between adults and youth permeated our dynamic as we moved from training young people in the various research methods to co-designing our study. All members were expected to contribute their ideas; however, one cannot expect youth and adult team members to participate fully without developing a shared knowledge base. Our team spent time in the beginning of our project collectively outlining our goals as well as the expectations of our grant, learning together about ACS and DOE history through scavenger hunts and cell phone surveys, and participating in research training so all members could weigh in on the research design. There is no way that the people in our group, both adults and youth alike who were newer to research, could have weighed in on our research design if they had not been given a sense of the possibilities of research methods from which to choose.⁵

Scaffolding Roles and Responsibilities

Adults scaffolded leadership opportunities at the beginning of this collective process. For example, at the beginning of our summer institute, adults recruited participants, created the initial agenda for the group, scheduled the meetings to accommodate the schedules of the young people, organized logistics, and conducted training in research methods. Gradually, after a bit of modeling, youth members began to share roles and responsibilities. Team members signed up to facilitate and co-lead parts of the meetings.

Power-sharing among adult and youth members continued to shift as we added new members to the research group. These moments of regeneration became opportunities to enact what had been modeled in previous iterations of the work. For example, youth and adult researchers recruited new group members, reviewed applications, and created an onboarding process the second time around. All team members oriented the new researchers through team building activities and talking through the goals of the research. Team members from the Summer Institute taught newer members the research skills they had developed like coding, analyzing, and so forth. This process modeled shared leadership between youth and adults in our group for new members. Having young people teaching other youth or teaching newer adult master's students who were coming into the program deepened the egalitarian feel of our partnerships.

TRANSPARENCY

Adults in the group had to work to recognize and check the role that power inherently plays in the partnership process. This took place internally among the adults, and also in the research process with the young people. We wanted to make transparency a norm in the research process, which meant that we needed to both remain mindful of each evolving stage of the group process (storming, norming, etc.) and share ongoing happenings outside of the immediate research. For instance, the Director updated the team on CUNY developments. One of the adult researchers spent time walking the youth researchers through the bureaucratic process of payment at the institution. Time was taken to talk about these details so that each member of the group could better understand the full world of the research process.

In tandem with this, the adults and young people in the group were encouraged from the beginning to name that power in the room, and continue to address it throughout the partnership process. Because we truly believed that each member's ideas and perspectives were to be respected, we sought to continually cultivate an environment of deliberation rather than debate, where everyone could raise differences of opinions. One ICI youth member said:

> I think when you are in an environment where everybody [has] connected and wants to get things done, there is no fear of speaking your mind. You know if I sa[id] "I disagree," there wasn't a problem. We were very comfortable with each other.

Feeling comfortable with recognizing and speaking back to power dynamics is a difficult task for youth and adults alike, but one that is important to developing strong partnerships.

Adults and young people who are interested working in partnership would benefit from developing the muscle of critical transparency. Critical transparency includes being transparent about issues related to power in its many forms (race, class, gender, age, sexual identity, etc.). In the ICI, this type of transparency was essential to developing a research project about systemic issues steeped in racial and class inequity, and it was equally important when bringing together such differently positioned researchers. For example, in one of our team building activities, we designated each wall in our room as a representation of different identity categories, such as race, gender, and age. When the facilitator of the activity read out a scenario, we would go to the wall that represented the particular aspect of our identity that was most salient in responding to the scenario at hand. Through these kinds of activities, we created opportunities to reflect on the multi-faceted identities of our team, deepen our relationships, and be transparent about how our identities and life experience influenced our approaches to the research and to interactions with other team members.

We were also transparent about money in this project (see Figure 9.2), which is often an untouched part of Y–A partnerships and generally reserved for the adults to determine. The quote below from one of our team members illustrates how we played with a modified participatory budgeting process as we were spending down a grant, and had decisions to make about our priorities:

> One of the things that adults and youth did together that was different for me than other PAR projects I had done in the past was a mini participatory budgeting process. Armed with sticky notes representing $5,000, $1,000, and $100, our team of youth and adults decided where we wanted to spend our money for the coming year. We made wish-lists, calculated costs, and decided

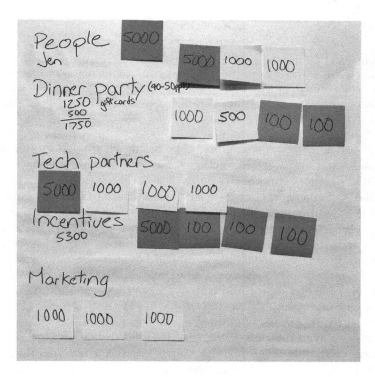

Figure 9.2 Youth–adult participatory budget.

our financial next steps jointly. I loved being transparent about our finances and having the group decide how money should be spent instead of doing that on my own as I had in other projects. (Adult ICI Member, 2019)

Even though budgeting this way could be considered a given based on our participatory approach, being transparent about how much we had to spend, who was getting paid and how much, as well as jointly deciding how to spend our funds, was a potentially difficult task we only ventured into after many other experiences practicing collective decision-making. The transparency of participatory budgeting required that we not only build the capacity of our group to deliberate over the dollar amounts, but also wrestle with the factors, priorities, and tensions of our group. People on our team who had never done budgeting at all, and especially not with thousands of dollars, found the process of discussing the sums really interesting. People who had done lots of budgeting, but not really with others, found the process of mulling difficult decisions equally engaging. Participatory budgeting built upon our group's commitment to transparency and participatory decision-making at all levels.

COMMON GOALS

Youth–adult partnerships can be described as equally balanced. Youth and adults partner in order to fulfill a mutual goal. No one person has a bigger role nor say in a matter. It is a method that's created in order to work collaboratively, giving each member an equal opportunity to share ideas. (Youth ICI Member, 2018)

Our partnership was strengthened by having clear goals around which we coalesced. Our project's initial goal was to research the impact of ACS and DOE practices and policies on the lives of the youth in their care. We all came to the table not only to study the issue, but to try to do something about it. Yet within that larger umbrella goal, there was still plenty of room for us to set goals together. We had to determine how to design our research study, and once we had completed data collection and analysis, we had to figure out how we wanted to take action and disseminate our findings.

We found it helpful to lay out a set of goals for the year and then articulate plans of action that would take us through the next few months. We were at our most productive when we had a set of concrete tasks on which we would focus. At the same time, while structure felt necessary, having some flexibility to respond in real time to opportunities or current events that arose felt imperative. The day we presented our research findings to the ACS and DOE Data Sharing Committee, one student who had repeatedly been a victim of bullying stabbed another student in a high school in the Bronx. Our team drew on our research to write an editorial as city officials and city residents debated employing metal detectors, counselors, and disciplinary practices in response to this tragedy. Our monthly timelines could not get in the way of our larger shared goal of using our research to take action.

CARING RELATIONSHIPS

We are inspired by Grace Lee Boggs' (2011) reminder that "'this exquisitely connected world,' the real engine of change is never 'critical mass'; dramatic and systemic change always begins with 'critical connections'" (p. 50). We are also inspired by adrienne maree brown's (2017) invitation to "see our own lives and work and relationships as a front line, a first place we can practice justice, liberation, and alignment with each other and the planet" (p. 53). In the ICI, we committed ample time and energy to building relationships. Developing strong relationships within our research collective was key for our research work as well as movement building, so our first three meetings focused on building community, values, and trust. The icebreakers used in that initial phase focused on getting to know each other's names and shaking up dynamics between youth and adults. One activity had youth and adult group members get into pairs and teach each other something new in two minutes. We made it very clear that everyone in the group had something to teach and contribute, and that we would all be learning from each other as the project proceeded.

Check-ins at the beginning of our meetings helped people bring their whole selves into our space. Our collective worked to maintain a mutually supportive space from our very first meeting, when one of our youth members had to leave because they found out their mother had been diagnosed with cancer. These check-ins continued through data collection, when one of our youth members had to miss afternoons to attend court-mandated programming, and through data analysis, when an adult member lost a family member. Building relationships where we can reveal our vulnerabilities with one another takes time, but the trust and care we built with each other in ICI made it possible for the team to figure out how to make accommodations, and support members to stay part of the team and continue the work. Our respect and genuine affection for our team members was palpable most days, as is captured by this reflection from one of our youth members about the feeling in the group:

> I love being here and working with everyone, I feel a calm here that I don't really feel anywhere else, and today was no different! We are doing some amazing and absolutely interesting work and I'm glad that I got this opportunity. Asha and I finished coding the Focus Group B transcript with the current codes. Amazing day with amazing people!

Youth members identified that building trust and having patience was important to their ability to engage in partnership with the adults. Trusting adults was not automatic; in many cases, adults had violated the young people's confidence before. Adults in our group had to earn trust by following through on tasks, caring about young people's lives outside of the work context, and proving they were strong collaborators. Moving past these barriers was critical to our ability to be productive together.

REFLECTIVE PRACTICE

Through a constant process of dialogue and reflection, any group of people can devise relevant and appropriate actions as solutions to their problems.
—Koirala-Azad & Fuentes, 2009/2010, p. 1

Another strategy that we used to support Y–A partnerships in ICI was writing daily reflections after each one of our sessions, from the first team

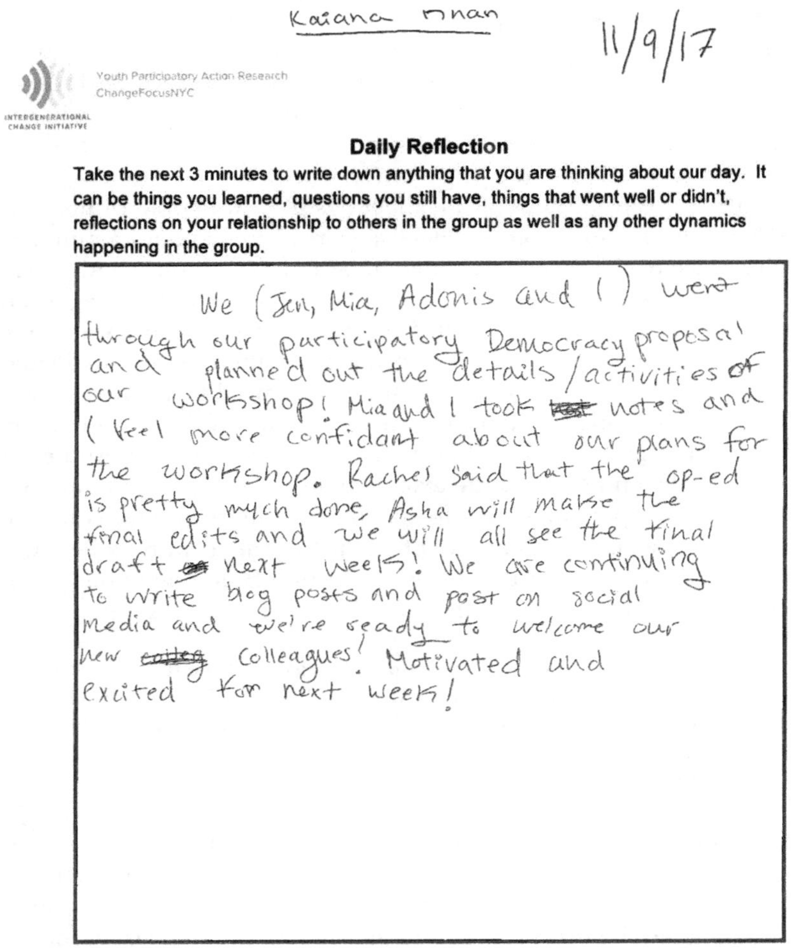

Kaiana Mnan

11/9/17

))) Youth Participatory Action Research
ChangeFocusNYC

INTERGENERATIONAL
CHANGE INITIATIVE

Daily Reflection

Take the next 3 minutes to write down anything that you are thinking about our day. It can be things you learned, questions you still have, things that went well or didn't, reflections on your relationship to others in the group as well as any other dynamics happening in the group.

We (Jen, Mia, Adonis and I) went through our participatory Democracy proposal and planned out the details/activities of our workshop! Mia and I took notes and I feel more confidant about our plans for the workshop. Rachel said that the op-ed is pretty much done, Asha will make the final edits and we will all see the final draft next week! We are continuing to write blog posts and post on social media and we're ready to welcome our new colleagues! Motivated and excited for next week!

Figure 9.3 A daily reflection sheet completed by one of our members.

building meeting to conference presentations (see Figure 9.3). This was a reflective tool that was not just used "on" youth, but one that the whole group engaged in as a ritual to help deepen our learning and document our process (Zeller-Berkman, 2007). These simple sheets, of which we now have hundreds, are a repository and collective timeline that documents which sessions felt productive, which felt frustrating, and even how the collective was able to lift spirits even when someone had come in overwhelmed by school or work or various life challenges. Reflections from our weekly planning meetings offer glimpses into the magic that happened when we knocked a task off our list or got completely derailed by a conversation related to the political climate—which at times seemed surreal over the course of 2017–2019. Our group had lively conversations about current events; news of technology companies violating our data privacy, the separation of children seeking asylum, and youth activism leading a nation-wide gun reform movement whirled around us. Our daily reflections allowed us "meta" moments to reflect on what was going well in our partnership and what needed shifting as a research group and as an intergenerational society.

In addition to daily reflections, we debriefed after our focus groups to explore what went well and what required shifting. These reflections about our data collection efforts supported members to give and receive feedback that helped sharpen their research skills. Lastly, we collectively reflected on current events that related to our work to see if there were ways we could use our data to speak back to issues that were bubbling up. This prompted us to write an opinion article about how schools deal with bullying, submit a public comment to changes to DOE policies, and join in the activism that was spreading from Ferguson, Missouri to Broward County, Florida, to NYC and beyond.

TENSIONS AND CHALLENGES

Tensions

Having youth and adults engage in deeply participatory work is both enriching and difficult. One of the more difficult collaborative efforts was writing this chapter. We had calls, exchanged multiple comments on Google Docs, and contributed reflections and literature on partnership to a shared drive. A few questions surfaced as we worked in our Google Doc which hadn't come up for us before: *Whose words get quotations and whose will be seamlessly woven in? How do we deal with authorship—is it who contributed most as first author or just alphabetical? Who gets to delete, curate, and edit other people's work? Should we parse out and attribute quotes to youth or adult ICI members or does that type of analytic slicing reify the differences when we worked so hard to ameliorate? Can effort really be really equal if some people have been privileged enough to have spent years studying intergenerational partnerships?* We discussed and addressed some of the issues related to authorship, editing, and attribution in one of our calls but tensions related to reification of difference and privilege are still somewhat enmeshed in these pages.

In general, tensions between adults and young people in our research collective were few and far between. However, a tension did arise with the city leaders who were part of the data-sharing initiative. Although all the adults in that group seemed genuinely committed to supporting the CPAR project and individually wanted to use the data to inform the larger initiative, a few issues hindered progress on these goals. Firstly, the larger data-sharing initiative became stuck in a legal limbo. This pause, which lasted more than two years, made it hard for the city agency leads to maintain momentum, and their group stopped convening until recently. Their loss of momentum meant that our allies—those who we thought would help put our research directly into practice—effectively disappeared. This lack of followthrough made our group feel that although there is an appetite for youth voice in city government in NYC, adults still need to commit to actually *listen* to the recommendations and enact them in partnership with youth. While ICI members had assured skeptical research participants in our focus groups that city agencies like DOE and ACS had a genuine interest in what youth had to say about their experiences because they were our partners, it became harder over time to be so sure. Too often, those in power ask the underrepresented for their opinions and then ignore the responses; this is a recipe for apathy and mistrust. The failure of adults to be consistent in doing what they say they will do makes building successful youth–adult partnerships more arduous. Although, we have just started meeting with the ACS/DOE data sharing group again as they just got approval to move forward from their legal teams, we re-enter this partnership wary and wiser.

In the interim years, we found multiple audiences for our work besides the agency officials in this group. In the past year, we presented at nine different events catering to a wide variety of audiences, including policy makers, city planners, youth activists, youth workers, academics, and more. We continue to be hopeful that we will come back together with the members of the data-sharing initiative to look at our research alongside other types of city data, and engage other community members in developing proposed solutions.

Another tension that comes up in our work is the desire by many to capture data on the youth and not the adults in our collective. In addition to researchers, audience members have asked our youth members to articulate repeatedly how our project has changed their lives, as opposed to letting them share their recommendations for systems change. There was another incident when a staff member on the marketing team changed what was supposed to be an interview with youth and adults about the partnership into the adults interviewing the youth about how it has changed them.

In and of itself, it is not unreasonable to want to know how intergenerational research collectives impact youth empowerment, critical thinking, resilience, or leadership as a result of the partnerships.[6] Yet when it is not coupled with a desire to find out how being on the research team has changed adults in the group, we slip back into positioning young people as objects of development or as vessels to be filled—not people in transformation, as we all are.

While we are not advocating for the use of the same measures—given that there may be very different takeaways for the adults—asking only young people what changed for them via the partnership makes assumptions about who needs to change and who has the capacity to change whom.

Challenges

For both youth and adults, there are multiple challenges that can impact someone's ability to commit to this type of work. If we want to thoughtfully engage young people who have been impacted by oppressive forces in this type of intellectual labor, we must create an environment that makes the commitment easier for the young person. This means adequately compensating someone for her/his/their time, providing a means of transport, providing food, and consistently acknowledging the value the young person brings to the work. Successful Y–A partnerships require that each person in partnership understands the process, and the majority (or all) can agree to decisions. Utilizing a more egalitarian approach to the work means each action will take more time, which can be a challenge. This constraint should be understood by those wanting to engage in Y–A partnerships, as well as those funding this type of work. Funders may also want to allow for flexibility for the group to alter the initial proposal and revisit the outcomes after the group has had time to build relationships, outline common goals, and develop a plan of action.

Possibilities

Youth have a perspective that [is] different than adults but can be used for the betterment of youth across the board. They experience things in the current era, things that an adult from another era may or may not understand. They are more likely to be blunt and vocal in expressing these thoughts. These abilities are what bring light and awareness to malfunctions all across the board in relation to youth experiences. Whereas an adult who has more wisdom, knowledge, can direct, guide, and teach young people on how to use their ideas, experiences, and voices in order to implement and fulfill the goal they want to achieve. One can't work effectively without the other. (Youth ICI Member, 2018)

In this chapter, we have outlined strategies that supported us in our process as the ICI, as well as raised tensions and limitations of our Y–A partnership work. We would like to leave the reader with a sense of the possibilities when Y–A partnerships are done well, as we believe they are key to charting a more just course in our country.

Throughout our experience in this collective, we learned that power-sharing, transparency, caring relationships, common goals, and reflective practices support productive Y–A partnerships. We believe that partnerships between young people and adults, grounded in social justice commitments, are not only impactful for the people in the project, but help build intergenerational equity. Given that young people are considered a low power group in this country (Coleman, 1974; Costin, 1982; Dollar, 1975; Zeller-Berkman, 2011), it seems critical that if we are going to challenge status quo for youth, it would have to be in partnership. Zakia Carpenter (2008) laments:

> My concern is with the lack of support my millennial generation is getting. This disconnect frightens me because it takes both leadership and support to change the world. We cannot do this alone. Therefore, how do we integrate the past and present so that fellowship between generations not only thrives but also transforms society? (para. 2)

Our theory of change includes youth and adults working together to change individuals, but also communities, institutions, and societal

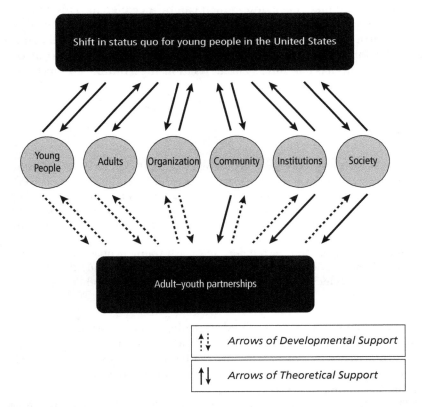

Figure 9.4   Theory of change (Zeller-Berkman, 2011).

perceptions of young people (see Figure 9.4). Impacting multiple levels of change through critical, transparent, constructive, and respectful Y–A partnerships is the promise of this type of approach.

What does this look like in practice? For our project, it looks like youth and adults gaining skills, engaging in transformative dialogue, and learning lessons from our research participants—but not stopping at the level of personal transformation. It looks like presenting our work at a conference, and inspiring a woman from the Bronx Office of City Planning to use intergenerational PAR in her next planning study for a Bronx neighborhood. She is now working with her leadership and partners at the NYC Department of Health and Mental Hygiene to integrate intergenerational community researchers into planning and resource-allocation processes for various neighborhoods in NYC. It looks like continuing to partner with activist and advocate allies to promote using PAR data to help reevaluate policies and practices, and collectively imagine a better future.

Even with what seems to be increased interest in Y–A partnerships and a long history of demonstrated impact (Zeldin, McDaniel, Topitzes, & Calvert, 2000), public perceptions of young people's capabilities have lagged behind with consequences for youth policy advocates. It seems that a vicious cycle is at play where negative perceptions prevent young people from being seen as capable of engaging with adults to impact the issues that shape their lives; this then promotes more siloing of groups by age, and less opportunities to prove how transformative these intergenerational partnerships can be. Besides supporting more widespread use of Y–A partnerships to promote change at multiple levels, intergenerational equity would be further promoted by using media savvy to shine a spotlight on the good work being done in these collectives. Delving even deeper, we posit that changing perceptions is important, but making youth participation a *right* would further ensure that it is not up to the good will of adults to "allow" young people to take a seat at the table.[7] Together we will build our own tables.

ACKNOWLEDGMENTS

We would like to thank all the team members of the Intergenerational Change Initiative, youth and adults, who helped make our work possible. We would also like to thank our partners at the Administration for Children's Services and the NYC Department of Education as well as our funders, the Young Men's Initiative, the Center for Economic Opportunity, and the Ford Foundation. Lastly, we would like to thank our colleagues and mentors at the Public Science Project at the CUNY Graduate Center.

NOTES

1. For more about ICI or our Institute, visit http://www.intergenerationalchange .org
2. Center for Economic Opportunity and Ford Foundation funding supported this project.
3. See the Public Science website for more on the principles of CPAR: http:// publicscienceproject.org/principles-and-values
4. While we know that the skills (such as active listening, etc.) and attributes (being caring, open, etc.) of youth workers and organizational infrastructure are important to the success Y–A partnerships, in this chapter we will focus more on practices that supported the partnership. The adults in our team were master's students, doctoral students, or professors who were also youth workers steeped in a critical youth development approach taught in the Youth Studies Program at CUNY SPS. Their prior knowledge of adultism, youth development principles and practices, critical theory, and prior experience working with young people helped the ICI start at a high level of partnership without needing substantial training for the adults.
5. Please see https://bit.ly/2QQjuFX for a link to a video about our summer training institute.
6. These are requests that our director has received from adults doing participatory action research in partnership with youth.
7. A rights-based approach to youth participation is promoted by the United Nations Convention on the Rights of the Child and implemented in many other countries besides the United States.

REFERENCES

Boggs, G. L., & Kurashige, S. (2011). *The next American revolution: Sustainable activism for the twenty-first century.* Berkeley: University of California Press.
Brown, A. M. (2017). *Emergent strategy: Shaping change, changing worlds.* Edinburgh, Scotland: Ak Press.
Carpenter, Z. (2008). *Youth-adult partnerships and growing communities.* Retrieved from http://boggscenter.org/youth-adult-partnerships-and-growing-communities
Coleman, J. (1974). *Youth: Transition to adulthood: Panel on youth of the president's science advisory committee.* Chicago, IL: University of Chicago Press.
Costin, K. (1982). *Youth participation in youth advocacy: A practical guide for developing programs* (Prepared for the U.S. Office of Juvenile Justice and Delinquency Prevention). New York, NY: National Commission on Resources for Youth.
Dollar, B. (1975). *Youth participation: A concept paper* (A Report to the Department of Health, Education and Welfare, Offices of Youth Development). New York, NY: National Commission on Resources for Youth.
Koirala-Azad, S., & Fuentes, E. (2009/2010). Introduction: Activist scholarship— possibilities and constraints of PAR. *Social Justice, 36*(4), 1–5.
Torre, M., Fine, M., Stoudt, B., & Fox, M. (2012). Critical participatory action research as public science. In P. Camic, & H. Cooper (Eds.), *APA handbook of*

research methods in psychology (pp. 171–184). Washington, DC: American Psychology Association.

Torre, M. E. (2014). Participatory action research. In T. Teo (Ed.), *Encyclopedia of critical psychology: Vol. 3* (pp. 1323–1327). New York, NY: Springer.

Zeldin, S., McDaniel, A. K., Topitzes, D., & Calvert, M. (2000). *Youth in decision-making: A study on the impacts of youth on adults and organizations.* Madison, WI: National 4-H Council.

Zeller-Berkman, S. (2007). Peering in: A look into reflective practices in youth participatory action research. *Children, Youth, and Environments, 17*(2), 315–328.

Zeller-Berkman, S. (2011). *"So what I got a mouth!": Reclaiming attachment and active citizenship through adult–youth partnerships* (Doctoral dissertation). Retrieved ProQuest Dissertations and Theses Database. (UMI No. 3460280)

TO PARTNER WITH US, TRUST OUR IDEAS

Washington Heights Expeditionary Learning School Educators' Support of Youth Researchers/Activists

Yohely Comprés

In Washington Heights Expeditionary Learning School (WHEELS), it's common for students to develop relationships with their teachers through work outside the classroom. This is visible in all of WHEELS' activities and clubs, especially the Critical Theory and Social Justice (CTSJ) club and our chapter of Million Hoodies Movement for Justice. Through my 6 years at WHEELS, it has been in these two clubs where I have felt the most empowered. These clubs have had a special influence in shaping who I am today.

Critical Theory and Social Justice was started by Daniel Morales-Armstrong and WHEELS students to learn about Afro-Latinidad in our community of Washington Heights, NY and internationally. During our weekly meetings at CTSJ, we build background knowledge about Peru, specifically the Afro-Peruvian community in Peru. We read articles, interviewed Afro-Peruvian people, tried Peruvian food, and built fundraising campaigns in order for us to go to Peru. The CTSJ's international research expeditions

At Our Best, pages 179–181
Copyright © 2020 by Information Age Publishing
All rights of reproduction in any form reserved.

have been to Cuba, Peru, and Puerto Rico. In CTSJ, I have also been able to dive into my Afro-Dominican identity and learn about the legacy of the African diaspora in Latin America. Daniel's story of self-identity inspired me to analyze my own identity and proudly identify as an Afro-Dominican. Traveling through Peru, we had the ability to lead conversations and teach our peers back home strategies to talk to our families about colorism. After our trip, we organized a presentation at our school based on our experiences. Daniel guided us every step of the way, and also found other opportunities for us outside of school to develop our learning and our success. Daniel dedicated his time at WHEELS to guarantee our success and expand our knowledge, and he continues to do so today while acquiring his PhD in Pennsylvania. Thanks to Daniel and the relationship we were able to build, I am writing about my experiences for this book.

I started the WHEELS chapter of Million Hoodies with two friends in 2017. This organization focuses on developing Black and Brown leaders through campaigns to end systemic racism. With the help of Mr. Voulgarides, our soccer coach, we were able to launch the first high school chapter. I believe Million Hoodies wouldn't have been the same without the support of Mr. Voulgarides. When Million Hoodies at WHEELS was just an idea, Mr. Voulgarides approached us to offer his help to start the chapter. It was only right for him to also become our chapter advisor. It was essential in the building of our chapter to have an adult who would help us every step of the way, and who could find opportunities for us that we wouldn't have had access to otherwise. Since then, we have organized a student walkout for the victims of gun violence, and have had a member speak on NPR's *On Point* about this same issue. We were also featured on a five-word speech video about gun violence during the Webby Awards. All of our success has been a result of Mr. Voulgarides' support and encouragement.

Because my peers and I were doing work that we could identify with and that mattered personally to us, we succeeded in our research and activism projects. In these programs, our teachers worked with us to bring our own ideas to life, so we were even more committed. Our teachers were able to get us life-changing opportunities that we wouldn't otherwise get. Just like Daniel and Mr. Voulgarides did, other adults should trust and support the ideas of students to create work that matters in their communities. I believe change can come from students if they are offered the support of an adult at their school. Building a relationship with a teacher encourages us to succeed and guarantees that our voices are heard to create change in our communities.

Bio: Yohely Comprés was born in the Dominican Republic and came to the United States in 2012 with her mother and brother. Yohely is currently a senior at Washington Heights Expeditionary School in New York City. Yohely has committed to joining the class of 2024 at Wesleyan University.

Per Yohely: I enjoy doing math and writing, as well as painting and drawing. I am a very active member of my school through clubs such as Million Hoodies (which I am chapter leader of), Critical Thinking Social Justice, Girls' Varsity Soccer, and the National Honor Society. I am interested in politics and the way minorities are portrayed in the media. I plan to go to college and continue to work for my communities both in the United States and the Dominican Republic. I want to use my experiences and successes to change my communities' perception of Afro-Latinidad, womanhood, and success.

CHAPTER 10

HIP-HOP MUSIC-MAKING AS A CONTEXT FOR RELATIONAL EQUITY AMONG YOUTH AND YOUTH WORKERS

Erica Van Steenis
University of Colorado, Boulder

Ben Kirshner
University of Colorado, Boulder

For many young people, writing and recording hip-hop music can be a culturally sustaining activity that emphasizes self-expression and storytelling (Ladson-Billings, 1995; Paris & Alim, 2014; Stovall, 2006). The music genre, comprised of sampling, beats, lyrics, dynamic range of voice, and looping melodies, originated in African American and Latino communities in New York city in the 1970s, and has since gained cultural significance and popularity with youth across racial, socioeconomic, and national lines (Alim, 2007; Bradley, 2017; Chang, 2007). Because of its relevance, hip-hop music is a promising curricular tool to use in educational spaces (Ladson-Billings, 1995;

At Our Best, pages 183–198

Morrell & Duncan-Andrade, 2002). Teachers and afterschool programs have used hip-hop music to develop young people's music production skills, literacy skills, and critical consciousness (Alim, 2011; Morrell & Duncan-Andrade, 2002). Such activities also enable educators to better connect with youth across lines of difference and support the cultural practices of youth communities (Morrell & Duncan Andrade, 2002; Paris & Alim, 2014; Stovall, 2006).

A small but growing number of youth development programs, called youth media arts organizations (YMAOs), have adopted hip-hop music production as their main programmatic feature. Although gaining attention from practitioners and educators, fewer academic researchers have investigated hip-hop music making in out-of-school spaces. Research on youths' participation in hip-hop music-making alongside adults adds to the conversation about how community-based educators can use varied modalities to partner with young people and support their development (DiGiacomo & Gutiérrez, 2015; Kirshner, 2008; Larson, Walker, & Pearce, 2005; Penuel & DiGiacomo, 2018; Zeldin, Larson, Camino, & O'Connor, 2005).

In this chapter, we draw on ideas and lessons from qualitative case study research of a YMAO in the San Francisco Bay Area called Horizons Youth Services (HYS; pseudonym), carried out by first author, Erica Van Steenis. Van Steenis's fieldwork explored how youth workers used hip-hop as a pedagogical tool to engage youth participants' passions and interests. This chapter highlights the design features of HYS that used hip-hop production as a context to facilitate equitable relationships between youth and adults.

HORIZONS YOUTH SERVICES

Horizons Youth Services is a nonprofit organization in the San Francisco Bay Area founded in 1993 by two community members interested in making a difference in the lives of underserved youth throughout the city. The organization offered case work, culinary arts, life skills workshops, and financial advising sessions. In addition to these programs, youth interested in hip-hop music came to HYS to access the digital media arts lab where they pursued their interest in music production alongside more experienced peers and youth workers.

At the time of this fieldwork, the digital media lab was equipped with a recording studio, professional grade digital audio and film production equipment, and desktop computers with ProTools, a computer program for composing beats and mastering music. Within this space, youth had access to workshops run by youth workers who were trained in digital arts and music production including writing, recording, and editing processes.

In the lab, the goal was (and is) to turn young hip-hop enthusiasts into skilled users of digital technology. As young peoples' skills advanced and they became more expert, HYS hired participating youth to run an in-house record label called Dream Records. This component of the program offered financial compensation to youth for their artistic contributions and facilitation of recording sessions for other youth in attendance. Employment with Dream Records deepened not only young peoples' hands on experiences with recording, mixing, mastering, releasing, and distributing music, but also helped them develop skills that would help them when they joined the workforce.

PARTICIPANTS

This study focused on 12 youth: three female and nine male identifying, who were 17–21 years old. Eight of them identified as African American, three as Latinx, and one as White. These youth were recruited for the study because they consistently utilized the digital media lab to pursue hip-hop music production. All of these youth were involved with HYS for at least 1 year, helped run recording sessions, composed their own music, worked for the record label, and helped peers learn how to use the equipment in the studio. The youth collaborated with 6 youth workers, including co-founders Diane and Jon, head caseworkers Lisa and Moses, and digital media arts lab leaders Leo and Emily. Leo and Emily both came to HYS with music production skills and expertise in various genres of music that they had developed over many years, positioning them well to scaffold and engage in pedagogical tasks with the youth. Observations focused on collaborations between youth and Leo more specifically because he connected most often with the 12 youth who frequented the recording studio.

HIP-HOP AND YOUTH MEDIA ARTS

YMAOs emerged in the 1990s and captured the interest of youth development practitioners and scholars. They became popular spaces for youth to engage their passions and interests in digital arts including, but not limited to, radio journalism (Chávez & Soep, 2005), filmography (Blum-Ross, 2015), and spoken word (Watson, 2012). Participation in digital media arts facilitates youths' ability to tell their stories using cutting edge mediums (Blum-Ross, 2015; Chávez & Soep, 2005; Goodman, 2011).

Youth media arts organizations often exemplify contemporary principles of *connected learning*: they are production centered, peer-supported, and interest driven (Ito et al., 2013). Chávez and Soep (2005) describe the type of learning that takes place with digital media as a "cycle of production" characterized by stages of "planning, practice, performance, and reflection" that allow youth to take on various roles and responsibilities (p. 417). Youth are encouraged to create artistic products that are relevant to topics that they want to explore and share via digital media; this work is usually done in tandem with adults and peers.

Research on YMAOs exists throughout a wide range of disciplines (Chávez & Soep, 2005). Youth Radio and Chicago Public Library's YouMedia are two programs in which practitioners and scholars have taken an interest. Both programs stand out because of their dedication to youths' positive development through participation in digital media arts. As part of Youth Radio, youth participate in the many stages of journalistic production, including learning basic media skills and creating sophisticated news stories for broadcast radio. At YouMedia, multifaceted program offerings allow youth to choose from a variety of digital media tools, enabling them to try out three forms of engagement, which Ito and colleagues (2013) have called "hanging out," "messing around," and "geeking out." Each stage exemplifies a different level of participation from a more socially focused use of digital media to advanced stages of use, including producing music or making documentaries (Barron, Gomez, Martin, & Pinkard, 2014).

Intergenerational Relationships in Youth Media Arts Organizations

Many studies trace the positive effects of youth's participation in digital media arts, including the role intergenerational relationships play in youths' learning and development (Soep & Chávez, 2010; Zeldin et al., 2005). Eccles and Gootman (2002) found that positive relationships with adults can provide youth guidance, support, and a sense of belonging. In YMAOs, youth–adult relationships are often characterized by more symmetrical interactions in joint activity, which is not accidental, but rather a key feature of programmatic design.

Common to YMAOs, young people and adults depend on each other's skills and commitment to jointly collaborate on projects. Though some adults are recruited for their track records as artists, they bring a pedagogy that emphasizes collaboration on tasks in ways that works to shift power and responsibility to youth (DiGiacomo & Gutiérrez, 2015; Halpern, 2005; Richards, Gomez, & Gray, 2014; Soep & Chávez, 2010; Zeldin, Christens, & Powers, 2013).

In their examination of Youth Radio's approach to producing journalism stories, Soep and Chávez (2010) describe a collaborative form of engagement between youth and adults called *collegial pedagogy*. Collegiality is characterized by joint work on projects with consequential expectations and outcomes, shared collective responsibility, youth-led inquiry, and distributed accountability on projects consequential for both parties. Chávez and Soep (2005) found that adults took a supportive position as they collaborated with youth on stories about topics ranging from youth's views on abstinence to freedom of speech in schools. At Youth Radio, the young people pitch their stories, drive the research process, and deliver the story through their own perspectives and voices. Although inquiries are youth led, they take shape with adult expertise and guidance throughout the process (Penuel & DiGiacomo, 2018). Adults work side-by-side with youth to help youth frame the stories they want to tell and to navigate barriers that arise. Intergenerational collegial relationships at Youth Radio demonstrate how adults follow instead of lead, positioned as learning from youth rather than teaching youth.

Youth practitioners who are a part of the Digital Youth Network (DYN), a hybrid out-of-school and in-school program, also approach joint production with youth in ways that position them more equally by uplifting their voices and expertise (Gomez, Barron, & Pinkard, 2014). Digital Youth Network in Chicago was created for a diverse community of youth interested in the skills associated with technology and digital media production. As part of the program, youth have access to their own laptops, studio spaces, production tools like video cameras and musical instruments, and expert mentors. Digital Youth Network plays an important role in addressing disparities in access to digital technologies by offering access and scaffolded learning opportunities using new technologies (Gomez et al., 2014). When youth participate in DYN, they work alongside student peers and professionals in their fields who act as mentors in various digital media practices like videography and music-making. Interactions between youth, their peers, and mentors are significant because through those connections youth's social capital increases as they develop both relationships and skills (Gomez et al., 2014). Although DYN mentors are experts in their fields, they prioritize youth interests, exposing youth to digital media tools they may not have otherwise explored on their own. Adults help youth build the confidence to "put in the work to deepen their digital media skills, and when ready, to showcase their work to peers, mentors, and teachers" (Pinkard & Austin, 2014, p. 16). The intergenerational relationships present at DYN lead youth to showcase their work; when adults position themselves in a support and guidance role, they allow youth to reach their broader goals.

An emerging framework for understanding intergenerational relationships in positive youth development settings is *relational equity* (DiGiacomo & Gutiérrez, 2015, 2017; Penuel & DiGiacomo, 2018). Relational equity, which draws on prior theories of guided participation (Rogoff, 2003) and youth–adult partnership (Zeldin et al., 2013), foregrounds *relationship in activity* as the unit of analysis to explore how intergenerational relationships foster youth agency and expertise through horizontal forms of collaboration (Edwards, 2011; DiGiacomo & Gutiérrez, 2015, 2017). This work builds on the above examples with its more explicit resistance to the historically dominant idea that adults are experts and youth are novices in any given practice (DiGiacomo & Gutiérrez, 2017, p. 44). As a construct and in practice, relational equity problematizes the traditional teacher-to-student hierarchy in which teachers engage students in adult-led tasks rather than more symmetrical joint production (Penuel & DiGiacomo, 2018). It also challenges some normative youth development practices where adult staff assume a position of savior or program leaders fail to incorporate youth perspectives into programming (Baldridge, 2014).

Designing for relational equity means that adults must position and reposition themselves to recognize their power, and value youth's expertise and agency in joint activities. In doing so, adults can humanize youth by working to engender more symmetrical relationships through purposefully negotiating, reflecting, and renegotiating interactions with youth (Halpern, 2005; DiGiacomo & Gutiérrez, 2017). As shown in the examples of Youth Radio and DYN, YMAOs are well positioned to develop and refine collaborative pedagogies among youth and adults. Youth media arts organizations emphasize "low barriers to entry, joint production, and shared, networked connection and expression" and offer "alternative participant structures in learning activity with the potential for more symmetrical participation among adults and youth" (Penuel & DiGiacomo, 2018, p. 6).

Hip-Hop Music-Making

Scholarship has described how hip-hop culture and music offer texts that enable young people to develop a critical lens for analyzing the circumstances of their lives and develop new literacy skills (Alim, 2007; Duncan-Andrade & Morrell, 2005). Common in the research on youth and hip-hop music, particularly in the field of education, is research on the use of critical hip-hop pedagogies in school settings and as a tool for youth identity development (Duncan-Andrade & Morrell, 2005; Emdin, 2010). This research includes how the use of hip-hop texts acts as a tool for literacy development (Duncan-Andrade & Morrell, 2005) and science learning (Emdin, 2010). Contemporary education scholarship also highlights how hip-hop can be a vehicle to engage young people's intellectual strengths and cultural assets

(Alim, 2014; Hill, 2009; Love, 2013, 2016; Nzinga & Medin, 2018). There has been comparatively less research, however, about how young people learn to write, record, and produce hip-hop songs, particularly in organized after-school contexts (see Flores-Gonzales, Rodriguez, & Rodriguez-Muniz, 2006; and Dimitriadis, 2001; for two articles that get close to this topic). This is an area that merits more research, given the recent growth of organizations devoted to music-making with youth.[2]

Given the promising nature of YMAOs, we draw on fieldwork from HYS to develop initial claims about the kinds of intergenerational relationships that are both possible and situated within hip-hop music production. Guiding the analysis of this case study are two research questions: (a) How do youth and youth worker's joint participation in hip-hop music production, within the context of a YMAO, demonstrate intergenerational relationships rooted in equity? (b) How does hip-hop music production between youth and adults, within the context of a YMAO, allow youth to gain access to new types of networks, tools, peers, and mentors in their communities?

FINDINGS: DESIGNING FOR YOUTH–ADULT PARTNERSHIPS THROUGH HIP-HOP MUSIC PRODUCTION

Van Steenis's ethnographic research with HYS found that the activity of hip-hop music production engendered collegial, partner-like relationships between youth and adults, which offered a sharp contrast to traditional understandings of adult–youth relationships where adults act as experts and youth are positioned as novices. This process was not accidental, but instead an intentional design feature of HYS. To make space for equitable social relations between youth and adults, HYS youth workers designed three main programmatic features. First, they provided high levels of accessibility to music-making resources, reducing barriers to the recording studio. Second, they prioritized joint work characterized by high degrees of both relational/social and material feedback where youth saw the process and the product as they participated in hip-hop music production. Third, invited youth to give input and collaboratively resolve recording studio-related dilemmas that emerged. The following examples illustrate how these design features led to intergenerational relationships that positioned youth as agentic in their own process of developing expertise in hip-hop music-making.

Access: Joining for the Studio, Staying for the Relationships

The no-cost aspect of the HYS recording studio and its high quality equipment drew youth to the center. Moreover, prior knowledge or evidence of talent and expertise were not requirements to participate in the space; instead, HYS was about playful exploration alongside others. These intentional design features allowed the youth to access equipment that they otherwise could not afford; youth traveled far distances across the city to write, record, and master their music. Youth's interest in using the recording equipment led to deeper relationships between peers working on music together, and also between the youth and youth workers, with whom they interacted daily. Across interviews with 12 youth, participants mentioned numerous times that the quality of the recording studio and the fact that it was free were big draws.

Several students spoke explicitly about the importance of the studio equipment in their experience of HYS. Devin, for example, told Van Steenis that he first started coming to HYS because he had a friend who told him about the free studio. Similarly, Adrian, who participated in HYS for 3 years, said that access to high quality recording allowed him to pursue his interests. Noting his passion for making music videos, he explained: "I can't go buy like a $2,000 camera. Like, I can't afford that." Trayvaughn's enthusiam for listening to music was long-standing, but before finding HYS he never got to *create* music; access to the recording studio enabled him to finally write and record his own hip-hop songs.

The youth explained that access to high quality studio equipment facilitated relationships with expert youth workers who were also passionate about music-making. Observations showed that, over time, youth who came in with more personal goals, such as to record a song or improve their lyrics, often stayed because of the relationships they formed.

One youth worker, Leo, stood out. Youth developed trusting relationships with Leo through making music together. Adrian called Leo his "mentor" and appreciated how Leo worked alongside of him in the studio recording sessions. He noted, for example, how Leo would explain the process of making a beat or laying down a track. Adrian would watch what he was doing and then Leo would hand over responsibility to Adrian. Adrian reflected:

> He would tell me what he was doing and he would let me track it and then I would kind of get the hang of it and he would be like, "Do you want to try it?" And, I would be like "Oh okay, alright, I'll do it," and I tried it and then I picked up some of the stuff he does. You know, he has kind of just been there like a mentor so he has taught me pretty much everything I know.

Devin similarly explained that Leo was his mentor; he attributed his own knowledge about producing music to Leo's guidance. Devin said that he initially found HYS because of the studio, but that he stayed because the youth workers and youth "all work together." Trayvaughn, who also worked for HYS in the recording studio, described Leo as a friend rather than an authority figure: "It's like when I talk to Leo, I am not even talking to a boss. It's like I am talking to somebody that is my friend." Trayvaughn's slightly different take on Leo as a friend rather than mentor, as the other youth described, shows how Leo was an approachable and personable adult figure in his life.

These examples exemplify that the no-cost access to high quality recording equipment created an appealing context that drew young people to participate. This draw was an important motivator, which was then augmented and strengthened by the kinds of skills they could develop and social connections they could form while creating music with others.

Joint Work: Youth–Adult Collaboration in the Hip-Hop Production Process

In HYS, hip-hop music production offered a context for joint-work between youth and adults and skill development. Throughout the course of observations at HYS, there were multiple instances in which adults partnered with youth in producing music throughout different stages of the process. For example, Michael, who had attended HYS for 2 years, described the place as one where everyone worked hard to collaborate on shared goals.

Consider this in-depth example observed several months into Van Steenis' weekly observations. One evening, Van Steenis joined Leo, a youth worker, and Bree, a youth who had attended HYS for 1 year. It was early evening and the recording studio was bustling with activity. Multiple youth worked in the space, one rapping in the recording room, while others worked on the sound board to select audio settings for the track. Bree sat next to Leo in front of a large Apple computer screen and worked on a program called ProTools to create beats to put with the lyrics she had just written. Leo was teaching Bree how to play beats on the keyboard and modeled an example for her. He showed her the different keys to press on the keyboard and the types of sounds she could create. Bree watched intently and followed his example eventually, mimicking the process but stringing together her own beats. Leo commended her for on-point timing, a skill he noted is hard to develop, and a unique sound. Then, without pause, Leo praised her, calling her a "boss," a natural at producing beats. She smiled, stating out loud to herself that she is a "boss."

During another observation, a 15-year-old participant named Selena joined Leo to work on writing lyrics for a song that she wrote. She shared with Leo that she could not figure out what to write about and that she was stuck. She wanted a song, she explained, that was in her own voice that captured the experience of young mothers who choose to share their stories. Leo encouraged her to write in her own voice, drawing on her passion about the topic. Selena came up with lyrics about her own personal experience of losing her baby in a car accident when she was pregnant; she explained to Leo that she wanted her song to help others who had been through something similar. They brainstormed ideas together, such as that teen moms are inspiring and hardworking, and that Selena wants them to be strong and not give up. Once they talked about the lyrics of the song, Leo focused on one particular element of songwriting: the chorus. Selena was reluctant to get started; she insisted that she was not a good writer. Leo suggested that they work together to write the words and melody of the chorus. As they wrote the chorus words, Selena added melody.

In both examples, Leo worked alongside youth in ways that expanded their sense of expertise and agency in the practice of music-making. He provided focused feedback and suggestions as they collaborated through the writing and recording process. He positioned the youth as agentic in their creative process, meaning that they were invited to choose or generate lines, beats, or melodies, even if some of the brainstorms or ideas were created together. Trayvaughn shared that when he had "an idea about a video or a picture or something like that, [Leo] would always listen before he made his move." Leo did not pressure the youth to like his ideas; instead, he would offer different ways to approach a song and let the youth choose what direction to take it in. For example, Bryan said that when he was worried about his album cover, he asked Leo to do it for him, but instead "he taught me the software and enabled me to do it myself and then if I had any questions he just answered them for me." Leo's positioning of himself as supportive and there for guidance, but not to tell the youth what to do, allowed the youth to develop confidence in their abilities to make their songs, and ultimately, to celebrate the end results.

Collaborative Visioning: Critical Conversations About Gender

Youth workers at HYS were attentive to issues of equity and invited critical conversations about gender, race, socioeconomics, and sexuality in their routine interactions with youth. For HYS youth, these issues were central to their lives, because they experienced discrimination and oppression in multiple forms every day. Gender dynamics, in particular, came up in several observations. These conversations emerged through the types of songs written and music produced, but also in the everyday interactions taking place in the context of HYS. Consider the following example:

> When I [first author] walked into the pizza place, there were 10 youth sitting around the table next to Leo and Lisa, two youth workers. When I entered, everyone was eating pizza and discussing gender dynamics within the organization. CJ, an African American youth, was first to speak, and he reflected that he did not expect female participation at HYS but that there were quite a few female participants. Initially, the youth around the table noted that female participation was going well, but as they continued to talk, they realized that girls were more hesitant to use the recording equipment. At this point, Lisa asked the boys if they had ideas for how to invite female participation. David thought female participants could have their own time in the studio without male participants present. Angel echoed that they could have a girl-day, and CJ said that was the best idea he had heard yet. Leo closed the conversation asking everyone to be mindful of inclusiveness so that girls also felt comfortable using the equipment.

In this interaction, Leo and Lisa brought the male youth into a conversation about how to structure the studio in more equitable ways. They invited youth to reflect on and talk about social interactions and opportunities for girls to participate. Lisa and Leo asked questions that gently encouraged those around the table to be more self-critical about the space and how they could encourage everyone's participation. In this sense, Leo and Lisa modeled how important it was to attend to power dynamics in terms of both interpersonal relationships and the broader structures of the setting. Even though they aspired for the learning space to be open and equitable, they observed that it often fell short and worked with the group to change its norms and practices related to gender and hip-hop. As demonstrated, they did so by collaboratively visioning with HYS youth instead of making the decisions without consulting them.

DISCUSSION

The youth–adult partnership literature often focuses on programs where youth and adults make joint decisions and participate in a level of shared governance. Zeldin et al. (2013) define youth–adult partnerships as:

> the practice of: (a) multiple youth and multiple adults deliberating and acting together, (b) in a collective [democratic] fashion, (c) over a sustained period of time, (d) through shared work, (e) intended to promote social justice, strengthen an organization and/or affirmatively address a community issue. (p. 388)

Zeldin et al. (2013) cite examples of partnerships, often housed within city government or community organizations, that have contributed to sustained youth participation in local governance or community planning. Other scholars, such as Mitra (2004), have developed this partnership metaphor to characterize shared leadership and governance opportunities for students and teachers in schools.

Youth media arts organizations offer distinct contexts from those typically discussed in the youth–adult partnerships literature. Horizons Youth Services, for example, did not design formal decision-making structures, such as a governance council or youth-adult advisory group. HYS used their music projects to address unjust policies or community issues; their work did not usually channel into specific community improvement projects or policy aims. Moreover, their most common types of youth–adult interactions were dyadic, rather than as a collective. Youth–adult interactions often exemplified deeper forms of one-on-one mentorships and a type of joint production that emphasized apprenticing the youth into music-making.

Nevertheless, we argue that the language that young people used to describe the work of music production, as well as the observations Van Steenis documented in fieldwork, show the ways in which the core elements of youth–adult partnerships, such as youth and adults deliberating over shared issues and projects with the intent to promote equity, were present. Van Steenis often observed shared music production between Leo and a single youth as he taught them a specific skill or helped them construct lyrics. Shared music production also occurred in a deliberative, community-based fashion where many HYS youth workers and youth collaborated on a song. Often the youth's music touched on provocative topics intended to engage an audience in more deeply understanding their experiences. There were also multiple examples of Leo producing music jointly with young people, while still prioritizing or privileging the learners' ideas and experiences as youth of color growing up in the San Francisco Bay Area. As the young people wrote and recorded amongst their peer community, their lyrics and messages often shared themes related to a common social justice analysis, and they communicated ideas for how to change the world through their music. Finally, although not as formal as a youth council, HYS youth and adults demonstrated a strong sense of being a collective, with shared goals and values. In the example from the pizza shop, we saw Lisa and Leo encourage a group discussion about what kinds of norms they wanted for the space and how to think critically about gender equity for girls.

Taken together, these examples show how HYS youth workers were doing more than just teaching youth the skills associated with making music. Instead, they engaged youth in positive intergenerational relationships that prioritized youths' experiences and expertise, demonstrating what it means to be in equitable youth–adult relationships. Given this, we can see the skillful guidance offered by youth workers such as Leo and Lisa expanding models of partnership in artistic spaces. Their approach shares elements with what Soep and Chávez (2010) call *collegial pedagogy* and DiGiacomo and colleagues call *relational equity*, in that it emphasized respectful and symmetrical interactions, while still embodying an intentional practice to foster youth's learning and development (DiGiacomo & Gutiérrez, 2015, 2017; Penuel & DiGiacomo, 2018). The example of HYS, however, further emphasizes how the youth workers made explicit efforts to position HYS youth's ideas and expertise as equal to those of adults. We do not take casually the exceptional degree of skill and care demonstrated by Leo and Lisa. This is not easy work; they had honed their approach over many years. Moreover, they had to both have some artistic talent, for songwriting and rapping, as well as pedagogical insight about how to guide and scaffold novices.

As advocates continue to build the field of youth work, particularly in emerging domains of media and music creation, we encourage attention to the partnership practices visible at HYS. As we conclude this chapter, we find ourselves left with various inquiries about the scalability of models like HYS. This study also raises debates in the field about how far to go in formalizing and institutionalizing youth worker training to learn the skills employed by Leo. We believe there is much value in the relational approach they take and that it ought to be formalized and taught to others. While we do not necessarily have set answers to these larger questions, we see value in sharing examples like HYS as a way to show the promise of digital media artistic spaces for expanding our conceptions of partnership pedagogies.

NOTES

1. The types of critical scrutiny vary. Some critiques are thinly-veiled expressions of stereotyping and racism. For others, particularly from feminist perspectives, it is based on concerns about the violence and misogyny that shows up in a subset of rap and hip-hop music. Still others raise concerns about the corporate influence on hip-hop as it has shifted from its early days as an underground movement (Watkins, 2005). Some social scientists have studied whether hip-hop and rap music are associated with drug use, crime, and violence against women, and this body of work has been challenged by recent scholarship (Nzinga & Medin, 2018; Rudman & Lee, 2002).

2. An in-depth scan of the web led us to identify several programs and organizations that engage youth in recording music. Some examples of programs include: The Living Remix Project, which provides youth a pathway to gain digital media, storytelling, and collaboration skills through the process of writing and producing hip-hop music (https://thelivingremix.bandcamp.com). Building Beats, which teaches youth about DJ and digital media production through music-making (https://buildingbeats.org). And Youth on Record (YOR) in Denver, Colorado (https://www.youthonrecord.org), which

partners with the local music community and public schools to give access to and uplift youth through the musical arts. This is not a comprehensive list. There are other programs that are exclusively hip-hop focused or incorporate hip-hop music production as part of their offerings.

REFERENCES

Alim, H. S. (2007). Critical hip-hop language pedagogies: Combat, consciousness, and the cultural politics of communication. *Journal of Language, Identity, and Education, 6*(2), 161–176.

Alim, H. S. (2011). Global ill-literacies: Hip hop cultures, youth identities, and the politics of literacy. *Review of Research in Education, 35*(1), 120–146.

Baldridge, B. J. (2014). Relocating the deficit: Reimagining Black youth in neoliberal times. *American Educational Research Journal, 51*(3), 440–472.

Barron, B., Gomez, K., Martin, C. K., & Pinkard, N. (2014). *The digital youth network: Cultivating digital media citizenship in urban communities.* Cambridge, MA: MIT Press.

Blum-Ross, A. (2015). Filmmakers/educators/facilitators? Understanding the role of adult intermediaries in youth media production in the UK and the USA. *Journal of Children and Media, 9*(3), 308–324.

Bradley, A. (2017). *Book of rhymes: The poetics of hip hop* (Revised, Updated edition). New York, NY: Civitas Books.

Chang, J. (2007). *Can't stop won't stop: A history of the Hip-Hop generation.* New York, NY: St. Martin's Press.

Chávez, V., & Soep, E. (2005). Youth radio and the pedagogy of collegiality. *Harvard Educational Review, 75*(4), 409–434.

DiGiacomo, D. K., & Gutiérrez, K. D. (2015). Relational equity as a design tool within making and tinkering activities. *Mind, Culture, and Activity, 23*(2), 141–153.

DiGiacomo, D. K., & Gutiérrez, K. D. (2017). Seven chilis: Making visible the complexities in leveraging cultural repertoires of practice in a designed teaching and learning environment. *Pedagogies: An International Journal, 12*(1), 41–57.

Dimitriadis, G. (2001). *Performing identity/performing culture: Hip hop as text, pedagogy, and lived practice* (Vol. 1). New York, NY: Peter Lang.

Duncan-Andrade, J., & Morrell, E. (2005). Turn up that radio, teacher: Popular culture pedagogy in new century urban schools. *Journal of School Leadership, 15*(3), 284–304.

Eccles, J., & Gootman, J.A. (2002). *Community programs to promote youth development.* Washington, DC: National Academy Press.

Edwards, A. (2011). Building common knowledge at the boundaries between professional practices: Relational agency and relational expertise in systems of distributed expertise. *International Journal of Educational Research, 50*, 33–39.

Emdin, C. (2010). *Urban science education for hip-hop generation.* New York, NY: Sense.

Gomez, K., Barron, B., & Pinkard, N. (2014). Introduction: The digital media landscape. In Barron, B., Gomez, K., Martin, C. K., & Pinkard, N. (Eds.), *The digital youth network: Cultivating digital media citizenship in urban communities* (pp. 1–13). Cambridge, MA: MIT Press.

Goodman, S. (2011). Mad hard fun: Building a microculture of youth media in New York City transfer schools. In J. Fisherkeller (Ed.), *International perspectives on youth and media* (pp. 338–354). New York, NY: Peter Lang.

Flores-Gonzales, N., Rodríguez, M., & Rodríguez-Muñiz, M. (2006). From Hip hop to humanization: Batey Urbano as a space for Latino youth culture and community action. In S. Ginwright, P. Noguera, & J. Cammarota (Eds.), *Beyond resistance: Youth activism and community change* (pp. 175–196). London, England: Routledge.

Halpern, R. (2005). Instrumental relationships: A potential relational model for inner-city youth programs. *Journal of Community Psychology, 33*(1), 11–20.

Hara, A. F. (2012). RAP (requisite, ally, protector) and the desperate contemporary adolescent. In S. Hadley & G. Nancy (Eds.), *Therapeutic uses of rap and hip-hop* (pp. 45–68). New York, NY: Routledge.

Hill, M. L. (2009). *Beats, rhymes, and classroom life.* New York, NY: Teachers College Press.

Ito, M., Gutiérrez, K., Livingstone, S., Penuel, B., Rhodes, J., Salen, K....Watkins, S. C. (2013). *Connected learning: An agenda for research and design.* Irvine, CA: Digital Media and Learning Research Hub.

Kirshner, B. (2008). Guided participation in three youth activism organizations: Facilitation, apprenticeship, and joint work. *The Journal of the Learning Sciences, 17*(1), 60–101.

Ladson-Billings, G. (1995). Toward a theory of culturally relevant pedagogy. *American Educational Research Journal, 32*(3), 465–491.

Larson, R., Walker, K., & Pearce, N. (2005). A comparison of youth-driven and adult-driven youth programs: Balancing inputs from youth and adults. *Journal of Community Psychology, 33*(1), 57–74.

Love, B. (2013). "Oh, they're sending a bad message." *International Journal of Critical Pedagogy, 4*(3), 24–39.

Love, B. L. (2016). Complex personhood of hip-hop & the sensibilities of the culture that fosters knowledge of self & self-determination. *Equity & Excellence in Education, 49*(4), 414–427.

Mitra, D. (2004). The significance of students: Can increasing "student voice" in schools lead to gains in youth development? *Teachers College Record, 106*(4), 651–688.

Morrell, E., & Duncan-Andrade, J. M. (2002). Promoting academic literacy with urban youth through engaging hip-hop culture. *English Journal, 91*(6), 88–92.

Nzinga, K. L., & Medin, D. L. (2018). The moral priorities of rap listeners. *Journal of Cognition and Culture, 18*(3/4), 312–342.

Paris, D., & Alim, H. S. (2014). What are we seeking to sustain through culturally sustaining pedagogy? A loving critique forward. *Harvard Educational Review, 84*(1), 85–100.

Penuel, W. R., & DiGiacomo, D. (2018). Organizing learning environments for relational equity with new digital media. In J. Voogt, P. Resta & T. Laferrière (Eds.), *International handbook of information technology in primary and secondary education, 2ndedition.* New York, NY: Springer.

Pinkard, N., & Austin, K. (2014). The digital youth learning model. In B. Barron, K. Gomez, C. K. Martin, & N. Pinkard (Eds.), *The digital youth network: Cultivating digital media citizenship in urban communities* (pp. 1–13). Cambridge, MA: MIT Press.

Richards, K. A., Gomez, K., & Gray, T. (2014). iRemix Education: Engaging mentors as teachers. In The Digital Youth Network (Eds.), *The digital youth network: Cultivating digital media citizenship in urban communities* (pp. 48–72). Cambridge, MA: MIT Press.

Rogoff, B. (2003). *The cultural nature of human development.* New York, NY: Oxford University Press.

Rudman, L. A., & Lee, M. R. (2002). Implicit and explicit consequences of exposure to violent and misogynous rap music. *Group Processes & Intergroup Relations, 5*(2), 133–150.

Soep, E., & Chávez, V. (2010). *Drop that knowledge: Youth radio stories.* Berkeley: University of California Press.

Stovall, D. (2006). We can relate: Hip hop culture, critical pedagogy, and the secondary classroom. *Urban Education, 41*(6), 585–602.

Watkins, S. C. (2005). *Hip hop matters: Politics, pop culture and the struggle for the soul of a movement.* Boston, MA: Beacon Press.

Watson, V. (2012). *Learning to liberate: Community-based solutions to the crisis in urban education.* New York, NY: Routledge.

Zeldin, S., Larson, R., Camino, L., & O'Connor, C. (2005). Intergenerational relationships and partnerships in community programs: Purpose, practice, and directions for research. *Journal of Community Psychology, 33*(1), 1–10.

Zeldin, S., Christens, B. D., & Powers, J. L. (2013). The psychology and practice of youth–adult partnership: Bridging generations for youth development and community change. *American Journal of Community Psychology, 51*(3/4), 385–397.

VOILA!

Latifat Odetunde

Stage lights come on. The crowd awaits a life-changing performance, as the magician enters the stage.

The magician, knowing their power, casts a spell on the audience, preventing the watching eyes from blinking. Aware that Magic is about to begin, the magician fades to the background. As the audience witnesses Magic's force, their eyes—dry as ashy skin on a winter day—stare, hypnotized. Magic opens a door into a mystical space of vulnerability and its power manifests, building and taking over the stage.

Magic comes in various forms, such as the type that is in the sleight of a hand, or an optical illusion. But what is constant is that *all* Magic changes the lens that an audience sees through. The job of the magician is to captivate the audience, and lure them in. Done properly, the show is no longer about the magician, but about the Magic itself.

All youth have Magic within them. It increases in power as they learn about their capabilities and the areas of interest that best reinforce their skills. With the right adult ally—the kind of magician that can set the stage for youth to transform the space—young people can help erase the hierarchies of adultism. Behind the curtains, there is a surge of appreciation

At Our Best, pages 199–200

and an exchange of feedback. The magician offers new ways to increase the capacity of the Magic, and in return the Magic balances the power dynamic, telling the magician what it needs, and how the magician can effectively provide feedback. This debrief is what helps the pair grow as individuals. They exchange words that reassure each other of their unique magnificence, sealing their attachment as a team. Youth–adult partnerships create an equal playing field, where adults and youth uplift each other and work together to reach a common goal, while growing simultaneously.

Bio: Latifat Odetunde is a Muslim Nigerian activist dedicated to uplifting marginalized communities. Currently, Latifat is a first-year student at Boston College with a double major in sociology and African & African Diaspora Studies.

Per Latifat: My activist career blossomed in Providence, Rhode Island where I attended Classical High School. I participated in various organizations such as Oasis International, and the NAACP, while receiving awards such as Boys & Girls Club Youth of the Year and the Secretary of State Civic Leadership Award. Lastly, I was one of the core organizers of the school walkout that took place in 2017. Youth In Action was my main organization that molded my character and interest in social justice. The adults within the organization served as allies, that treated me as their equal through love and honesty, which led me to become confident in being a changemaker, while remaining unapologetically me.

CHAPTER 11

BUILDING THE BELOVED COMMUNITY

Intergenerational Organizing at the Highlander Research and Education Center

Jessica Tseming Fei
Harvard Graduate School of Education

with Nayir Vieira Freeman, Rush George,
Ash-Lee Woodard Henderson, and Allyn Maxfield-Steele

In this chapter, we explore the youth–adult partnership work occurring at the Highlander Research and Education Center in New Market, Tennessee. For decades, the Highlander Center has been a space of learning for youth and adults engaged in intergenerational organizing across the South and Appalachia. Given the focus of this book on the range of ways in which young people and adults build authentic relationships and partner towards shared goals, the book editors connected with staff members at the Highlander Center to learn more about their history, methodology, and

At Our Best, pages 201–217

pedagogy. We were especially interested in Seeds of Fire, an intensive training program that Highlander hosts for youth organizers every summer.

Over the course of two phone conversations in January 2019, Jessica Fei (book co-editor and chapter co-author) interviewed and facilitated dialogue with Highlander Center staff and Seeds of Fire alumni. Jessica then transcribed recordings of these conversations, co-edited them with the participants, and excerpted key parts for the purposes of this chapter. What follows is a selection of the perspectives shared by the four individuals who participated in these calls with Jessica: Ash-Lee Woodard Henderson and Allyn Maxfield-Steele, co-executive directors of the Highlander Center; Rush George, a youth organizer and member of the Seeds of Fire advisory committee; and Nayir Vieira Freeman, a young adult organizer and an adult ally for Seeds of Fire.

Our chapter begins with each of these individuals introducing themselves and then moves through their discussion of the work of the Highlander Center, focusing on the structures and strategies they use to support young organizers. Through this dialogue, we see how youth and adults at Highlander nurture intergenerational relationships that are rooted in shared understandings of history and shared commitments to the "Beloved Community"—Dr. Martin Luther King Jr.'s vision for a global society that is grounded in nonviolence and upheld by social and economic justice.[1] We gain knowledge about the transformative power of practices such as creating formal leadership roles for young organizers, drawing connections between issues of oppression across boundaries of time and place, and fostering collectives that honor all individuals as learners and as human beings. Ultimately, Highlander illuminates the power of humanizing out-of-school spaces that are co-created by youth and adults, where everyone invests deeply in their own and each others' education and liberation.

WHO WE ARE: AN INTRODUCTION TO THE CONTRIBUTORS FROM HIGHLANDER

Rush: I'm Rush, my pronouns are she/her/hers. I'm 16, and I've been working in organizing since I was 12. I started with the Deep Center here in Savannah, which is a writing and social justice advocacy organization. Through Deep Center, that's how I came up to Highlander and participated in Seeds of Fire camp. And then in the following year, I was part of the advisory committee.

Nayir: My name is Nayir; I use they/them pronouns. I'm one of two co-chairs for Young Democratic Socialists of America, and I'm vice president of community for Transcend at Texas

State, the first trans student organization at a public university in America. I also work with immigration justice and other queer trans justice work. I've been involved in [organizing] spaces for about 11 or 12 years now—ever since I was about 8 years old. My first organization that I came to Highlander with was YO Houston, dedicated to eradicating the school-to-prison pipeline, especially in Texas. I've since progressed from youth participant to youth advisory committee member, and from there I moved on to an adult ally in our Seeds of Fire advisory committee.

Ash-Lee: I'm Ash-Lee Henderson; I use she/her/hers pronouns. I'm the first Black woman to serve as executive director of the Highlander Center, which has been around since 1932. We're very Southern, very rooted in culture, very rooted in a social justice politics. I was introduced to Highlander's youth and intergenerational organizing work 12 years ago. I came through "Transitions," which was a program for young people coming into intergenerational leadership of organizations and movements that were and had been led by well-known and respected elders. So I cut my teeth on methodology here at Highlander.

Allyn: My name is Allyn, I'm one of the co-executive directors; in the last couple of years, I came alongside of Ash to do that. I served on the board before that, and served as an adult ally for Seeds of Fire before that—while also doing some other programs around emerging leadership at Highlander.

HIGHLANDER: CREATING AND CATALYZING A HOME FOR ACTIVISTS

Allyn: Highlander functions as a catalyst—working with grassroots leaders through educational processes to fight back and push forward and create something new. A conversation about fighting back and creating something new can't happen without young people, and without young people leading, because that kind of conversation is about centering the experiences of folks who are inheriting what we [as adults] are leaving behind. Doing that in partnership and in solidarity is part and parcel with Highlander's mission.

Ash-Lee: It's why we have specific programs for young people and over our history have had specific programs for intergenerational organizing. And I think that in this political present—we don't think it's a moment, we think it's a pendulum swing in a long history of resistance to oppression and the blowback that comes with victories—we're also seeing young people at the helm of transforming Appalachia and the South, this country and the world.

Highlander . . . is a place that helps to identify, develop, connect an intergenerational cohort of folks that will envision, sustain, and implement the next phase of the Southern Freedom movement, but . . . we also are not making the assumption that everyone over a certain age is a veteran of the movement. There are folks who are older who are coming into the movement fresh, and are looking to get trained up, and Highlander is a place where that can happen. So yeah, Highlander is both a physical place where people can come together across difference, and it's also a commitment to the beloved communities that practice these methodologies—intergenerational organizing just being one of them.

Rush: What Highlander does is kind of like waking people up, or giving people the resources they need so they don't have a defeatist mindset.

Every morning that we wake up, that's resistance. With being in the South—and I'm from Georgia, the deep South—every day, it's kind of like, why even bother? You're seeing your family and friends getting killed by officers, and people being locked out of resources . . . [but] it's just kind of [about] remaining vigilant and remaining steadfast in the work that needs to be done.

Highlander to me was a really life-changing experience. There aren't a lot of movement-oriented things within my city other than the organization that I'm a part of, so it was refreshing to be around other people who have the same passion. And seeing that and looking at the history as we were on the Seeds of Fire tour, it kinda refocused me. When I joined the advisory committee for Seeds of Fire, I was able to learn more about the methodology and the rituals and staples and things that make Highlander, Highlander. Its connection to grassroots movements within the South. It's kind of a home for activists within the Southern region.

Ash-Lee: When I think about the South, I think of it not as a monolith——I think of it as a very dynamic and abundant place. And that with the investment of our time, and energy, and resources, and love, and principled struggle, that "as goes the South, so goes the nation" is not just an opinion. It's actually a quantifiable fact. And that the Southern Freedom Movement, by being committed to this work and to do it and to win, will be changing the entire dynamic of this entire country.

Allyn: I think that sometimes the South is defined by people's perceptions of it. And so when we talk about the work and some of what we do in this particular political present, it's about turning the camera back on who is creating the narrative about the place. Or, turning a camera on who's actually creating the story of the place.

Ash-Lee: We literally are the embodiment of the Highlander Folk School. That was our origin—it was that of the folk school movement. And because we were doing intersectional work and bringing people together—particularly Black and White people—the state of Tennessee kicked us off our first home almost 60 years ago. Our name changed when we restarted in Knoxville, and then we ultimately landed in New Market, but we're very much still functioning as a place that centers popular education and intergenerational organizing and being that catalyst for social movement.

Highlander is rooted in a Southern way-of-being, and to fight for and train up young people in the South and to allow for them to have space to be autonomous and learn how to fight for themselves. Because they can, and they do. Every day. Every day they wake up and are resisting, in the fight for liberation.

Rush: Highlander is a place where people are able to just be free. And be themselves completely, and they don't have to worry about whatever other labels they might have in other spaces. Yeah, Highlander is where I feel the most whole and the most myself.

SEEDS OF FIRE AND HIGHLANDER'S APPROACH TO SUPPORTING YOUNG ORGANIZERS

Rush: Seeds of Fire is a program during the summer, and it basically brings different youth—like two or three representatives from different youth-led organizations—from across what we call the South and Appalachia. We bring them all to Highlander to crowdsource, get ideas, and come together. We see what's working, where people are, and what are some different things that we can bring back to our respective communities. It's also a fellowship—a time to be in fellowship with each other, and learn, and create bonds that last for a lifetime.

In years past Seeds of Fire has been a camp; in some recent years, it's been a tour . . . it just depends on what the vision is for each year. The first year that I was a part of Seeds of Fire, it was a tour, so we started off on Highlander ground for 2 days. And then we started travelling across Tennessee and Texas and the total duration was about . . . 10–14 days. And with the tour, each day looked different from the other, but certain Seeds of Fire rituals were held constant. For example, when we get up in the morning we'll eat breakfast, then we'll do "Blacked Out History" and then we do "Beautiful Solutions." So that for every problem we see, there are beautiful solutions for it. Different organizations, programs across the entire world that have uplifted and shaped and changed an issue that was found within that person's area. At the tour, after that morning ritual, we would get ready to go to whichever site we'd be at for the day—whether that's us visiting the U.S.–Mexico border, us going to a museum to look at history in that sense, or going to somebody's Center, that focuses on LGBTQ and Latino rights . . . One day we focused on food justice, another day we focused on immigration rights, and then we did Black history, and we visited the Lorraine Motel.

This past year, we did the Seeds of Fire camp. We partnered with another group—the Donkeysaddle Project. And one of their directors, Jen Marlowe, she has a play that she wrote based on Land Day in Palestine, where a young man named Aseel was shot and killed by Israeli police forces while they were peacefully protesting. So the play is about Aseel and his family and mainly his sister—his older sister—and how they coped with Aseel's death. It has before and after scenes. And so this past year . . . we did the play as well as our Seeds of Fire rituals.

And throughout Seeds of Fire, the advisory committee is really there to structure the day, but it's really up to the participants. The participants host different workshops based on what they concentrate on. My organization, the Deep Center, we did a writing workshop with interviewing and getting to how to provoke answers from people in a real authentic way. We had people from Atlanta talk about the National Students' Bill of Rights. Children's Camp, they did a workshop on adultism and how we cope with it and deal with it.

The first time I went to Seeds of Fire, honestly, initially I thought it was going to be very "Y'all do that and we'll do this and that's gonna be that." Like, very separated. But, my expectation wasn't reality. It's not just adults chaperoning and being there for legality purposes. Like, we were all learning from each other. And even on Advisory Committee—which is all former participants and also adult allies—I thought it was going to be kinda that same thing, where it's like: "We know more than you guys do, because we've already done it, and gone through it." But it was still like a learning between and across generations. And like seeing that continue on into this year's advisory committee and this year's camp: that running theme of breaking that expectation of those -isms being in place.

Nayir: Highlander is just a huge melting pot where we are explicitly, constantly saying—over and over again, like NO, you cannot—in this space—allow for these -isms and phobias to continue to exist. Because if we can't do this in our own spaces, then how the hell are we supposed to do it in someone else's space?

I also want to speak back on my first experience at Highlander. I almost want to say we had a perfect [Seeds of Fire] tour. We had a huge group of maybe 30 people participating. And I think we had somebody who was around 12 or 13...and then the oldest person was I believe in her 60s or 70s, and she was the mother of one of the participants. So we had like a 50-year gap. And it was a complicated situation...but our biggest collaborations are spaces where the people that create our structure are a blend of youth and adults.

From the blend of youth and adults we have to selectively customize work we do between each and every organization that comes through Highlander. We have to connect these people who have different levels of experience and different types of work that they're doing, and connect it back to the Highlander methodology and pedagogies that people had invented from scratch and that had been working since the 60s. [In addition] each and every one of the ideas that the advisory committee comes up with is then altered by the youth and adults that are participating in our group. As soon as people meet each other, they start clicking. And they start creating entirely new ideas. This group clicked so well that there were about...I want to say that there were maybe seven workshops that were not put on by the advisory committee explicitly.

At that Seeds of Fire tour, I instantly connected with a mentor [whose] work was so strong, and it was so amazing to me—meeting another Black, older, queer, non-binary person with these strong ties to their family but also a lot of trauma there, and who just understood me on an intrinsic level. Meeting these people through Highlander gave me the space to be safe while also teaching the adults about things that I still knew.

Ash-Lee: I think there are just so many ways that Seeds of Fire is impactful. One of the ways that sticks with me the most is, you know, Highlander is an active member of the movement for Black lives. And a few years ago, we had a national convening that ended up being an international convening of Black people from all over the diaspora in Cleveland, Ohio after Tamir Rice was murdered... There were about 2000 people from all over the world there, all Black people. Alicia Garza and I were co-facilitating a People's Movement Assembly, a Black People's Movement Assembly. And I look down in the audience and there was at least 900 of the 2000 people just in this auditorium alone. And I see all these familiar-looking young people!

And... what we're doing at the time is this radical Black history timeline. We're talking about Harriet Tubman, Sojourner Truth. We're talking about Ida B. Wells; we're talking about the United Negro Improvement Association. We're talking about Fannie Lou Hamer... and I looked down and with this sea of young people that I recognize, I also see Fannie Lou Hamer's niece. And it hits me that the Seeds of Fire youth have brought their delegation of Black people to the convening! And that Fannie Lou Hamer's niece was an adult ally for Seeds of Fire at the time. So we not only got to see family showing up for family; we literally created an opportunity for me to be able to honor Fannie Lou Hamer through a recognition of her niece and her relationship to Seeds of Fire and Highlander.

Seeds of Fire shows up off the physical property that is where Highlander is located. It shows up *everywhere* where young people and their adult allies do their work, right? Because that's literally the point. It's for them to come together, to build relationships with one another, to become comrades and a generation or cohort of Southern freedom fighters who will come together and throw down for each other. And then to go and spread the word—the gospel of the Southern Freedom Movement. Seeds of Fire literally does that. Its name talks about *planting*, right? Literally these seeds go out all over the region and then blossom into these incredible campaigns that win and change people's material conditions.

Allyn: There is some other youth-oriented work at Highlander, although Seeds of Fire is the one that's most focused on working with youth leaders from youth-led or youth-serving organizations across the region. We have a separate program that focuses on a different experience of youth, which is more around children ages 6–12 and the families or guardians or folks responsible for children, caretakers. It's called Children's Justice Camp and it's traditionally led by former participants; someone who was a participant as young as age eight and is now in her late 20s or 30s and is now the director of the camp.

There's also a range of other ways that we support young people through more administrative and strategic guidance around fiscal sponsorship . . . so there are a range of other affiliations that you can have with Highlander as a youth organizing group or youth-oriented group, and it's happening year-round.

Ash-Lee: And I think the other thing that's interesting about the way we do it at Highlander is that it's not just like a summer program and then we don't talk to these young people again. Literally there are young people who are now in their 30s who continue to be in the movement and when they need support, they call Highlander. Or when we hear about something going on in the neighborhoods that they live in, we can call them and be like, "Hey what do y'all need? How can we support?" So it's lifelong leadership development and building that Beloved Community that will last beyond the time that they're of age to be in the program.

Allyn: What I think makes Highlander unique is the way we try to do things. Our board reflects our commitment to intergenerational work. We have someone as young as 23, and we have someone as old as 80 on our board. And they're equally holding leadership roles on the board. So the governance of the organization is one way to understand it.

I think the staff function similarly. We have a range of age on the staff, and if you look at organizational leadership right now, Ash and I are both in our 30s, and I just tipped over 35, just tipped into the older adult realm. But that's a really substantive thing, that is in the DNA of the organization. The founders of the organization, in the 1930s, were in their 20s. So I think it's hard to talk about programming separate from the fact that we want to govern ourselves also as an organization in the same way we're training people to be in the world. That's where there's a world that we inherited that exists, and then there's the one that we want to get to. And we're working our way there, day-by-day.

"I HAVE A ROLE": STORIES AND STRATEGIES OF ALLYSHIP IN INTERGENERATIONAL SETTINGS

Rush: What's different about Highlander is definitely that humanization, validation, and honoring people or respecting people. The spaces where that's not happening a lot are . . . church and school and definitely home—where there's that power dynamic between elders and young persons, especially if it's a caretaker. And youth are being talked at and not to. And decisions are being made for you because you're a child and children don't technically have rights. And because you're just a child you have to go along to get along and you know, survive. And just to be able to continue on.

In school . . . our teachers are very—"This is your club, y'all run it, I'm just here because the state requires it." But even that—even things like that, where they let you run it yourself, that's not always a healthy model because there are still experiences and things that youth don't have. And it's still also that adults and people who are supposed to be allies aren't learning in the space as well.

Allyn: The adult ally idea is that we have a role to play too, as folks who are on this continuum of what it means to be a person and a whole person. And we have different assets that we can leverage and we have different roles that we can play in terms of supporting youth leadership. So one thing I remember distinctly about Seeds of Fire when I was part of it as an adult ally—before I was on board, before I was on staff—was that we had our own track within the week that we were a part of the camp. So it sort of functioned as a pocket, an autonomous space for adult allies to talk about what are the things that we need to be doing differently, what are the things that we're learning, what are the things that we experience as people who work in support of young people. I thought that was one of the more powerful pieces of the camp—not experiencing it as a young person, it was helpful for me to actually have a space to not just be a depoliticized person in the space. I'm not just a "chaperone." I have a role—I have a political role to play as an older person to support young people in this liberation work that we're all talking about.

And like I said, there are some concrete roles to play around you know—what are the politics of being someone who can drive a rental car? [chuckles] As someone over the age of 25, that's one way I can support young people, I can provide transportation. So there are ways that are mundane but are actually really real, in terms of doing this kind of work. And it ranged from that all the way to what does it mean to run block for young people as they're pushing a particular campaign, or leverage fundraising resources for young people as they are trying to raise resources and learn how to do fundraising stuff for their work.

Nayir: A lot of my experience with adults has been a little more threatening, outside of Highlander. We do a lot of holding older people accountable and by the neck. But I do feel like Highlander holds a very healthy space where . . . some of the more senior members of our spaces—or the people who are more connected to Highlander—they allow themselves to be checked. Which I think is really, really important in being an older ally. And it's a complicated thing, because I don't want to discredit ideas and mentalities of our older community—and I also don't want to discredit younger community. But I feel like in most spaces, youth have the ideas and adults have the power.

Every time we come together at Highlander, it requires that we view each other on equal levels . . . and to an extent, while respecting experience, we also have to respect the work put in. Because a young person who has been doing that work for 5 years since the age of 15, that's an entire third of their life. So it feels like a long time to that person.

Allyn: I think that there are always challenges in holding older people accountable too—just like not letting White people off the hook—with "I'm human too." It's like actually, you still have to reckon with your identity as being a dominant identity.

The challenge of youth work, from an adult perspective, can be in really continuing to absorb what I think Rush was saying, a really humanizing experience of being held accountable for your own dominant cultural habits.

Rush: A successful example of youth–adult partnership that I have experienced was the first Seeds of Fire tour I went to in 2017. We were visiting the U.S.–Mexico border in Laredo, Texas. And the night before we had a briefing, so everybody could be prepped on all the possibilities of what could happen. And for us—a bunch of Black and brown youth in this daunting situation—it was kinda scary. They were preparing us for what could happen between border patrol and more. And from that, there were other tensions and things that were going on within our group and it all came to a boil that night. There were things going on with people's food situations, and rooming, and people feeling like they were profiled, within our group. And a lot of other things that were going on.

And that night, there were not just youth comforting other youth, but also adults comforting other adults. It was across—intermingling, everyone helping one another heal from the microaggressions that occurred while we were on our tour. And that was very real. I still remember that night, and how much it impacted the rest of our tour.

As far as concrete strategies, [it's important] to always listen with intent to understand each other instead of listening to each other just to respond when we're communicating . . . and to value and validate other's experiences—as much as you would your own.

In my intergenerational organizing spaces we start with that basic tenet of honoring each other, by first sharing names and pronouns and what people want to be called and go by. Because that has caused a lot of trauma for other people, it's important that we are making sure that what we call you is respectful and humanizing. And then continuing on from there, building the relationships. If there is something going on and you don't feel comfortable, then that'll be brought up and dealt with through our community agreements and things like that.

Nayir: Like Rush said, we try to have a humanizing space, but one thing we do is explicitly define our space as a space to learn. Highlander obviously has gone from the Highlander Folk School to the Highlander Research and Education Center. So it started as a school, and through that, implies that this is a space that is defined for learning.

There are certain things that we do—one thing that comes to mind is clap for understanding. So if someone has the courage to ask a question—like "hey, I don't know what this is"—we applaud them. Like, learning is a good thing and something to be commended. From there, we utilize the idea of a community space, or even in big boy communist terms, "the collective." [chuckles]

One of my favorite community agreements to use is called "step up, step back"—so those who have been speaking more and taking or holding a lot of space [are] stepping back for those who are maybe more nervous about sharing space with other people, more nervous about sharing their ideas. Allowing them to step up and allowing [others] to step back and remember that we're not the only ones, just because we're the loud ones or you're the person at the front in the pictures or speaking at our press conferences. If it's just you alone, you couldn't do the work. So, celebrating as a collective, making decisions as a collective, coming back to this idea of the collective being what we do what's best for.

Rush: At the Deep Center, where I work in Savannah, we have things like "don't yuck my yum" which is like, if I like something and you don't like it you don't have to down or demean what I like; we can just agree to disagree. And "one mic"—one person talks at a time, and we all police each other on that. Whether it's a youth or adult breaking the rule, we all hold each other accountable. So setting community agreements that everybody agrees on—that helps set the stage for how you want your space, our spaces, to be.

We also have a "joy-bringer," one youth who will have a game to get everyone pepped up and ready to do whatever it is we have planned. And then we have a "music-maker"— the person in charge of the aux cord. And then someone for our closing ritual as well, which is normally a breathing exercise or exercise of that nature, to calm us down because we go over heavy stuff and things that might be triggering for our youth . . . things like that to bring everybody back in, all things opened up—to bring those in and be closed. And be ready to go back out and face the world. Those are our rituals. And then we play it by ear.

Nayir: You have to allow yourself to be somebody who is open not just to new ideas but also open to being wrong . . . and then from there, not like "oh them kids got it, y'all good, I'ma step away." Not that, but

I have stepped back, I recognize that I have power, and I am going to utilize that power in your favor, because I actually do genuinely support you. And if I think something you're doing is not necessarily going to work or isn't right, if you're doing something that's not going to work for you, I'm not just going to say, "We're not doing that;" I'm gonna say, "Hey, here are some things I've seen in my own life that have caused these things."

So say if you're presenting a plan and say, "We're going to do XYZ and when we execute X we're going to do 123." I can be like,

Cool I like this plan, here are the things I see about it, and I think you're doing a really great job. However, point 2 on X, I've done that before in my life and here's where it went wrong. I'm not saying it's going to go wrong for you all, but I want you all to be careful and to be vigilant about this thing.

You step up and you do those things. But you can only do that if you've earned the respect. Everybody is deserving of respect, obviously but there are different kinds of respect. There's respect, such as "I'm going to treat you as a human with rights and things you deserve because you are a human being." And then there's "respect me, treat me like someone who has experience and authority etcetera, etcetera." And everybody does not deserve that second type of respect. I don't think it's implied that even like a parent deserves that, intrinsically. Yes, you deserve maybe honor for maybe holding me in that space and raising me . . . but that person does not know everything. That person is not all-knowing, all-seeing.

The adults I've grown attached to and seen as both mentors and people I could genuinely see as people who are safe for me to have questions with—they made themselves safe, they made themselves vulnerable, and they made themselves open to me. Because if you aren't willing to be vulnerable with the youth who are inherently vulnerable to you, then there's never going to be that trust.

Rush: In addition, every youth is a different individual and what works in one space might not necessarily work in another all the time. School is definitely a different setting than let's say the Deep Center or being at Highlander or being at your university. Every youth has their own backstory and history and things that they're coming to a space with. Just be mindful of that, and always hold space for that, because we never really know what people have come from.

Allyn: For me, some of the best examples of youth–adult partnership—or intergenerational educational work—come from giving the time to the issue that it deserves, because of the way that it will help everybody take major steps forward toward liberation work. So it's like, we are on an urgent scale and an urgent pace, and we're learning that the kind of work that we want to do requires deep attentiveness. It snaps open the parentheses that sometimes camps can bring to people's lives—like, "Well you came here, you were here, then you left."

No, we are in a community here. And this is the kind of thing that will continue beyond our time together. That's what makes it no longer a parenthesis, no longer a liminal moment.

EMBRACING AND LEARNING FROM IMPERFECTIONS: CLOSING THOUGHTS

Ash-Lee: Intergenerational organizing is a gift that keeps on giving. Because it's impacted my life, now I'm helping raise my 6-year-old niece and this was the first year that she's old enough to attend Children's Justice Camp. So [we are] literally building a tradition of Southern folks getting their friends, their family, their committee members, neighbors, the folks they worship with, the folks they kick it with at the bar, or the baseball field...it's a community of people, related to this place, that just keeps on getting bigger and bigger.

I don't want us to come across as though intergenerational organizing is just the easiest thing on the planet. In any sort of work where we're building relationships, especially relationships that have to acknowledge power differentials, and acknowledge that we live intersectional lives...oppression can exist in those spaces. There are interpersonal challenges, there are ways in which those with power embody it and internalize it and use it—or abuse it, in ways that harm people within our community.

But what's also real to me is that...especially for those of us that are Southern, of color, working-class...we've had to be in relationship, nine times out of ten, in order to survive capitalism and White supremacy, heteronormativity, all of these systems of oppression that harm our people. So I think about, "Who does it serve for elders and young people to not be in right relationship?" It's the people who want to concentrate their wealth and power, and who need us to not be together in order to not see that concentration.

For me, intergenerational organizing is about literally being able to build the Beloved Community that will liberate this place that I live and love in. And . . . the majority of the people that tell me that there's a problem between young people and elders—are not people that are trying to build that Beloved Community . . . It ain't nothing but systemic oppression that's keeping intergenerational organizing from getting the goods and liberating our people.

Nayir: Highlander is obviously not a perfect space. There is no perfect space of course . . . we've had spaces where the people who are in charge at Highlander were not always in the right. It's happened to me multiple times as a nonbinary person—that I've had to check people about my pronouns and also as a person who looks very young—like revaluing my position and recognizing that no, everyone who is in a position is not necessarily going to look like you, is not necessarily going to be who you expect.

So, you need to be keeping your mind open to these new possibilities and ideas. You need to be recognizing that the younger folk—they kind of have a hold. They know what they're doing. They really know what they're doing! Maybe they don't have all the pedagogy or maybe they don't have all the text or the words. But that's when you give them those words. That's what you're supposed to do, if you're one of the people in the older generation. What you're supposed to do is give these people this toolbox and these words and lessons so they can take them and if need be, destroy them. And you can't be too attached to those.

I also want to say that before anything else—be kind. Remember the kindness that has been afforded to you. Remember to hold that and afford that to others. From there, I'm echoing what Rush says—every person is an individual, and every individual brings something different to the table. Not only should we acknowledge that, but we should honor that. Even bad experiences are foundational to a lot of people. Especially in activist and leftist spaces, a lot of people are there because of a trauma they've endured or because of the life that they live being tied intrinsically to the difficulty that exists within living in the world that we live in. So, uphold that. Lift it into the space. Accommodate for that.

Remember that you, as an adult ally, also are deserving of rest. You are not—you don't have to be, at all times, a pillar of strength. And many times your youth will respect you more for admitting that you are not infallible. Remember being a youth. Remember that, hold in your heart—that there will always be things that you don't know.

One of my favorite stories is—I can't remember what culture it comes from—but there are certain times when you weave a basket, you don't weave a basket perfectly, you always make sure there's room for error. Because once you've woven the perfect basket, then is there a reason to create more? Is there a reason to grow? Is there a reason to learn if you've done it perfectly and know everything from there on? No. There should never be a time when you stop learning. And, there is no shame in learning. There should never, ever be shame in learning.

NOTE

1. For more on Dr. Martin Luther King Jr.'s concept of the Beloved Community, please see http://thekingcenter.org/king-philosophy/#sub4

SECTION IV

ON THE COMPLEX ROLE OF ADULTS

FAILED BY THE SYSTEM

Emmylou Nicolle

At Our Best, pages 221–222

My biggest pride when it comes to adult–youth partnerships comes from my relationship with my aunt. Although many young people I know are not really close with their aunts or uncles, I'm really close with mine. My aunt almost raised me and my brothers, and is more like a second mother than an aunt for us. When I was 17 years old, she helped me to install my very first exhibit, entitled "Not your Pocahontas," in her restaurant.

The exhibit was a series of 35 watercolor portraits, each with a story written on the back. Thirty-five interviews and portraits drawn from the shared experiences of 35 beautiful, resilient, and intelligent indigenous women from all ages and all nations. This idea came to me during a trip, as a way to give thanks and honor all the strong indigenous women who helped me to grow as an adult. It was really important for me to share their voices instead of claiming to "be a voice for them." The experiences of indigenous women are incredibly diverse, complex, and sometimes difficult to articulate.

I worked on this exhibit nonstop from February to October 2017, and my aunt was here to support me during the whole process. She was way more knowledgeable than I was when it comes to creating exhibits, because she had hosted many in the past. She helped me to promote the exhibit and to collect the money raised through selling the paintings. The proceeds were sent to Arming Sisters, an organization led by Patty Stonefish (Lakota), with the goal of teaching self-defense, not as a tool of prevention but as a form of healing. I met Patty online, and as she shared a bit about her story for this exhibit, I became really interested in her nonprofit.

This project was the result of a collaboration with so many women who accepted my invitation to share their stories, and trusted me to paint them in a way that was true to their vision. But I know I wouldn't have been able to share all of these stories without my aunt and her endless support. By providing me with a positive experience of my very first exhibit, she allowed me to feel confident enough to pursue my painting journey, and she opened the door for so many other experiences. Sharing my journey with this project brought me an online platform where I now share my artwork and share issues that are important to me. It also helped me to realize the importance of collaborating with authentic voices when I want to deal with a complex subject that I'm not directly affected by.

Bio: Emmy is a 20-year-old aspiring artist and curator. Her hometown is Naoned but she has had the opportunity to call many other places home. She is currently studying history of art and Spanish literature at Università di Pisa and hopes to become an art curator, an artist, or a professional translator in the future.

CHAPTER 12

HOW DO WE HEAL TOGETHER?

Unlearning Trauma in a South Asian, Diaspora, and Indo-Caribbean Youth–Adult Partnership Space

Melissa Kapadia
University of Pennsylvania

Anika Kabani
Institute of Ismaili Studies

Nudar Chowdhury
Stockton University

Formal education spaces can be contentious and systemically violent toward youth of color (Jordan, 1988; Ladson-Billings & Tate, 1995). This is true for South Asian, Diaspora, and Indo-Caribbean (SADIC) youth who experience nuanced discrimination like alienation, orientalism, invisibility, Islamophobia, and policing. Out-of-school spaces can provide alternative

At Our Best, pages 223–239

learning environments for youth who experience marginalization in traditional contexts. Within these spaces, youth–adult partnerships can be useful tools for deconstructing hierarchical models of learning and re-centering youth experience.

This chapter focuses on East Coast Solidarity Summer (ECSS), a summer program for SADIC youth across the East Coast of the United States. We describe the left-radical pedagogies that have framed ECSS's work and examine ECSS as a youth–adult partnership program that aims to serve SADIC youth via a nonhierarchical, agency-building model.

We write as two former participants (Nudar & Anika) and a former organizer (Melissa) of the ECSS program. Nudar Chowdhury is a sociology and anthropology student at Stockton University in New Jersey. Anika Kabani is a London-based graduate student at the Institute of Ismaili Studies; she graduated from Washington University in St. Louis in 2017. Anika and Nudar were first-time participants in ECSS 2018. Melissa Kapadia is a radical educator/organizer from Philadelphia, who works with the Radical Asian American Womxn's Collective (RAAWC), Asian Arts Initiative (AAI), and Philly South Asian Collective (PSAC), and teaches in the University of Pennsylvania's Critical Writing Program. Melissa spent 3 years as an ECSS organizer.

This chapter is informed by our conversations with each other and others who attended ECSS in the summer of 2018. Our aim is to examine ECSS's ability to meet its goals of offering an affinity, healing, and education space. Our writing comes out of both a deep love of our own SADIC communities and a desire to better conceptualize how to create spaces that support learning and healing.

EAST COAST SOLIDARITY SUMMER: AN OVERVIEW

Although ECSS is 6 years old, it is the third iteration of leftist SADIC youth programming that began in New York in the 1990s. The first iteration was Youth Solidarity Summer (YSS), a grant-funded youth conference organized by a collective of organizers and academics including well-known Indian Marxists Vijay Prashad and Biju Mathew. Youth Solidarity Summer used a 2-day conference format of workshops and panels on topics like South Asian identity, gender and sexuality, power and privilege, capitalism, and labor struggle.

East Coast Solidarity Summer is a community-funded, 5-day overnight camp that combines radical education with activities like pool time, bonfires, and tie-dyeing. Because of a rotating organizing team, ECSS's mission changes slightly year-to-year, but the overarching goals are to: (a) provide left-radical political and identity education, and (b) offer a space of community-building and healing to SADIC youth. Participants are drawn to ECSS because of its focus on understanding SADIC identity and experience, combating White supremacy and anti-Blackness, centering queer and trans experiences, and crafting tools for leftist organizing in local communities. East Coast Solidarity Summer attempts to use a nonhierarchical, distributed labor structure in which a group of 11–20 organizers, aged 15–35, work over a full year to plan the camp. Similar to its predecessor, YSS, which recruited approximately 30 youth aged 17–23 per year, ECSS recruits about 20–24 participants, ages 15–23. One interesting facet of the program is that ECSS often sees an overlap in age among participants and organizers, most of whom are between 19–24 years old. Both YSS and ECSS use a combination of word of mouth, social media, college networks, and community networks for recruiting.

Pedagogical Frameworks

Historically led by educators and social workers, ECSS has evolved into an activist-oriented education space guided by radical and Black feminist ideologies.[1] The summer retreat begins with a welcome workshop, which serves as a starting point for sharing ECSS's values and modeling nonhierarchical community decision-making and consensus-building. Here, we describe ideologies that have influenced ECSS's design and practice.

Non-Hierarchy and Trauma-Informed Practices

As a radical, queer,[2] SADIC education space, ECSS engages a critical pedagogy, divesting from hegemonic banking models, in which teachers act as depositors of information and "the scope of action allowed to students extends only as far as receiving, filing, and storing the deposits" (Freire, 1970, p. 58). Along these lines, the ECSS space is shaped by the concept of education as the practice of freedom, and a desire to distribute power equitably, centering participants' experiences in conversations about the conditions of their own oppression (Freire, 1970; hooks, 1994). Given this, organizers put many hours of front-end labor into designing workshops that offer facilitated community learning, model nonhierarchical dialogue, and provide loosely-guided activities. Per hooks' (1994) notion of an engaged pedagogy, emphasizing the holistic well-being of learners and teachers has also influenced the inclusion of healing and wellness spaces during ECSS. For example, trauma-informed therapy is available throughout the retreat, there is unstructured recovery time between workshops, and programming includes workshops on mental health, intergenerational trauma, healthism, and the like. In each of these spaces, participants' own lives and experiences are the materials to be "studied," and unlearning and healing are the primary learning objectives.

Femme-Centering and Counter-Hegemony

Few radical SADIC spaces exist for youth in the United States, especially ones that are femme-centered,[3] are queer- and trans-inclusive, or work to decenter Indo-Pakistani centrism and dominant caste hegemony.[4] The intention behind centering diasporic, historically-silenced communities is to bring their experiences to the forefront in order to combat systemic erasure, and generate a more diverse and inclusive vision of liberation. The goal of building community among a group of people whose experiences are so marginal in a larger context is best described by Lorde: to

> [build] genuine networks of support for each other and our communities, so that wherever, however, whenever we are functioning within this system which cannibalizes our loves and our lives... we work to bring about more humanity and more light for each other and for those who, like ourselves, have felt the keen edge of rejection. (Byrd, Betsch Cole, & Guy-Sheftall, 2009, p. 227)

East Coast Solidarity Summer offers workshops like "Queer & Trans Liberation" and "Diaspora at the Margins" to center these values and narratives. We also use these ideologies to reimagine what activism looks like, moving away from prioritizing masculine models of activism like direct action or civic- and government-focused work, and reframing community engagement, (un)learning, and self-healing as important, feminine models of activism. We also practice these ideologies by working to defeminize traditionally feminine labor, such as kitchen, cleaning, and organizing/management labor (although this practice is usually reiterated throughout the retreat, in the 2018 year, it was less explicitly emphasized to participants).

Anti-Carcerality and Justice

East Coast Solidarity Summer has theorized carcerality in two ways: (a) the retreat's relationship to and desire to divest from carceral state structures like police, and (b) the carcerality of interpersonal relationships. In the 2018 welcome workshop, the group built consensus on the decision not to call the police during situations in which individuals might traditionally call police, such as nonemergency medical situations, alcohol- or drug-related situations, or escalated personal conflicts.[5] The explicit goal was to solve problems through non-carceral means like restorative justice facilitation. Abolishing the carcerality in interpersonal relationships, though not discussed explicitly, came up organically in conversations about "cancel culture" and the tendency in radical organizing spaces to socially ostracize, shame, or dispose of those who misspeak or have ill-informed opinions rather than engaging with or supporting their learning; this is a relationship that mirrors the anti-rehabilitative interaction between the carceral state and the "problematic" individual. While some organizers engaged "teachable moments" or incorporated challenging moments into workshops, we found that—despite good intentions—many organizers and participants upheld carceral values by replicating dismissiveness or disposability, in essence reproducing "cancel culture." We describe this in more detail below.

SHIFTS IN VALUES AT EAST COAST SOLIDARITY SUMMER

East Coast Solidarity Summer's work is primarily shaped by domestic leftist movements (including East Coast SADIC activism, Black Lives Matter, responses to Islamophobia and policing, #noDAPL, etc). These recent movements have contributed to shifts in thinking about activism in general. Specifically, the availability of activist and leftist conversations online has shaped ECSS's organizing practices, including the potentially problematic expectation that organizers and participants bring prior experience and prerequisite knowledge about activism and radical thought with them. One example of this is an unintentional/organic shift toward recruiting more organizers with activist backgrounds rather than education backgrounds, meaning that many organizers come into this work without teaching experience or familiarity with education philosophies.

Over the last 2 years, returning organizers, specifically those with educational backgrounds, have expressed concern about whether expectations of prerequisite knowledge for participants are incongruous to ECSS's educational and political goals. Because, like all spaces, organizing spaces can be classist, this practice tends to favor well-educated and wealthier applicants. This has brought up the question of whether ECSS is an education space or an organizing space. This tension impacted ECSS 2018 participants' experiences: Whereas education spaces seek to prioritize forgiveness and (un) learning, organizing spaces can default to "oppression Olympics" and performativity in a way that hinders learners' experiences.

In the remainder of this chapter, we discuss a key incident from ECSS 2018 in which this dynamic played out. Specifically, this incident highlights tensions around the different purposes of our space (education/organizing), the gap between intent and impact, and power dynamics between organizers and participants. After telling our story, we reflect back on it, together.

Tensions Between Organizers and Participants: Our Story (Anika and Nudar)

During the summer of 2018, in order to facilitate participant agency, our ECSS organizing group gave participants debrief time after every workshop. The goal of this time was to reflect on community agreements, share our feelings collectively, and offer feedback to workshop organizers. Certain workshops, including one on mental health, left us feeling heavy and vulnerable. Others, like one on state surveillance, militarism, and imperialism, ended in conflict and tension, leaving participants unsettled. In each of these cases, the unstructured reflection time was intended to help us move the work forward.

Sometimes, however, our reflections did not go as planned, as was the case when we reflected on the surveillance and militarism workshop. During this workshop, the three workshop organizers wrote terms like "state surveillance" and "neoliberalism" on large pieces of paper and asked participants to write their definitions, thoughts, and reactions to the words on the pieces of paper. After the individual writing piece, the group came together to discuss what was written and create collaborative definitions for the terms. The workshop felt rushed, like we were trying to cram hours' worth of conversations into a short workshop. Participants felt disappointed as the workshop ended because we'd only discussed the concepts at an arm's length instead of interrogating how state violence impacted everyone in the room in similar and disparate ways. Recognizing that the workshop had felt incomplete to us, one workshop organizer commented flippantly while leaving the room that they'd do the workshop better next year, which felt dismissive.

In our debrief, participants expressed remorse that this topic, which was deeply personal to many of us, felt like it hadn't been taken seriously; we hadn't gotten a chance to delve into the shared experiences of surveillance and policing of our bodies and our families. One participant shared frustration around the casualness and depersonalization of the workshop as compared to others, wondering if it was a result of participants' collective distance from experiencing surveillance and militarism. As Muslims, we two (Nudar and Anika) personally disagreed with this because our communities regularly experience state surveillance, but we agreed that the topic deserved to be handled with more seriousness.

Participants wrote a list of ways we hoped to do better as a community, such as by centering Black liberation more actively and being more vocal about workshop pedagogies that weren't particularly engaging to us (such as writing definitions for phenomena we personally experience). We then invited organizers to view our list, hoping to involve them in our attempt at holding ourselves more accountable to our collective values.

As we shared our observations, agreements, and commitments with organizers, one of the workshop organizers began to cry. We realized that our message wasn't being received as we'd intended. Although our goal was to communicate what was working for us pedagogically and what was leaving us unsettled, it felt that many organizers were receiving our message as a direct attack on them and their work. One reason our message was received this way was that two of the workshop organizers came from communities that have experienced or reside in active militarized zones, and are also directly impacted by militarism and policing. They received our feedback as implying that they were not concerned enough with these issues.

The next morning, a group of organizers called youth participants together for a meeting—the two workshop organizers mentioned earlier did not attend (nor did Melissa). The organizers in attendance explained that the two workshop organizers were extremely hurt by participants' feedback, and that participants needed to apologize. They added that our intentions in sharing our observations the day before were irrelevant, as it was important instead to center the impact on the hurt organizers. After what felt like a scolding lecture, in which one organizer said that "it was no one's job to educate each other" and that participants could "just Google it" if they had more questions about workshop topics, we were asked to go around in a circle and say in one word how we were feeling. This, again, felt dismissive of participants' feelings and reactions, as we could not express ourselves. Further, we were told that the two organizers would not be accepting hugs or physical contact from participants during our apology. Although we did apologize, organizers and participants were even more divided afterwards. Just a couple hours later, the retreat was over and we all went back home, feeling supremely unsettled and silenced.

EXAMINING EAST COAST SOLIDARITY SUMMER THROUGH A YOUTH–ADULT PARTNERSHIP FRAMEWORKS: REFLECTIONS

It has become clear to us over the course of writing this chapter that our work with ECSS 2018 brought with it quite a bit of trauma for all three of us. One of the most valuable parts of working on this piece has been our capacity to offer each other space to process our trauma collectively; this has also involved asking big questions about what is possible in radical queer SADIC spaces, and what work still needs to be done. For Melissa specifically, as an educator-organizer who views these two arenas of work as intrinsically tied up with each other and who has engaged many discussions about the shifting mission of ECSS, hearing participants' retelling of the meeting described above has been frustrating and disappointing.

In our attempts to examine the dynamics and questions described above, we have found Zeldin, Christens, and Powers' (2012) framings of youth–adult partnership helpful. The authors describe youth–adult partnerships as, "the practice of: (a) multiple youth and multiple adults deliberating and acting together, (b) in a collective [democratic] fashion, (c) over a sustained period of time, (d) through shared work, (e) intended to promote social justice, strengthen an organization and/or affirmatively address a community issue" (p. 4). Below, we use these four concepts: youth voice and agency; mentorship; community-building and engagement; and reciprocity to examine our ECSS 2018 experiences as participants (Anika & Nudar) and organizer (Melissa).

Youth Voice and Agency

Zeldin, Christens, and Powers (2012) have explained that encouraging youth agency can be a key to empowerment, allowing youth to gain sociopolitical awareness. As described below, each of us experienced feelings of agency—and, specifically, the focus on youth voice and agency—differently over the summer of 2018.

> **Anika:** I appreciated organizers' intention to cultivate youth voice and agency at the start of the retreat, their stated intent not to lecture and teach in a dominating sense, but to guide conversations so participants would be able to understand our own experiences in a politicized and historically-informed manner. I also appreciated the invitation for participants to reflect after every workshop and assess how we (as participants) and organizers had stayed true to the community agreements we'd co-constructed on the first day of ECSS. Feeling like I had a voice in building and critiquing the space was important to my engagement and empowerment.
>
> **Nudar:** From the beginning of the retreat, it was clear to me that the organizers wanted to create a space in which we could feel comfortable partaking in the various planned discussions and activities. Participants and organizers alike came up with a set of community agreements on the first day of the retreat, aimed at holding each other accountable so that organizers did not have to play the authority figures and participants were encouraged to speak up in times of discomfort. This was one of very few spaces where I felt so easily connected to the people sitting in the room with me and one in which I felt encouraged to share my thoughts.
>
> However, there were also times in which the equity in the room was tested. After the incident described above, it truly felt like our voice and agency had been taken away. There was no discussion following this moment as it felt like there

should've been. To me, it felt like a lot of miscommunication had happened and it was important to create clarity for everyone. Not apologizing did not seem like an option to us participants. For me, these events re-instilled a hierarchical structure within the space, as many participants felt quite traumatized by a forced apology to what seemed like a forced end to the discussion and situation.

Melissa: Looking back, I think the 2018 organizing team struggled to craft a space for youth voice and agency. Although we plan activities and workshops around the values of non-hierarchy, this is often challenging to practice once we are actually in the week-long camp. This is partly due to the exhaustion organizers face because of the retreat's high labor demand and the unfamiliarity of being in an all-SADIC queer left space, often for the first time in our lives.

One factor that comes up in SADIC organizing spaces is a desire to save face: Our organizing team faced a lot of internal conflict and dysfunction that most organizers were not comfortable discussing even with each other, let alone with participants. Although organizers typically have nightly processing meetings, these meetings were not well-facilitated or "safe" spaces for discussion because of the ongoing tension among organizers during the 2018 camp.

I believe sharing our own conflict and asking participants to help us problem-solve could have been a good way for them to engage some of the concepts they were learning about in a safer space. It would also have provided participants a glimpse into the messiness of organizing work, and offered them an opportunity to engage non-hierarchy by supporting us. However, even retrospectively, I don't think our organizing team would have been comfortable making ourselves vulnerable in this way. We missed many opportunities during the camp, and my understanding now is that many participants came away from the week feeling disempowered because of various moments in which they felt their voices were taken away from them. As discussed more below, I'm relieved that I continue to have mentorship relationships with many participants, so that I can support them in processing their experiences, and extend care beyond the space of the retreat.

Mentorship

Zeldin, Christens, and Powers (2012) suggest that offering judgment-free engagement and compassionate interest in youth experience are key characteristics for adult mentorship (p. 8). In our reflections of the summer, we recognized this as an intended but unachieved practice of the ECSS 2018 organizers.

> **Anika:** Given the time constraints of ECSS, it felt unrealistic to be able to develop close mentorship relationships with organizers. Despite that, I feel there were organizers who were invested in the growth of participants both during ECSS and afterwards, and I felt very lucky to build relationships with those organizers. Even some of the organizers I didn't build relationships with impacted me by virtue of being queer, nonbinary, radical SADIC folks: Representation that is very uncommon for me in my communities.
>
> Thinking about Zeldin and colleagues' (2012) framework, however, one of the defining characteristics of strong mentorship is being nonjudgmental and forgiving toward participants; this is an area in which ECSS fell short for me. Although a handful of organizers seemed to view participants as learners, others were often unforgiving. I remember feeling shamed for not having a strong background in caste-ism and for the feedback that participants gave on the aforementioned workshop. This made me feel stripped of the opportunity to engage in conversations around where my education fell short.
>
> **Nudar:** It's difficult for me to reflect on how ECSS embodied mentorship because the camp was only 5 days long. However, I think mentorship could have been more evident in smaller ways. For example, during meals or downtime, some organizers would sit amongst each other to allow participants to get to know each other, but we would have liked to sit together. Because mentors and participants are supposed to be allies to each other's thinking and growth, I think it would have been significant for organizers to sit in on at least a couple of the reflection sessions we had so that when we wanted to bring up ideas or issues, they would have better understood where these thoughts came from and how they evolved.

It's also important to feel like those who seem mentor-like are our equals and that we as mentees have something to offer to their growth. There were times when one specific organizer, who designated herself as the retreat "aunty," became snappy and authoritative with participants. This showed me that those who proclaimed themselves as "mentors" did not embody the positive practices that such a label entitles.

That being said, I do feel that a few organizers took on very mentorship-like roles throughout the retreat without taking on aspects of superiority that can be typical to mentors. These organizers were judgement free and provided guidance in moments when I needed it. They also have been a distant support, since camp ended. I find comfort in knowing that such loving and compassionate folks exist and are happy to be contacted. They have continued their mentorship to me in both obvious and less obvious ways and for that, I am so grateful.

Melissa: As Nudar and Anika describe, mentorship is not an explicit goal of ECSS. While organizers discuss, both in planning and practice, the desire to craft safer spaces for queer, brown youth at ECSS, mentorship capacity doesn't factor into organizer recruitment, nor have we discussed explicitly what it looks like to model mentorship or what types of behaviors and values are required in cultivating a culture of mentorship. Age can also be complicated at ECSS, since organizers and participants often overlap in age.

While I agree that 5 days can feel short for developing mentoring relationships, my personal interest in cultivating one-on-one relationships with participants comes from wanting to engage a starting point for building relationships that will extend beyond the retreat. Because organizers were experiencing so much internal tension in the 2018 year, I found myself drawn toward more conversations with participants. This enabled me to have closer mentorship relationships with participants than in prior years. My ongoing relationships with participants post-retreat have been rewarding and have taught me a lot about sustaining long-term mentoring relationships as an educator. They have benefited my own learning deeply.

Community-Building and Engagement

Zeldin, Christens, and Powers (2012) have described community-building and engagement as the practice of supporting youth in thinking about organizing beyond the immediate learning space (p. 9). This part of the work feels central to ECSS, and yet, we recognize the ways in which the events of 2018 may have negatively impacted some participants' understandings of organizing spaces.

Anika: Though ECSS was my first engagement with a radical SADIC space, it was a space that had moments of trauma. The way the retreat ended left me feeling upset and unheard, and processing after the fact with other participants made me feel resentful about what the space could have been and wasn't. While we did build a community of sorts, I feel that my community was made up of participants more so than the organizers, and many of the relationships built over the course of those 5 days were grounded both in a shared trauma related to our identities, and the hopes and at times disappointments over what we imagined such a space could be.

Nudar: Prior to this retreat, I had never experienced a space like this, and it was one that I had not realized I needed as much as I did in the larger world of radical organizing. For those 5 days, participants and organizers alike became a small community in the larger SADIC community. I wasn't particularly sure what to expect when going into this space but regardless, once I was immersed in this community, I felt regretful; it could have been much more. Although we created community agreements as a means of being accountable to one another, the space seemed to lack accountability in many ways, especially in the distinction that existed between participants and organizers. I believe that due to our proximity throughout the retreat, we as participants were able to build lasting relationships with each other. I became comfortable with many of the other participants quickly. I knew that there was possibility here that would expand beyond the retreat, whether it be appreciation, support, or more organizing.

Regardless of my other expectations coming into ECSS, I expected compassion and understanding, and I feel I got this from other participants and some organizers. Although it's possible all organizers had the best intentions for the space, many did not always reflect this in their actions. It's important to note that many of us left the retreat with discomfort, trauma, and aloneness. For me, that's important to reflect on: Although this space showed me the importance of being with other SADIC folks, in future organizing spaces I hope that we can hold each other accountable for what we felt and experienced at the end of the week.

Melissa: In prior years, I felt ECSS organizers were able to cultivate community among participants that extended beyond the retreat space, enabling attendees to build connections post-retreat, with various other networks, and across other parts of the country. This was not true in 2018. I believe the lack of community and collective respect among organizers ourselves translated into the space we created for our youth. I feel strongly that while educators can often work to hide dysfunction from the youth they serve, it can be challenging to keep the dysfunction from spreading into the work we do. Given this, I was not at all surprised when many participants reached out to me post-retreat to talk about various moments that had made them feel unsafe, unwelcome, or silenced.

Keeping in contact with participants post-retreat has enabled me to hold onto positive feelings about the work we did. Communicating with a handful of organizers post-retreat and processing with them has helped me to understand the ways we might heal and shift practices in future work. My biggest takeaway in terms of how to cultivate the spirit of community when working with youth in the future is to be more transparent about how adults and educators occupy a space—learners can feel educators' tension, and they react and respond to those tensions in ways that can shape the education space as well.

Reciprocity

Zeldin, Christens, and Powers (2012) have defined reciprocity in youth–adult partnerships as the intentional shifting of power in the learning space to the learner (p. 10). Perhaps more than any other aspect of the work, we felt reciprocity was lacking in some of our interactions during the 2018 summer.

Anika: In the very structure of the space, I think there were limitations in how reciprocal relationships felt between organizers and youth. I want to center what I believe were good intentions from the organizers, although I think there was a fundamental disconnect between organizers and participants because of unequal divisions of labor, agency, and planning. To me, an important cornerstone of reciprocity is everyone equitably taking care of the people around them. Doing labor for others and putting effort into noticing each other's needs are important ways in which I demonstrate that I care about the people around me. I think shifting power and responsibility towards participants would have included involving us more in the labor processes.

Nudar: I felt that reciprocity was an area of struggle at ECSS. Throughout the retreat and especially towards the end, it did not always feel like we were allowed to contribute to other aspects of the retreat besides insightful comments and discussions. As described above, even when some of those insights were given, they were not received well. Personally, it felt like we did not have much to offer to the organizers, or we were not given the opportunity to offer it. I think a space that values reciprocity should allow participants to take on tasks and leave space for them to take on more initiatives throughout the retreat.

Melissa: I believe participants made an effort at engaging in what they perceived as organizers' openness to reciprocity through their sharing of concerns with us about ways certain workshops failed to meet their learning needs. Similarly, they took initiative in making suggestions for activities and offering support with meals, planning, and so on. In these ways, they were modeling many of our organizing and teaching values and practices in their own delivery. In reflecting on this, I wonder how organizers and educators can better receive the ways youth ask for, model, and attempt reciprocity, especially given the larger goals of out-of-school spaces to provide safety and affinity from traditional, often oppressive and violent spaces. It's understandable that adults/organizers can at times feel defensive about feedback, but this defensiveness stems from a hierarchical, one-directional view of teaching ("I own the knowledge and you receive it") and part of our work as organizers is to challenge ourselves when we feel that defensiveness slip in.

HEALING TOGETHER

Even in writing this chapter, we have admitted to each other that we have stifled our own voices, writing with fear that those at ECSS 2018 with whom we disagreed might further alienate or invalidate our experiences were they to read this piece. This unsettles us, but it is something we continue working through as radical SADIC community organizers. Because our community is small and we are actively working against disposability, it is important to us that we both maintain our truths and stay committed to the work being done by others in our community(ies).

In questioning whether ECSS is an education space, an organizing space, or both, we note the importance of balancing comfort and growth for organizers and participants. Many organizers felt that if the space was re-traumatizing to them, or replicated the oppression that they experienced in the world, it was no longer their duty to educate participants. We problematize this: while educators do deserve spaces in which they feel safe and seen, adopting a *believing* and *forgiving* stance is key to doing radical education work. Further, youth–adult partnerships should require that those responsible for the "teaching" view learners as intellectual equals with the capacity to make mistakes and learn from them, and offer opportunities to extend learning beyond pre-planned objectives. In this way, we believe that programs must work to balance comfort and growth for both youth and adults, participants and organizers.

An understanding that comes up in radical organizing spaces is that we are all traumatized by our experiences as marginalized people, and it is inevitable that we will replicate unhealthy or oppressive practices even in spaces of affinity. How, then, do we make space for processing collective trauma as we are replicating it? In what ways can we learn to practice justice and understanding when we are enacting trauma and injustice on each other? Partnership spaces can support this work by acknowledging from the beginning that spaces of healing are spaces of trauma; in other words, healing is ongoing, extending beyond the learning space, and collective healing is about investing in each other's healing long-term.

Despite the challenges of ECSS 2018, we believe radical education spaces that prioritize youth voice are well-suited to offer marginalized communities opportunities for collective healing. Viewing participants as agents in healing work can enable them to feel ownership for their and organizers' learning and healing, which is critical to radical community work. Further, acknowledging that hierarchies exist, even in spaces that aim for non-hierarchy, can support (un)learning because conversations about power and hierarchy are made explicit in the work.

NOTES

1. Framings of thinkers like Angela Davis, Assata Shakur, bell hooks, and Audre Lorde have helped to shape the work of ECSS—these thinkers situate education and feminism in the experiences of people of color, and in global contexts in general. Their ideas are described more in the next few sections.

2. Throughout this chapter, we describe ECSS as a queer space. This does not mean that all participants identify as LGBTQI, but rather that ECSS actively works to decenter cisheteropatriarchal ways of knowing and learning. That said, a majority of applicants (who become organizers and participants) tend to identify as LGBTQI, and many actively seek out this space because of its centering of queer perspectives and experiences.

3. The terms "femme-centering" and "femme-centered" originated in conversations that took place among a group of women and nonbinary organizers of the PSAC in March 2016. This group, of which Melissa was a member, was concerned about the ways PSAC's organizing work was replicating traditional gendered labor patterns that are often present in patriarchal and SADIC communities. In the process of teasing out ideal models of labor and organizing, this group began using the term femme-centering, that is, the process of decentering masculine supremacy, masculine value systems, and masculine models of organizing. One example of a masculine model of organizing and labor is that women might do the back-end labor of organizing and planning a meeting and men might facilitate the conversations at that meeting. A femme-centered approach would acknowledge this dynamic and ask that men take on more back-end labor, and so on.

4. South Asian, Diaspora, and Indo-Caribbean organizing spaces tend to center the experiences and voices of North Indians and Hindus. East Coast Solidarity Summer makes efforts to shift this tendency via focused recruitment of non-Indo-Pakistani South Asians and Indo-Caribbeans. East Coast Solidarity Summer's work aims to understand and unlearn casteism and leans on the work of Dalit activists and thinkers to shape these efforts (Soundararajan & Varatharajah, 2015).

5. The primary goal of this decision is to preserve the privacy of those dealing with such situations and conflicts, especially since many of our communities are heavily policed. Maintaining this practice further enables us to protect those with varying citizenship status, healthcare access, and identities that might be policed or problematized in medical situations (e.g., fatness, gender identity). Further, this is a way to decenter traditional carceral models in which alerting police is the norm.

REFERENCES

Byrd, R. P., Betsch Cole, J., & Guy-Sheftall, B. (2009). *I am your sister: Collected & unpublished writings of Audre Lorde.* Oxford, England: Oxford University Press.

Freire, P. (1970). *Pedagogy of the oppressed.* New York, NY: Bloomsbury.

hooks, b. (1994). *Teaching to transgress: Education as the practice of freedom*. New York, NY: Routledge.

Jordan, J. (1988). Nobody mean more to me than you and the future life of Willie Jordan. *Harvard Educational Review, 58*(3), 363–375.

Ladson-Billings, G., & Tate, W. F. (1995). Toward a critical race theory of education. *Teachers College Record, 97*(1), 47–68.

Soundararajan, T., & Varatharajah, S. (2015, February 10). Caste privilege 101: A primer for the privileged [Blog post]. Retrieved from http://theaerogram .com/caste-privilege-101-primer-privileged/

Zeldin, S., Christens, B. D., & Powers, J. L. (2012). The psychology and practice of youth–adult partnership: Bridging generations for youth development and community change. *American Journal of Community Psychology, 51*(3/4), 385–397. https://doi.org/10.1007/s10464-012-9558-y

HELPING HANDS

Gassendina Lubintus

Recently, I was notified about an upcoming college interview for one of the eight Ivy League schools. When I received the email, my stomach was quivering in fear. I had never been interviewed before, and my teachers at school had failed to mention college interviews to me. I shared the nerve-wracking news with my parents and my teacher at Workforce, my after-school program. They all reassured me by saying that I have nothing to worry about, since this is a great opportunity to showcase myself as a diligent scholar and person. Bryan Zuluaga, my teacher, told me: "From time to time, you managed to handle school, clubs, chores, and jobs well enough to not let it affect your grades. I've never seen anyone do it better. It'll be alright, because you are going to ace this interview."

With that in mind, we figured out a plan to prepare for this interview. Bryan had a lengthy conversation with me about the whole situation. Together, we researched more about the college and the interviewer. Along with that, we talked about what to wear, what to bring, and body language. Even though my parents were extremely busy working, they conducted several practice interviews with me. They were patient and truthful with their responses, since they always stopped to explain my mistakes. At these

At Our Best, pages 241–242

moments, I felt lucky to have people I can talk to when I'm in a somewhat stressful situation. Additionally, I have adults other than my own parents who are supporting my dreams and who want me to be ahead of the game.

The day of the interview arrived rapidly. At first, I was so nervous, but then I shook it off due to the help I received in a time of need. As a result of that, I went into the interview with an open mind, and with faith. I had faith in myself to do well because I had practiced numerous times for this moment, and I was not going to let doubt get the best of me. I reached my goal by simply advocating for myself to the adults in my life. In any event or crisis, I know I have a few people in my circle who will support me unconditionally, and who can lend a helping hand.

Bio: Gassendina Lubintus is a freshman at the University of Massachusetts Amherst. Born in Port Au Prince, Haiti, Gassendina moved to Cambridge, Massachusetts at the age of one.

Per Gassendina: Being Haitian has always been important to me, especially since my ethnicity and culture defines who I am. Currently, I am a full-time college student. When I am not vigorously concentrating on school, I love to read and watch videos in my free time. Additionally, I love writing. I usually write fan-fiction, but I never post my work online. In the future, I hope I can publish more of my own books, such as novels and short stories.

CHAPTER 13

TENSIONS OF PURPOSE

Strategies to Strengthen Partnerships and Overcome Barriers Between Youth and Adults and Advance Transformative Social Change

Samantha Rose Hale
The Center for Teen Empowerment

Heang Ly
The Center for Teen Empowerment

Nathaniel McLean-Nichols
The Center for Teen Empowerment

Carrie Mays
The Center for Teen Empowerment

Before there was an adult, there was the youth. What is an adult without their youth?
—Gabriel Petit

Youth and adults have much to learn from one another and together. Regardless of our age, we never stop growing. Yet despite the inherent interdependence of young people and adults, a myriad of factors can separate

At Our Best, pages 243–257
Copyright © 2020 by Information Age Publishing
All rights of reproduction in any form reserved.

us and prevent us from collaborating with one another. In this chapter, we focus specifically on tensions of purpose, using the combined lens of four co-authors, each of whom is a current or previous employee of the Center for Teen Empowerment (TE). Together we believe that through uncovering and addressing the deeply complex layers of tension that can arise in youth–adult partnership, youth and adults can better tap into each other's humanity, and develop deeper understandings of how to authentically and collectively move toward shared goals.

INTRODUCTION

Founded in 1993, the mission of TE is to empower youth, in partnership with adults, to lead their communities to achieve peace, equity, and justice. With this purpose, TE hires and employs Youth Organizers[1] to identify, analyze, and advocate for pressing issues of racial equity in their communities; these intersecting issues include violence, mass incarceration, mental health, poverty, education, and other social inequalities. We strive toward youth voice and empowerment by rejecting pervasive social stigmas, celebrating the skills and strengths of youth and their communities, and building youth leadership. By working together to unearth the realities of historical oppression, make connections to the immense disparities within today's society, and decentralize and redistribute power fairly, we provide and enact a vision for real, positive, and sustainable social change. The three key areas of TE's change strategy are facilitated public dialogues, community advocacy events, and social justice and community organizing through the arts (e.g., music, dance, visual arts, spoken word, and theater).[2]

The co-authors of this chapter met through working at TE in Roxbury and Dorchester, Massachusetts.[3] We are thought partners, and we have worked closely together at TE in several different iterations. While TE is the glue that brought us together, our perspective is also informed by a breadth of personal and professional experiences in a range of different settings. We are a diverse group in age (18–41 years old), race (Black, Asian, and White), gender identity (male, female, and nonbinary), education, and training. Carrie is a current youth organizer and has worked with TE for 4 years; Nate is a former youth organizer and is currently an assistant program coordinator, totaling 3 years at TE; Samantha is a former employee who worked at TE for 6.5 years, beginning as a program coordinator and then becoming assistant director of Boston programs; and Heang is a former employee who worked at TE for 13 years, first as a program coordinator and later as director of consulting and training.

As co-authors, we believe that the TE model can effectively empower and give voice to those who have been historically oppressed. At the same time, while TE aims for reciprocal and balanced partnerships between youth and adult practitioners, it is not impervious to systems of oppression that perpetuate an unjust social order; it is a microcosm of our society. In this chapter, we illustrate tensions that surface in the diverse and intergenerational partnerships we seek to foster. Furthermore, we demonstrate how authentic youth–adult partnership can transform tension into possibility. In tension, there is a powerful opportunity for adults and youth to grow, improve, and discover new strategies towards a shared purpose.

CONCEPTUALIZING TENSIONS OF PURPOSE AND AUTHENTIC YOUTH–ADULT PARTNERSHIP

We define *purpose* as the meaning, the motive, and the reason that guides action. Purpose is informed by lived experiences. When two or more stakeholders strategize together towards an agreed-upon and shared purpose, a partnership is formed. Informed by our experiences with TE, we believe that *authentic* partnership must include a dedication to achieve a diverse, equitable, and inclusive space. In addition, it must be based in a shared belief that the intersection of lived experiences, identities, and positionality holds possibility for something greater than we could ever imagine on our own.

However, even in the shared purpose to effect community-wide and institutional change through youth–adult partnerships, priorities can diverge and compete with one another during the planning and implementation process. Unaddressed, these tensions can result in cascading consequences that ultimately create a barrier for the collective to successfully work towards their agreed-upon purpose. We believe that it is imperative that all constituents are in constant individual and collective reflection about the tensions and challenges that arise in this work. In this way, a collective can seek to ensure that they are ever-evolving to best fulfill their purpose. Working through these tensions of purpose can carve a pathway to hope and the foundation for action towards a just and equitable world. Through this iterative reflection process, our core belief, and thus practice, holds constant: *Authentic youth–adult partnership* is essential to transform society.

As co-authors, we have spent significant energy and time reflecting on the relationship between tensions of purpose and authentic youth–adult partnership. This chapter reflects our beliefs that

1. tensions of purpose are inevitable in youth–adult partnerships;
2. to address tensions of purpose, it is essential to deeply consider the contributing factors that precipitate tensions in youth–adult partnerships; and

3. TE's strength-based approach to youth–adult partnerships enables the embrace of tension as a vehicle to change harmful or oppressive social constructs that have existed for generations.

In the following sections, we draw from our own experiences as well as from the perspectives of our youth and adult colleagues at TE,[4] to demonstrate how we work with tensions of purpose through TE's core philosophical and programmatic framework. We begin by sharing a scenario in which a tension of purpose arose at TE, and then discuss the strategies that youth organizers and adult staff used to address the situation. Next, we identify and discuss the complex and interconnected factors that contributed to the tension, with the goal of deepening understandings of the issues that can arise in collaborations between adults and youth. We conclude the chapter with recommendations for navigating tensions of purpose, and supporting authentic youth–adult partnerships across settings.

CONTEXTUALIZING TENSIONS OF PURPOSE: COMPLEXITIES OF YOUTH AND ADULT PARTNERSHIPS

At the beginning of each academic year, TE Boston hires youth organizers and forms two youth organizing groups, each composed of 14 youth from the communities in and surrounding the local neighborhood. Each led by two adult program coordinators, these youth organizing groups work as a cohort from October through the end of May. Throughout this time, the TE program director and executive director are available to support the youth organizers and adult program coordinators. During the first 2 weeks of employment, the two youth organizing groups participate in an intensive training on issues of racial equity and community organizing strategies, sign an employment contract, and develop a combined action plan for the academic year based on shared goals of community-wide and systemic change.

In the fall of 2015, directly following the hiring process for youth organizers, the adult program coordinators and several youth organizers attended a public panel discussion and dialogue convened by students and faculty at a university just outside of Boston. The youth organizers in attendance at the event represented approximately one third of the total group of youth organizers hired that year. Upon arrival at the event, these youth organizers were struck by the absence of people of color from their home communities. In a predominantly White academic audience at a resource-rich institution, TE youth organizers were the only youth of color present.

Of their own volition, the youth and adult staff met in the parking lot of the university to discuss the event after it concluded. They were inspired by some of the content and at the same time critical of the effectiveness of the event due to the lack of diverse representation and the lack of opportunity for the audience to actively participate in the conversation. One youth organizer posed a question to his youth colleagues: "What would it be like if we were able to facilitate a dialogue on racism in our community?" Excited and empowered, the small group of youth and adult staff collectively agreed TE should hold an interactive intergenerational dialogue on racism in their community.

In the weeks following the event, however, the demands of TE's packed schedule began to take precedence over the planning for the dialogue on racism. With the intent to avoid overworking the youth, TE's adult staff met separately from youth organizers—without their knowledge—to discuss and design the event. The adult staff included the program coordinators who worked directly with the youth organizing groups as well as members of the management team, who were experienced youth workers who had minimal interaction with the new youth organizing groups at the time of the planning process. They ranged in age, gender identity, and race: a White male in his 60s, a Black female in her 50s, an early 30s White female, a mid-20s White female, and an early-20s Latinx male.

Conversations between these adult staff were laden with disagreement on core aspects of the event, including whether TE should move forward with the event, how to frame and facilitate the conversation, and who to invite. Time was limited and meetings were rushed. At the end of one particularly challenging meeting, a White staff member shared an observation that White staff often dominated these planning discussions for the dialogue. The other staff members in the meeting said little in response. At the time, they did not seem ready to discuss the racial dynamics and workings of power in their own group. Instead, the adult staff resumed discussion about the racism dialogue, made the decision to host it, and compromised—with some apprehension—on a structure that was similar to the dialogue held at the university.

About a month prior to the anticipated date of the dialogue, the adult staff presented their proposal to the youth organizers. All adult staff attended this session, and a White staff member presented the proposal. The first youth responses consisted of a series of questions: "Who came up with this?"; "Do we have input on ways to change it?"; "Is there even time to change it?"; "How do you expect us to develop content for this event and at the same time do outreach for it, with only weeks to prepare?"

One youth organizer expressed that the format and content of the proposal did not align with the needs or interests of their peers and community. Others declared that no one they knew, especially their peer groups, would want to attend this event. One by one, the youth organizers rallied to support one another and agreed that the event was adult-centric. They believed that the adults were using them to spread an agenda to which the youth never agreed. They related their exclusion from the planning process to the external systems that subjugate youth of color to oppression and deny them opportunities to positively contribute to society. A youth organizer we will call Javiar,[5] became extremely upset and abruptly departed from the group for the day.

As the work day neared its end, everyone felt exasperated. Although some adults and youth expressed that it might be best to cancel the event, ultimately the group agreed to continue their conversation the following day. Once the youth organizers departed, adult staff remained to discuss what had unfolded during group time. They sought to make sense of how a process that began with excitement and an aligned sense of purpose with the youth organizers had made a turn towards division and mistrust, hopelessness and anger. Why did this happen?

REPAIR AND RE-VISIONING: STRATEGIES TO ADDRESS TENSIONS OF PURPOSE

In their debrief meeting, the TE adult staff admitted to feeling overwhelmed by the emotional and physical demands of the work schedule. They also reflected upon the need to unpack the racial dynamics and inner power structure of their group. After an initial emotional and nuanced conversation, they recognized characteristics that make up White supremacist culture surfacing throughout the planning process for the racism dialogue, including the sense of urgency, paternalism, individualism, perfectionism, and more.[6] When a predominately White group of adult staff members created the proposal without representation from the youth and without amplifying the voices of staff of color, the outcome was a reproduction of the White savior narrative. Furthermore, in marginalizing the youth organizers, the adult staff unwittingly reinforced negative beliefs that youth are not capable of thinking critically about issues most salient in their lives and in society. At the same time, they fell into stereotypes of adults as being close-minded, out-of-touch, authoritative, and dismissive of youth needs. At the end of their meeting, and with guidance from a lead staff member, they reaffirmed their care for one another and their dedication to create empowered communities together with youth.

With the renewed understanding that the best decisions are informed by a group that includes diverse representation and equitable participation of those most impacted by the outcomes of a decision, adult staff at TE committed to renegotiating their proposal for the racism dialogue, and to including the youth organizers in the planning process. They took the next week to repair trust within the group—seeking to reestablish TE's strength-based approach to authentic youth–adult partnership, resolve differences, and collaborate towards hosting a powerful, multidisciplinary TE event. As we illustrate in the remainder of this section, strategies included using balanced and transparent systems of communication, routines for feedback and accountability, consensus-based collaboration, and interactive spaces for teaching and learning.

First, the adult staff acknowledged and affirmed the concerns of the youth organizers, and were transparent about how the pressures of limited time and resources had led them to lean on familiar hierarchies and systems of power. In addition, the adults explicitly communicated their commitment to thoughtfully ensuring space and time for everyone—youth and adults—to reflect on the process that preceded the tension and to create steps to move forward together. For example, as an indicator of this commitment to collective reflection, the introduction to one of the group meeting agendas read:

> People are questioning this event, and we really want to explore (a) what we are doing; (b) whether or not we should do it; (c) if we are going to do it, how we should do it; and (d) if things should be changed. We want to have a free and open conversation about what our goals are and what we want to do be doing to best support these goals.

In subsequent conversation, some members of the group differed in their perspectives on the types of initiatives that would best support progress on TE's mission to create community-wide change toward peace, justice, and equity. Adult staff expressed that it was important for youth to participate in critical conversations and be part of institution-level change, while some youth organizers expressed a preference for smaller, youth-centric social events that emphasized community safety, such as a basketball tournament, an open mic and talent show night, a youth dance party, or a movie night. Differences in youth and adult cultures were acknowledged. With this honest communication about priorities—and with the encouragement of the youth organizers who attended the original dialogue on racism—a new baseline strategy organically emerged: The group agreed to hold a dialogue on racism that highlighted artistic performance.

With this consensus, the group brainstormed the following goals for the event:

- Gain understanding. Bring a diverse group of people to offer different perspectives, new possibilities, and share stories that build relationships. We want to understand each other's privilege, move beyond statistics, and show that we are not in a post-racial world.
- Demonstrate strong youth leadership and collaborate with other youth organizations.

- Create a safe space. Demonstrate empathy, respect, honesty, caring; be open; don't attack the person but rather the idea; use your freedom to speak.
- Engage political figures around issues that impact communities of color, and address the policies that directly impact those issues.
- Educate people about the solutions that can create change and build a movement. Because we are all in this together, we must teach about how to become involved, take action steps, maintain a sense of urgency, and inspire others.
- Be real about race and class, and represent TE and the community in a powerful way.

After reviewing the goals to the entire group, each staff member met with a small group of youth organizers to discuss the following questions:

1. Are these the right goals for you?
2. If no, why? And how would you change them?
3. If yes, what are we doing to meet these goals? What else should we do to meet these goals?
4. What is your role in the event? Are you comfortable with what you are doing to meet these goals? If no, how should it change?

Each small group was responsible for reporting back on their discussion to the larger group, and answering questions from their peers and the adult staff. Each report back generated conversation to get to the heart of their message, and suggestions on the format and content that could best meet the collective's goals. As lead facilitators in this conversation, youth experienced a strong sense of agency in creating the vision and purpose of the event, which ultimately helped decentralize power in the group.

In the days to follow, each session began with an honest reflection on the previous day, including the tone of the meetings and the group's perceived challenges and successes. The daily group agenda integrated previously shared feedback from both youth and adults on how to best move forward. Adults also facilitated a group feedback session designed to help individuals communicate their experiences with one another, and address overt and covert tensions specific to the dialogue on racism in a manner that was caring and constructive. It was important to create an equal exchange between youth and adults, and to ensure that youth felt empowered to give adults grounding and honest feedback. At TE, feedback structures are used on a weekly basis to enable youth and adults to actively participate in one another's growth.

Through these practices of feedback and reflection, the group came to an understanding that a panel discussion carried inherent risks of reinforcing restrictive and hierarchical notions of expertise. Youth organizers continuously voiced their desire to structure an event that was inclusive and participatory, and to bring White people into the room—specifically, *the ones who needed to hear their message,* or individuals who have limited engagement, experience, understanding, and awareness of issues of racial equity. During one group conversation, a youth organizer thoughtfully reflected that he never considered the culture in which White people were raised and how it created unconscious bias that ultimately supports a racist system. He inquired of his White staff about what their parents told them about race. His question, and the conversation that followed, led the group towards a clearer vision of the racism dialogue.

Ultimately, youth and adults agreed to host an intergenerational dialogue on racism between urban and suburban communities led by youth, supported by adults, and inspired by artistic performance. In lieu of a panel, each attendee would be invited to actively participate in a series of paired conversations on specific questions presented by young people. A youth facilitator would direct participants to move one seat over following each question, so that they were paired with someone new to help ensure diverse pairings. Attendees would also have the opportunity to actively engage in a large group speak-out on four specific topics, facilitated by a youth and an adult. The question "What did your parents tell you about race?" would become a central discussion point and a platform for entering deeper conversation about the internal and external structures that uphold systems of oppression and racism. Throughout the dialogue, youth would provide speeches and perform artistic pieces specific to each topic to help get to the heart of the topic and provide an entry point for conversation.

Finally, to best fulfill the mission of TE, the youth and adults agreed it was important to integrate youth leaders of color and White youth allies from organizations doing related work into the planning and facilitation of the event. From this point on, the process continued as true to the TE model, involving extensive research on chosen topics to assist in the development of content, practice and rehearsal, weekly constructive feedback, discussion of possible challenges during the event, implementation of the event, debrief and evaluation, and recommendations for the future.

This is not to say that further competing priorities did not come up throughout and following the repair process. Differences between youth and adults around content and censorship routinely caused tension in the group. For example, one youth organizer was passionate about giving a speech that was fully "real" while adult staff expressed a need for content that the audience would be willing to receive and engage with, pointing out that attendees would include funders, city leaders and officials, and White adults. Another youth organizer felt equally passionate about performing a spoken word piece that included use of profane language about the "White man" that some adult staff thought would be considered inappropriate by the standards of the dominant culture and/or by other adults. These two youth organizers felt it essential to preserve their original content to authentically articulate, capture, and relay their message.

Transparent conversations—that often involved referring back to the agreed-upon goals for the event, which were written on a large sheet of paper hanging on the wall—were key to addressing conflicting priorities in the development of content. They also helped maintain the overall health of the group. Defined censorship guidelines signed by both youth and adult staff at the beginning of the year were also key in the final decision-making process. Adult staff were able to agree to include concepts that pushed far outside their own comfort zones, while youth were able to agree to exclude the use of profane language.

It is also important to note that throughout the process of planning, repairing, and re-visioning TE's dialogue on racism, adults also checked in individually with youth who had been particularly triggered by the tense atmosphere that was created when the adult staff initially proposed their ideas to the youth organizers. This included check-ins with Javiar, the young person who walked out the day that the adult staff shared their proposal, and who had been in jeopardy of being fired due to his behavior. It was unclear whether Javiar would be able to fulfill the expectations of his work contract while still maintaining the overall health of the group and the success of the dialogue. At the same time, the adult staff understood that a multitude of intersecting factors impacted his daily lived experience. False internalized narratives, cultural beliefs, and a lack of resources prevented him from getting the immediate and long-term wraparound services that he needed to address toxic trauma, the experience of poverty, long-term struggle with mental health, daily encounters that target and criminalize him as a Black male, and more.

With the belief in young people's capacity to use their strengths to positively impact their environment when they have access to resources and legitimate sources of power, the adult staff met regularly with Javiar and, in mutually respectful conversation, agreed on the importance of doing everything possible to keep Javiar on staff. Driven by this commitment, everyone was able to support one another to meaningfully contribute to (and participate in) this important event. Because youth and adult staff were able to engage with their competing priorities on a very dense and complex subject matter, the result was a profoundly moving and empowering event that served as a springboard for all future events that year, as well as the years to follow. As a whole, the experience showcased that without the voices of both youth and adults held in equal esteem, progress is sure to be halted and respect is bound to be lost.

AN EXAMINATION OF FACTORS CONTRIBUTING
TO TENSIONS OF PURPOSE

Multiple intersecting factors influenced the way that individuals navigated and made meaning of the scenario we discuss in this chapter. As co-authors, we sought to uncover the systems of power, privilege, and oppression that formed the backdrop to the tensions of purpose that arose in that experience. While the specific behaviors and interactions in this scenario were unique to this moment in time, they parallel other experiences the co-authors have had in youth–adult partnerships. We found that our experiences of tensions of purpose have been shaped by the same set of contributing factors, which we name and define below:

1. *Biases, assumptions, and stereotypes*—or the preconceived, unconscious negative beliefs passed down from generation to generation and perpetuated through policy and the media. They are systematically pervasive, and thus become part of our lived experiences and interpersonal relationships. They can inhibit progress by creating an environment of division, suspicion, and mistrust.

2. *Racial, ethnic, and cultural barriers* stemming from the different social identities that shape our experiences and thus influence our values, beliefs, expectations, and behaviors. History and present-day racism shape the way in which systems of power, privilege, and oppression are both enacted and perceived by different groups. When efforts are not made towards understanding one another across these axes of difference, tensions of purpose tend to increase.

3. *Collective strategy vs. individual needs*—or the tension that can arise when an individual's basic needs—including needs for housing, mental health, food security, and safe neighborhoods—must take priority over investing in a collective strategy towards community change. This reality can generate multiple competing priorities, especially in collectives where there are deep bonds between members, and in settings where wraparound services might be lacking.

4. *Lack of organizational resources*—or the limited economic resources faced by many small nonprofit and out-of-school time programs. Working within resource constraints requires immense emotional and intellectual energy. It can also provoke stress and hamper efforts to best prepare youth and adults for their partnership work. Authentic youth–adult partnerships require physical, temporal, emotional, and human resources—combined with the belief that young people are sophisticated and capable of real change.

Teen Empowerment's methodology to address tensions of purpose is clear and intentional. By working to minimize stereotypes, build understanding across barriers, address imbalances of power, and offer wraparound services, TE's strategies are designed to pinpoint and alleviate the tensions that often arise in youth–adult partnerships. Indeed, once we utilized these strategies during the repair and re-visioning process around hosting our own racism dialogue, we were able to hold space for the intersectional identities of youth and adult staff, and work as a collective towards shared visions for community change.

RECOMMENDATIONS AND CONCLUSION

Human relationships and behavior are complex. Even with a model that has been refined over the past 25 years by youth and adults working in partnership to address issues of equity and justice, there is always the possibility that we might fall back on the familiar oppressive systems and behaviors into which we were socialized. An important aspect of the scenario we presented in this chapter was the ability of adults and youth to see possibility, even in the face of conflict. This ability to see possibility enabled the group to reintroduce organizational strategies that had proven, over time and experience, to foster trusting and successful partnerships between youth and adults.

The process towards *authentic youth–adult partnership* is methodological by design and personal in nature. Based on our experiences, we believe that tensions of purpose can transform into positive results when youth and adults intentionally cultivate:

- agency to choose to participate in action steps toward shared goals,
- time and willingness to actively listen to and benefit from the perspectives and lived experience of others,
- a belief that everyone is considering the best interests of one another,
- an abundance of support and care for one another, and
- a group effort to build pathways of empathy toward collective power.

Most importantly, youth and adults need to share the understanding that one group is not superior to the other.

In authentic partnership, each individual takes responsibility for their growth edges while also investing in the strengths and growth areas of other people. Adults invest in youth and youth invest in adults. Pride and ego are constantly checked and rechecked and, at times, it might require losing a piece of individuality to meet the collective end goal. Yet when the setting makes it possible, youth and adults can find "home" with each other, developing and maintaining a bond through what at first may feel like irreparable differences. In this way, a new system—one that is more just and equitable than what we have inherited—can be created.

We suggest that program directors, education practitioners, researchers, funders, and administrators more deeply consider the intricacies of truly embracing an agenda towards justice. These stakeholders must dedicate their energy to imagining a society that is different than the adult-led world that currently exists, and to co-creating with youth a vision and strategy towards liberation. Such an agenda is intergenerational, as well as holistic (union of the mind, body, and spirit) and WHOLE-istic (multidisciplinary and inclusive). We caution against systems reflective of top-down hierarchical power structures, as they inevitably support an unjust and oppressive capitalist patriarchy. We also recommend that those in power (adults) remain cognizant of the risks of youth tokenism. Adults must ensure that youth are able to authentically articulate, capture, and relay their perspectives in the planning and implementation of intergenerational collaborations, such as the racism dialogue hosted by TE.

While there are many tensions that can arise when youth and adults work together in movements towards justice, fortunately there are powerful models that demonstrate how to authentically engage with tension. In addition to the organizational strategies to address tensions presented in this chapter, we further recommend the following to decrease potential tension and increase opportunity for successful partnerships between youth and adults:

1. Increase funding for opportunities and groups dedicated to supporting youth and adults in developing partnership skills.
2. Address the differing needs and interests expressed by youth and adults to ensure that the voices of those most impacted by issues of equity and racism are actively engaged in partnerships towards social justice. This includes utilizing practices of shared facilitation and public speaking, and prioritizing youth culture by integrating the arts, sports-related events, youth parties, and movie nights to engage a diverse contingent that includes those who struggle most with issues of violence and safety in their community. Increased funding could build capacity for organizations to provide culturally relevant, community-centered programming that engages a wide range of avenues for youth and adults to work in partnership towards justice and peace.
3. Provide youth and adults with professional development, supervision, and training opportunities led by qualified professionals whose sole focus is to ensure their immediate and long-term success. We define success as a person's ability to recognize his/her/

their potential in personal, academic, employment, and civic life; formulate personal goals; and take action to achieve such goals.

4. Formally integrate youth into all organizational structures to ensure authentic youth voices and youth–adult partnerships. For example, organizations should prioritize a direct link between youth and the board of directors, executive directors, administration, funding and budgeting processes, and programmatic and direct service team meetings. Defined systems of upward mobility and increased leadership for youth and adults who have sustained involvement in an organization will increase opportunities for leadership that is reflective of the communities served, and uniquely able to understand and respond to community needs.

5. Remind yourself and others of what is possible; to find hope when all feels hopeless. Recognize when mistakes are made, reassess, and try again.

The opportunity for youth and adults to work together does not often happen in our society; it is not the norm. In order for this work to be successful, it is essential to be transparent about tensions and committed to engaging with interpersonal challenges. At TE and in other settings, we have encountered the challenges of partnership and the various ways in which they play out in our daily work. We have also felt how deeply moving, spiritual, and liberating it is when youth and adults successfully align their abilities and discover new ways-of-being. True partnership between youth and adults is an incredibly powerful and humanizing experience that empowers revolutionized thinking and behavior. When we explicitly acknowledge what is challenging and claim space for possibility in tension, we can appreciate that what we have is both precious and magical. From this place of collective strength, trust, and wonder, we become capable of achieving a collective sense of purpose.

NOTES

1. Teen Empowerment's youth organizers are between the ages of 14 and 21, and are paid an hourly wage for their work. They are residents of the communities in which they work, and reflect the racial/ethnic demographic of these neighborhoods, which are predominantly Black or African-American, Latinx, Cape Verdean, Nepalese, and Caribbean.

2. Audio and visual examples can be found on YouTube (at TeenEmpowerment-TV), on bandcamp (TeenEmpowerment.bandcamp.com), and Facebook (@ TeenEmpowerment). More information on TE can be found at: http://teen-empowerment.org

3. Teen Empowerment also has programs in Somerville, Massachusetts and the southwest quadrant of Rochester, New York.
4. We would like to give our sincere gratitude to Shawn Brown, Taylor Copeland, Stanley Pollack, Sheri Bridgeman, Melissa Orasme, and Gabriel Petit for advising us through our questions to help us clarify our purpose for this chapter.
5. Pseudonym is used to protect the identity of the individual.
6. This conversation continued throughout the year and into the present, and provided some context for organization-wide action to reaffirm anti-racist practices.

IF THE GOAL IS GREATNESS, EXPECT GREATNESS FROM EVERYONE

Noelis Tovar

What makes group work between adults and youth difficult? Language barriers? A shortage of the word "rad"?

No, it's the space. Imagine this: You've come across an opportunity—whether by chance, invitation, or after a long season of searching. It's an opportunity to which you want to contribute your time, energy, and ideas. You take the plunge, you walk in, you sign up, you apply, and you make it to the first day—only to be met by faces sporting doubt and low expectations. A waste of time, right? *That* is where the problem starts.

A single coat of inadvertent condescension can make the difference between an imaginative, productive environment and an uncomfortable environment that results only in long summers and unimpressive project results. Creativity and innovation are not limited by time. They will never expire, and we have an array of minds to thank for this. We do not have to wait on the birth of inspiration because being a vessel for exceptional ideas

At Our Best, pages 259–260

is an open position for anyone. Unfortunately, that message is not always clear when you're a minor.

Young people, like all people, want to do well. They are motivated and qualified but if the leaders of these young people demean their motivation and capability with low expectations, the magic is gone. Just like that, what could have been a great moment for innovation is a thing of the past.

Community-based activities, programs, mentorships, and extracurriculars for young people all begin with the intention of encouraging productivity in a meaningful way. They are begun with the hope that a sense of unity will grow. And they *can* live up to these expectations. As long as young participants are treated like they are expected to do exactly what they came to do.

And that is to be exceptional.

Bio: Noelis Tovar is a Hispanic, African-American, cisgender female and aspiring writer. She is currently enrolled at Suffolk University as an English major and will soon be minoring in philosophy. In studying in these fields, Noelis hopes to strengthen her communication and problem solving skills because she believes that making connections in our shared world will save it.

Per Noelis: The projects, companies, and partnerships that have helped strengthen my belief in the power of connections are Kennedy Resource Center Renovation Project, Passport to College with Boston Herc, and BA-HEC. Thanks to them, I gained experience as an active and initiative-taking leader who wants to continue to find ways to bring people together in the best interest of us all.

CHAPTER 14

"WHY COULDN'T THAT HAVE BEEN ME?"

Reflections on Confronting Adultism in Education Organizing Spaces

Kristy Luk
Center for Youth & Community Leadership in Education

Noah Schuettge
Center for Youth & Community Leadership in Education

Keith Catone
Center for Youth & Community Leadership in Education

Catalina Perez
Center for Youth & Community Leadership in Education

AN IMPROMPTU DEBRIEF

The 3 days of nonstop action were coming to an end as we finished the closing session of the Youth Leadership Institute (YLI) 2018, a youth organizing

At Our Best, pages 261–276
Copyright © 2020 by Information Age Publishing
All rights of reproduction in any form reserved.

conference that brings together about 150 high school-aged youth and nearly 50 of their adult allies from across New England. Youth Leadership Institute often feels upbeat, spirited, and energetic—it's not unusual to see spontaneous dance parties with music blasting from portable speakers, or adult allies connecting at the snack stations. The theme of YLI 2018 was "Growing Our Power" and the conference included a range of youth-led workshops: For example, a group of undocumented young people living in Connecticut led a session on building a youth-led legislative campaign for financial aid, and a group of youth from Rhode Island (RI) created an interactive gallery on identity, social location, and intersectionality in education. There was also an adult affinity space and numerous social activities occurring outside of the scheduled program. Three of the chapter authors—Kristy, Noah, and Catalina—comprise an adult staff team who support youth organizing efforts for educational justice in New England as part of the Center for Youth and Community Leadership in Education (CYCLE), based at Roger Williams University in Providence, RI. Among these efforts is the annual design, planning, and facilitation of YLI.

As YLI 2018 began to wrap up, we felt fatigue; but at the same time, a sense of relief was settling in. The three of us looked at one another, and started to breathe, relax, and laugh. The last thing we had to do before packing up was hold a closing circle of affirmations and hugs with the Youth Planning Team (YPT), the group of twelve young people from around New England who helped plan YLI. That was when we started getting urgent texts on our WhatsApp thread from the YPT members. A few of the young people expressed that they needed to meet urgently, for more than just affirmations. We had planned for a debrief call with YPT for a week after YLI, but it was clear that they wanted to talk immediately.

What followed was an impromptu debrief with a clearly frustrated and passionate group of youth leaders who had put 9 months of work into planning YLI. While a few of the youth leaders felt excited and energized by the conference, one young person expressed dismay and confusion about her role at the conference itself. She voiced that she felt as though she was just another participant and rarely felt like a leader during YLI, and many of her fellow YPT members seemed to relate to that experience. After putting so much work into the planning of the conference, they told us, they were disappointed at the lack of clear leadership roles for them at the actual event. One YPT member asked why they weren't responsible for facilitating YLI teams—small breakout discussion groups that met periodically throughout the conference, and were facilitated by adults that we hired as "Facilitator Fellows." Basically she was asking, "Why couldn't that have been me?"

This was an incisive question, which we use as an entry point to explore tensions of power in youth–adult partnerships in this chapter. We were grateful that young people felt empowered to be honest and critical in their feedback about their desire for greater leadership and ownership over the space. Ultimately, their feedback gave our team an opportunity to recognize that we focused our energy on making sure young people were leading in the planning process, but that didn't translate into their leadership in the product or implementation of YLI itself. In our aspirations to develop the perfect planning process for YPT to step into authentic youth leadership, we lost sight of their leadership roles during the product: the actual 3-day event.

In this chapter, we first provide some context and background about the work our team and organization does before introducing a conceptual framework that guides our approach to YLI. Then, we dive back into the moment of impromptu debrief with YPT to explore tensions of power in youth–adult partnerships. Finally, we end with a discussion of the implications of this experience on our work with both young people and adults moving forward.

CENTER FOR YOUTH AND COMMUNITY LEADERSHIP IN EDUCATION AND THE YOUTH LEADERSHIP INSTITUTE

The work of YLI and the YPT sits within the work we do at CYCLE. At CYCLE, we partner with communities and school districts looking to build collective power through grassroots leadership, organizing, advocacy, and relationship building. We support youth, families, and educators—focusing on those most impacted by injustice—to fight for and win policies and practices that create equitable opportunities and outcomes for all students. We believe that when done right, our work supports groups and individuals engaged in educational justice organizing around New England to feel less alone in the struggles and joys that come with their work. Ultimately, connecting groups makes for a stronger landscape of youth organizing in the region, which will lead to more victories and a sustainable community of practice over time.

Youth Leadership Institute is an extension of CYCLE's commitment to educational justice organizing and is generously supported by the Nellie Mae Education Foundation. The goals of YLI are to build the connections that strengthen the field and to deepen the shared analysis, skills, and the relationships required to make change in the education system through youth-led organizing. The majority of these groups work with young people from historically marginalized communities, including high school students of color, immigrant and undocumented youth, and young people from both urban and rural contexts. In this vein, we believe out-of-school programs like YLI are important as a space to challenge the adultist structures often found in traditional schooling. These spaces are crucial for cultivating youth voice and dissent, and providing opportunities for young people to flex their creative muscles and to dream big without having adults stand in their way.

AUTHENTIC YOUTH LEADERSHIP
IN THE FACE OF ADULTISM

How do we build spaces for authentic youth leadership without reifying the same adultist structures and practices we seek to deconstruct? Our exploration of this tension of power in intergenerational partnerships is grounded in two key frames of reference: (a) understanding adultism as a system of oppression, and (b) using the "Levels of Youth Participation/Power" (see Figure 14.1) as a tool to measure authentic youth leadership. We define *authentic youth leadership* as young people having power and agency to make decisions affecting their lives and their communities. It assumes that young people are full human beings despite their ages; young people possess clarity about what they want and need, and should not be treated as mere

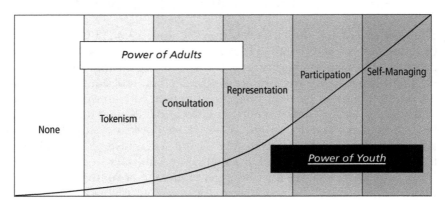

None	Youth are not included.
Tokenism	Adults set agenda and make decisions. One or two young people may be consulted or visible, but their views are not necessarily considered.
Consultation	Adults consult young people within adult parameters.
Representation	A select number of youth are put forward for their peers, in collaboration with adults.
Participation	Youth set agenda, decide on issues and activities, and have joint accountability with adults.
Self-Managing	Youth work with little or no adult authority.

Figure 14.1 Levels of youth participation/power. *Source:* Adapted from Northern Ireland Youth Council and BEST Initiative, Heath Resources in Action, 2011.

spokespeople for adults' interests. It is also an orientation toward actively centering the experiences and knowledge of young people as guiding wisdom. We believe centering young people is important not only because this process contributes to the dismantling of adultism, but also because young people are among those who have the most at stake in education, and therefore should lead any organizing, advocacy, or action for educational justice (Rojas & Wornum, 2018). This centering is both strategic and moral.

As a system of oppression, adultism (or young people's oppression) is based on the belief that adults carry wisdom and experience that young people do not have, and that is more valuable than that which is carried by young people (Bettencourt, 2018). Adults are assumed to be the right ones to make decisions and to take action, sometimes with the justification that their decisions are made in the best interests of young people. Like other systems of oppression, adultism has real material, institutional, and structural consequences and is perpetuated by myths and stories our society tells itself about needing "adults in the room" as responsible decision-makers who know what is best (Bell, 1995; Bettencourt, 2018). Adultism—especially as it intersects with other oppressions—means that young people are often treated as political pawns for adults' policy aims. It means that young people's ideas are dismissed because they are deemed developmentally immature, and that young people have no avenues for exercising political power, traditionally understood, until they reach the arbitrary age of 18. Thus, our conceptualization of authentic youth leadership is in direct contradiction to the societal adultist conception that young people have little to no experience and knowledge worth significant value compared to those of adults. Authentic youth leadership challenges the very foundations of this system of oppression that minimizes the power, agency, and wisdom that young people bring.

Often, as adults seeking to be in allyship with those most impacted by oppressive structures, we can be hindered by perfectionism. At times, shame, the fear that we are unworthy of connection or belonging (Brown, 2012), can lead to an inability to take action, because we don't want to take a risk and make ourselves vulnerable to criticism and maybe social alienation. In the field of Whiteness studies, there has been much discussion linking shame to the experience of the oppressor—both embracing the presence of shame as useful (Jacobs, 2014) and criticizing it as individualist and a stand-in for anti-racist action (Milazzo, 2017). Shame has been described as a way of hiding from deep pain or harm (Suchet, 2007) in a way that can ultimately uphold many systems of oppression. Reactions to shame often include attacking ourselves and others (Nathanson, 1992). In our work in adult affinity spaces, we have seen shame play a special role in upholding adultism. Adultism is a unique system of oppression because every adult individual has both been oppressed and oppressor, resulting in both internalization of young people's oppression as a young person, and acting on this internalization as we become adults. What does it mean when adults who work with young people look back on their own youth with so much shame? How do adults inadvertently project this shame on the young people we work with? How does it impact our relationships with individual young people, youth as a concept, and our perception of young people's potential to lead our communities in the direction of justice? These are questions that we grapple with and contend that every adult who works with young people should be asking of themselves.

One tool that helps concretize these questions and helps to apply a framework to this level of reflection is the "Levels of Youth Participation/Power" (Hart, 1992; Northern Ireland Youth Council as cited in BEST Initiative, Health Resources in Action, 2011). It presents a spectrum of ways that youth are invited to participate or hold power in what are often adult-dominated spaces. It is a tool that CYCLE uses as a barometer for how authentically youth-led our work is.[1] The different levels of the tool should not be thought of as static; instead, we believe they are best used as a way to reflect, and to aspire to new ways of being with young people. It also helps concretize the ideas underpinning adultism, demonstrating that the power adults have on a systemic level oftentimes comes at the expense of young people's access to power and decision-making. As adults relinquish power around decision-making, or voice and presence, there is greater space for youth power to move up the continuum. It becomes more possible for young people to move from a place where they have no power or role to play, to a stage where they are self-managing, working with little to no adult authority (see Figure 14.1).

Here it is important to note that the relationship between youth power and adult power is not linear, and power is not necessarily a zero-sum calculation. Indeed, intergenerational organizing is a beautiful example of what collective, generative power and action can accomplish. As a heuristic, though, the levels of youth participation and power succinctly illustrates what we believe to be a central tension of power in youth–adult partnerships—that in order to create authentic youth leadership, adults must cede power and support young people toward self-management. To be sure, there is intentional youth development work that must happen in between those stages. Just because adults step back does not mean that they do not have the responsibility to support young people's leadership. Authentic youth leadership is represented not by a space where youth are left to fight for their own liberation alone, but rather a space upheld by youth and adults between whom there is mutual trust.

The Center for Youth and Community Leadership in Education's imperatives include the deconstruction of adultism by focusing on process, and careful attention to how we support young people's growth and development as leaders in that process. We believe anti-adultism goes beyond merely being non-adultist, and necessitates a constant reflective process of evaluating and re-evaluating our own practices and beliefs to actively fight against and dismantle adultism, a process that Winchester (2018) calls "decentering adultism" (p. 32). Guided by these beliefs, we see YLI as an iterative project, each year presenting a chance to be more participatory, more authentically youth-led, and more reflective of the wishes and wisdom that young people bring to the space. In the remainder of this chapter, we critically examine how we have sought to create more space for authentic youth leadership in our work with YPT (the YLI youth leaders), while ensuring that we are supporting them to step into their power.

TENSIONS OF POWER

In this section, we return to the impromptu debrief described at the beginning of the chapter to parse out the tensions of power that transpired not just in that moment, but also in the process leading up to it. We lay out the logic for how we (as the adult staff supporting YPT) hoped to practice anti-adultism; we also interrogate the ways in which our hyper focus on making the planning process authentically youth-led ultimately enabled adultist conditions during YLI itself. The feedback we received from members of the YPT was humbling because youth identified a crack in the foundation we built as adults. They were shining light on that crack, urging us to see how much farther we could push to support the power of young people at YLI.

Emphasizing Process as an Anti-Adultist Practice

When we started YLI in 2012, there was no youth planning team and certainly no youth emcees at the front of the room during the conference itself. Over time, we have worked with YPT to push back against adultist values that emphasize cultivating professionalism, polish, or productivity. Freire's (1970) notion of problem-posing pedagogy, where people are "in the process of becoming—as unfinished, uncompleted beings" (p. 84), recognizes that challenging adultism might necessitate *slowing down* and focusing on the process of learning, instead of solely on the outcome or product. Similarly, adultism can manifest in ways that White supremacy culture does: Okun (n.d.) observes that a White supremacy culture is one in which "little or no value [is] attached to process; if it can't be measured, it has no value" (p. 3). For us, *slowing down* means entering a space of reflective process not always rewarded by society's goal- and product-oriented adultist culture. Oftentimes we do not slow down because we "don't have the time" or "have to get it done." The system is simply not designed to hold the complexity of an intergenerational space of equitable power distribution, where adults use their capacity and privilege in society (e.g., access to budgets, funding, networks, reputations in the field, etc.) to support and build new capacities for young people to step into the role of leadership.

Engaging YPT in planning YLI with an emphasis on process became a method to push back against the urgency of delivering a polished, professional product for the eyes and consumption of adults. We took projects that adult staff had managed in the past and handed them over to YPT. For example, the Facilitator Fellow role had become a crucial and transformative part of the relational and supportive culture of YLI. This group of educators, youth workers, organizers, and activists from around New England often modeled what support can look like from adults in their one-on-one interactions with young people at YLI. Young people interviewed and hired the Facilitator Fellows, and they selected workshop presenters using a rubric they designed. They also led parts of the training for the Facilitator Fellows they had hired. In these ways, we sought to create room for new possibilities of youth leadership and agency in the process of planning YLI.

In addition, we attempted to build a structure for YPT to take on planning for YLI 2018, in an effort for it to become a more self-managing space of authentic youth leadership. We increased the engagement of YPT from 4 to 9 months, kicking off with a 2-day retreat to bring all of the YPT members together. At the retreat, we spent a substantial amount of time delving into the specifics of how to create an agenda, how to debrief a meeting, and best practices in facilitating meetings over Zoom video conference software, because YPT members lived all over New England. After the retreat, we adopted an apprenticeship model through which young people would eventually be the ones to plan and facilitate all of the YPT meetings. Adult staff modeled creating agendas for meetings, facilitating the meetings, and debriefing how they went. Then, youth–adult pairs co-created and co-facilitated meetings, followed by a check-in to see how the process felt for youth leaders before having YPT members independently create, facilitate, and debrief team meetings. This apprenticeship model is outlined in Table 14.1.

By the end of the year, YPT had become a cadre of young people who felt confident in organizing and facilitating meetings that resulted in concrete next steps at each stage of planning for YLI. Ultimately, we felt successful in our effort to slow down in order to actively position the YPT to set agendas, decide the parameters of decisions to be made, and to own the YLI planning process from beginning to end. Young people who were in YPT for multiple years reflected that they felt better prepared to be able to facilitate these YPT meetings successfully. It felt like a victory as the YPT structure fell on the edge of the "Participation" and "Self-Managing" categories of the "Levels of Youth Participation/Power" spectrum.

TABLE 14.1 Apprenticeship Model for Agenda Setting and Zoom Facilitation Calls		
Task	**Youth Role**	**Adult Role**
In-person trainings on agenda setting, Zoom mechanics, and virtual facilitation	Practiced launching Zoom meetings and using different features, filled out agenda template, practiced facilitation	Explained Zoom platform, provided a template for agendas with critical elements, provided facilitation scenarios
1st Zoom Call	Observed agenda setting and facilitation	Set agenda and facilitated the call, led debrief
2nd Zoom Call	Set the agenda with support and co-facilitated call	Supported setting the agenda, co-facilitated call, led debrief
3rd Zoom Call	Set the agenda and facilitated the call, led debrief	Observed agenda setting and call facilitation with feedback

Adultism in the Product

For however much it felt like we supported YPT to be more authentically youth-led in the planning of YLI, the YPT noted during our impromptu debrief how their experience at YLI did not mirror a consistent level of authentic youth leadership. In this moment, even as we breathed a sigh of relief at the successful conclusion of YLI 2018, we felt a level of failure and shame upon receiving this feedback. Our team sat with the question posed to us by one of the young people talking about facilitation at YLI: "Why couldn't that have been me?" Indeed, we had asked and supported young people to set the agenda and facilitate most of the phone meetings in the planning of YLI, managing small working teams over the course of 9 months. So why didn't we turn to them for in-person facilitation at the event they worked so hard to plan? The YPT had written the application for Facilitator Fellows, they interviewed applicants and made hiring decisions, but that preoccupation with having youth lead the hiring process meant that both we and the YPT did not recognize the great opportunity we had to engage the YPT members as Facilitator Fellows themselves.

For the adult staff team supporting YPT, this realization signaled a larger pattern in our approach. Our preoccupation with perfecting the apprenticeship model led us to become so absorbed in ensuring that young people were supported in practicing their leadership in the *planning* of YLI, that we neglected to intentionally create space for them to practice self-managing leadership at the event itself. While we accomplished moving YPT towards "Participation" and "Self-Managing" in the planning stages of YLI, YPT's role at

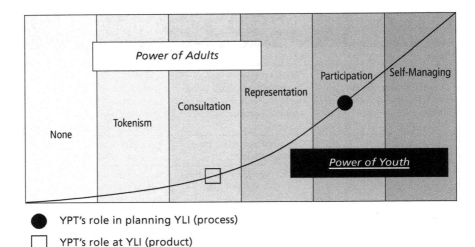

Power of Adults

None
Tokenism
Consultation
Representation
Participation
Self-Managing

Power of Youth

● YPT's role in planning YLI (process)

□ YPT's role at YLI (product)

Figure 14.2 Youth participation and power in the process and product of YLI.

YLI often fell squarely in "Consultation" given the parameters that adults had set around facilitation at the conference (see Figure 14.2). At worst, youth participation at YLI at times fell into the "Tokenism" level, as YPT became the face and voice of the conference as emcees but not as facilitators.

Consequently, there were several ways in which the implementation (or *product*) of YLI reflected adultism. Namely, our adult staff team was very concerned around the level of polish the event itself reflected. This preoccupation manifested in our choice to hire adults as Facilitator Fellows, our need for a tight agenda, and our concern with the "flow" of the conference. Through these choices, we reified some of the very values of adultism that we sought to push back against during the planning phase. Granted, there were real constraints we were operating under that led us to focus on the polish of YLI. The Center for Youth and Community Leadership in Education shares a common funder with all of the youth development and organizing groups that attend YLI, and that funder's presence at YLI inevitably creates a dynamic where it seems that the quality of the event could factor into considerations for future funding. Indeed, in 2016, YLI was held at a larger venue with a packed agenda, which led to chaos and disorganization as people got lost on the campus and did not know where they needed to go. The lack of contingency plans for outdoor activities in the middle of an August heat wave in New England put further pressure on the event. There were real concerns about the future viability of YLI, if we did not focus on the polish of implementation. Additionally, as noted earlier in this chapter, practicing anti-adultism requires slowing down. Unlike in the planning phase of YLI where we had 9 months to create the best possible conditions to support youth leadership in the process, YLI is a 3-day event, and we did not feel that we had the luxury of time needed to intentionally slow down. The interaction between these external factors and our preoccupation with process was only made plain to us after YPT members named the absence of authentic youth leadership in the implementation of YLI.

Despite these external constraints, the lesson our team has taken most to heart has been that in our efforts to become more process-oriented, we did not consider how process and product are not simply a binary, but rather are inextricably linked. We set process and product up as "either/or" (Okun, n.d.) choices, and failed to recognize that processes absent an eye toward product would invariably reproduce the very same adultist practices and structures we were seeking to undermine.

Implications for Youth Leadership Institution and Youth Planning Team Moving Forward

At the time of this writing, we are preparing for YLI 2019. While it is important to be critically reflective of our own practice, we know that reflection without action will not create change (Freire, 1970). We are fortunate to have support from CYCLE leadership and our funder to have freedom in our budget and programs to address youth–adult partnerships/relationships as they currently stand in order to enact change. In an effort to integrate feedback from YPT and an aspiration to move YLI closer towards a "Self-Managing" level of youth participation and power, we are shifting the roles and responsibilities of YPT from planners of YLI towards facilitators at YLI. We hope YPT's shift towards a focus on planning and facilitation at the conference will increase the capacity for authentic youth leadership in both the process and product of YLI.

This shift towards YPT as facilitators brings their role closer to that of Facilitator Fellows. Creating more crossover between the Facilitator Fellows and YPT also responds to feedback we received from them that they *should* be working more closely together. Indeed, in past conferences, these two groups had very little interaction, though both were integral to the leadership of YLI. At a conference where the goal is to grapple with the aspiration of youth–adult partnerships, we were not modeling this from the "front of the room." We hope this expansion of YPT's role will also have a significant impact on Facilitator Fellows' ability to model adult support within an authentically youth-led framework.

Instead of hiring an adult staff as the only facilitators, we will have a one-to-one ratio of YPT and Facilitator Fellows who will be co-facilitating significant portions of YLI. We are aware that this will require a major rethinking of the process to prepare the YPT for its role in both planning for, and implementing, YLI. We anticipate spending significantly more time on facilitation practice and building youth–adult partnerships grounded in an explicitly anti-adultist framing. Because of this shift, YPT will be paid more, bringing their stipends closer to that of the adult Facilitator Fellows. While Facilitator Fellows have become a crucial part of the culture of YLI and bring with them knowledge and experience in authentic youth leadership, this shift towards YPT taking on more facilitation in the implementation of YLI is necessary to move towards "Participation" and "Self-Managing" on the Levels of Youth Participation/Power. On the ground, this looks like reducing the number of Facilitator Fellows from 20 to 12, and inviting YPT to the 2-day facilitation training right before YLI so Facilitator Fellows and YPT can begin building relationships and hone their skills of co-facilitation. Table 14.2 shows, with changes reflected in italics, how the roles and responsibilities of YPT will shift in 2019 both in process and product, and how the Facilitator Fellow (FF) role will mostly stay the same.

TABLE 14.2 Roles and Responsibilities in the Process and Product of YLI 2018 and YLI 2019

| Role | YLI 2018 | | YLI 2019 | |
	Process	Product	Process	Product
FF	• Start in April 2018 • Attend YLI facilitation training in July • Connect with one home organization to begin action planning process	• Facilitate YLI teams (mixed groups) • Facilitate home organization breakouts • Facilitate some large group activities	• Start in April 2018 • Attend YLI facilitation training in July • Connect with one home organization to begin action planning process	• *Co-Facilitate YLI teams (mixed groups) with YPT* • Facilitate home organization breakouts • Co-facilitate some large group activities with YPT
YPT	• Start in November 2017 • Attend YPT retreat • Hire Facilitator Fellows • Plan themes and some large group activities at YLI • Oversee youth-led workshop selection process	• Emcee flow and agenda of the conference • Facilitate some large group activities • Oversee some social activities, such as open mic	• *Start in February 2018* • Attend YPT retreat in March • *Attend YLI facilitation training in July* • Hire Facilitator Fellows • Plan themes and some large group activities at YLI • Oversee youth-led workshop selection process	• Emcee flow and agenda of the conference • *Co-facilitate some large group activities with FF* • Oversee some social activities, such as open mic • *Co-facilitate YLI teams (mixed groups) with FF*

In addition, YPT will start their employment significantly later than previous years, illustrating an intentional shift away from *process* toward *product*. In doing so, we may lose the utility of our successful coaching model for facilitating Zoom calls, which required a significant amount of time and capacity early in the planning process last year. However, this same coaching protocol can be used for in-person facilitation, which is best trained in-person. Multiple meetings "in real life" will also lead to more community-building and tighter unity among our planning team and with FF before the conference, resulting in stronger youth–adult partnerships overall.

As we enact these changes, we recognize them as the latest iteration of YLI, and more specifically, how we partner with young people in the planning for YLI. These changes are not static, and we will continue to listen to YPT and FFs, and reflect using the "Levels of Youth Participation/Power." One of the biggest learnings from this year's YLI was the need to formalize debriefs and check-ins with young people as built-in feedback mechanisms. This year, we plan on introducing the "Levels of Youth Participation/Power" as a shared tool we can use to talk about how authentically youth-led YLI is feeling for the youth involved. The "impromptu debrief" with YPT this year showed us that YPT, and not just our team, need spaces for slowing down. Each evening at YLI, FFs are given space to check in on their feelings and how they think the conference is going, and YPT deserves a similar space.

CONCLUSION

In this chapter, we hoped to convey and model how we take this work of youth–adult partnership seriously. The work of rooting out adultism in organization practices is challenging and requires deep reflection, patience, and slowing down. The perfectionism lauded and perpetuated by our dominant adultist culture so often gets in the way of both deep anti-oppression work and quality organizing. We often think that if we don't have the perfect way for youth to be in the lead, then it is not worth doing at all. We wholly reject this notion of "perfectionism" and "either/or" thinking (Okun, n.d.). We believe that slowing down and reflection must also come with action in order for change to happen (Freire, 1970), which means imperfect iterations and implementation. In sharing our experiences of YLI with the YPT, we have been self-critical of our practices and approaches. In so doing, we hope to model the honest, vulnerable, deep reflection we think is necessary for the work to progress and transform.

The power of out-of-school spaces is in the experimentation and aspiration to model ways of being with young people that do not yet exist in other places, such as schools. In this striving towards a different way of being, we take our cues from the practitioners and organizers we partner with, who reorganize their boards to make more spots for youth, find new ways to support young people while removing adults from the limelight, and rethink "business as usual" to radically imagine the space and power that young people can hold in educational justice youth organizing work and in the world.

The Center for Youth and Community Leadership in Education holds a unique role in this community, as we receive funding to support organizing on the ground with both young people and the adults who support them, mostly outside of schools. Since opening a space for adult reflection and identity work at YLI 2017, groups have reached out to CYCLE to work with both adults and "mixed" groups of adults and young people to name, define, and resist adultism in this work. Early on in the process of writing this chapter, our team discussed including young people as co-authors, but decided against it. This chapter is our reflections and learnings from an experiment with setting up a space differently, and it is our work as adults to reflect, learn, and share our story with other adults who work and partner with young people to grapple with us. We believe affinity spaces for adults are needed for adults to dismantle the ways adultism shows up in our life and work—just as people who hold other identities with privilege and power, such as men and White people, need spaces to grapple, name, and dismantle their complicity in oppressive systems. We see this chapter as an extension of those spaces, and hope that it is a conversation starter and possibly a connecter between people who are actively thinking and feeling their way through this work. This work cannot be done in isolation. The more support we all receive in thinking through adultism, the better we are equipped to support young people in their organizing and activism.

We contend that the way out of adultism requires a way out of our individual shame. And the way out of this shame is community. Together, we must engage in sharing, affirming, critiquing, receiving, listening, and most of all, being vulnerable and taking risks—all while holding the belief that we are not as important as the work of liberation that is in front of us. We hope this chapter has been one model of this reflection and vulnerability, and a first step to continuing this conversation with other adults supporting young people in their organizing and activism. We encourage you to reach out to us with feedback, and to connect over this work: cycle_youth@rwu.edu

ACKNOWLEDGMENTS

We have access to this space of reflection and learning because of the generosity, experience, and knowledge of the amazing individuals and groups surrounding us in this work. First, we want to thank YPT for trusting us with their feedback, critique, and love—this chapter would not happen without you and all of the young people who showed up, led workshops, and held space at YLI this year. Dave Jenkins has pushed our thinking, analysis, programming, budgeting, and ways of being in the youth organizing world as adults. Much of our analysis around adultism, and the Levels of Youth Participation/Power tool, were shared with us by Dave. Thank you, Adeola Oredola, for your support and thought partnership in making YLI happen. Delia Arellano-Weddleton's consistent championing of youth voice and organizing has led to the Nellie Mae Education Foundation's commitment to YLI as a space to celebrate and support youth leadership. And, thank you to the organizations we partner with who model authentic youth leadership every day. We want to lift up the ways in which Providence Student Union and Students for Educational Justice have shared their processes and models of youth leadership with us, pushing our thinking on what is possible.

NOTE

1. In workshops, we often ask adults from different organizations to interact with a large poster of the "Levels of Youth Participation/Power" (see Figure 14.1) by putting blue stickers indicating "Where does your work currently sit?" and orange stickers to symbolize "Where do you want your work to be?" on this spectrum.

REFERENCES

Bell, J. (1995). *Understanding adultism: A major obstacle to developing positive youth-adult relationships* [Pamphlet]. Somerville, MA: YouthBuild USA.

BEST Initiative, Health Resources in Action. (2011). Retrieved from http://www .kdheks.gov/tobacco/download/2019_presentations/02-2_Cashin_Youth_ Adult_Partnerships_Handouts.pdf

Bettencourt, G. M. (2018). Embracing problems, processes, and contact zones: Using youth participatory action research to challenge adultism. *Action Research,* 1–18. https://doi.org/10.1177/1476750318789475

Brown, B. (2012) *Daring greatly: How the courage to be vulnerable transforms the way we live, love, parent, and lead.* New York, NY: Gotham Books.

Freire, P. (1970). *Pedagogy of the oppressed.* New York, NY: The Continuum International.

Hart, R. A. (1992). *Children's participation: From tokenism to citizenship* (pp. 1–38, Rep. No. 4). Florence, Italy: UNICEF International Child Development Centre.

Jacobs, L. (2014). Learning to love White shame and guilt: Skills for working as a white therapist in a racially divided country. *International Journal of Psychoanalytic Self Psychology, 9*(4), 297–312. https://doi.org/10.1080/15551024.2014 .948365

Milazzo, M. (2017). On White ignorance, White shame, and other pitfalls in critical philosophy of race. *Journal of Applied Philosophy, 34*(4), 557–572. https://doi .org/10.1111/japp.12230

Nathanson, D. (1992). Shame and pride: Affect, sex, and the birth of self. *Contemporary Psychology: A Journal of Reviews, 38*(2), 219–219. https://doi.org/10.1037/033089

Okun, T. (n.d.). *White supremacy culture.* Retrieved from http://www.dismantlingracism.org/uploads/4/3/5/7/43579015/okun_-_white_sup_culture.pdf

Rojas, C., & Wornum, G. (2018). Speaking up and walking out: Boston students fight for educational justice. In M. R. Warren (Ed.), *Lift us up, don't push us out! Voices from the front lines of the educational justice movement* (pp. 20–28). Boston, MA: Beacon Press.

Suchet, M. (2007). Unraveling Whiteness. *Psychoanalytic Dialogues, 17*(6), 867–886. https://doi.org/10.1080/10481880701703730

Winchester, C. (2018). Investing in critical leadership development with high-school students. *New Directions for Student Leadership, 159*, 27–40. https://doi.org/10.1002/yd20295

PAST, PRESENT, FUTURE

Eduardo Galindo

At Our Best, pages 277–279
Copyright © 2020 by Information Age Publishing
All rights of reproduction in any form reserved.

My artwork is a political altar, a statement, a creation that was possible thanks to the respect and belief that adults like my mother, teachers, and others have in me. They make me feel supported with the challenging art topics I select. I don't think I could have made this piece of art if I thought they wouldn't support my opinions, my worldview.

I made this artwork in the Multigenerational Afterschool Arts Program (MASA). To me, MASA is a place where I don't just hear "good job" or "that's good"; it's a program that pushes me in being truthful, and to be my most honest self, while I create art. And that is the best part of all because it really opens us to feel mutually empowered, to have a voice in creating new possibilities. The program gives us the confidence to trust the way we express complex thoughts.

MASA is offered by the University of California at Los Angeles and their Visual and Performing Arts Education (VAPAE) Program. The afterschool program occurs at the UCLA Community School, the school that I currently attend. The program is about expressing ourselves through art and evolving as creative human beings. Our parents are invited to join us too, which is very good. Being in the program has been an amazing bonding experience for me and my family. It has brought us closer to each other. Taking the time to make art isn't something I would normally do if it weren't for being in the program. It's fun to be able to have the space to do something like that. I have seen my mother be really involved in the program. She even makes art here at home. MASA is a wonderful space to be part of if you want to bond with other people while making art. Both spaces feel like home.

I consider an art project to be challenging if it requires something deeper from you, something that is hard for you to express, to bring out. Some of the art forms that I personally like are sculpting, which seriously grabs my attention, and self-portraits, which I personally find challenging. And I like weaving and knitting, because of the many possibilities you have with what you can create. When I was making this altar, I wanted to explore the idea of creating meaning through art. I know that art on its own creates meaning but I wanted to expand on that. I find that one of the greatest strengths that a human has is that of self-expression, but to some individuals, this task is hard. And it's hard for me too sometimes.

I used this altar to express my thoughts in the simplest way I could. I had half the face of Donald Trump combined with half the face of Hillary Clinton. Above that is written "DEATH," which I added not only because of the "Day of the Dead" theme, but also because during the 2016 presidential election, I often heard people saying that the lives they had would "end" because either one of the candidates could do something to harm their lives in this country. And this is a reference mainly to the many immigrant families in the country and in MASA. I combined the images of the candidates because I wanted to make people see that no matter who became president, it wouldn't stop us from having peace and sanctuary among ourselves. And the sun will still come up every morning, so it's not the end of the world. It's about having the strength to keep going and to have trust in the world. When it's not alright, we can make it right because that's why we exist, we have control over our lives. We can! That's what this altar means to me. It is the best way I have used art to express myself in a long time, which is why I consider it to be one of my greatest art works.

Adults have shown me support through their words. The fact that they like my art and accept who I am, creates the confidence that I have when it comes to showing people my work while just being me. One of the best examples of this is when my teachers allowed me to teach a class. I chose knitting as the topic for the class and it was fun. I really enjoyed having the opportunity to show everyone in the class something that I like. It empowered me and made me happy to know that I had that type of trust from my teachers and other adults in the program.

There have also been many times when the teachers personally challenged me to do something different—to "go the extra mile," as I like to say and as was said by my my inspiring teacher, Mr. Chen Feng, in the past. And that further shows me that being a member of MASA is like being part of a community—a sanctuary where my teachers will always push me to do my best because they believe that I have it in me. When you give space to young people, it really does empower and it brings out the best in us. And when we get to share our art and be proud of what we have created, it makes us feel good inside because everyone accepts what you did—and in doing so, they're accepting the entire you. No one judges you for your artwork. In that way, I see how the MASA's idea of sanctuary comes into play.

Bio: Eduardo is a sophomore at UCLA Community School and loves the school. He is always doing his best to get ahead of his education, through either taking college classes or AP classes.

Per Eduardo: I love math. If there's anything math related you need help with, count on me. If I can't help, I don't mind learning so I can be able to help. It's just what I do, and I love it. I am always focused on doing my very best so I can always have those straight As. I love technology, too. It's a part of me and I have fun with it. I am also part of an organization called Changeist, which is focused on getting youth to become leaders in their communities. I have enjoyed my experience in the program serving communities here in Los Angeles.

CHAPTER 15

FLIPPING THE SCRIPT

Leaving Room for Youth
to Grow Their Power

Thomas Nikundiwe
Education for Liberation Network

Who thinks we should wear our black fist t-shirts in court tomorrow?

There were a dozen or so of us in the classroom where we had been posting up during the first weeks of summer. It was 3 years into a campaign in which the young people in the Baltimore Algebra Project[1] (B.A.P.) were demanding the fulfillment of Judge Joseph Kaplan's orders that the state of Maryland pay the Baltimore City Public Schools the hundreds of millions of dollars it owed them.

The students had filed a motion in Judge Kaplan's court based on Article VI of the Maryland Constitution, which provided the right and the responsibility for the public to establish a new government "whenever the ends of Government are perverted, and public liberty manifestly endangered, and all other means of redress are ineffectual" (MD Const. art VI). The young people wanted to replace the Maryland Board of Education with a new

At Our Best, pages 281–286
Copyright © 2020 by Information Age Publishing

Maryland *Freedom Board of Education.* Judge Kaplan had granted a findings hearing to see if the argument had merit and invited the youth to testify.

As with most actions, major or minor, the young people were preparing—getting clear on the message, the plan of action, their different roles, contingency plans, where they would debrief. They had already decided who was to speak and we had heard their testimonies, doing the work of fine-tuning the points. The arguments were cogent and clear, and the young people expressed that they were nervous, but prepared.

All that was left to plan were the logistics. We would meet at the McDonald's across from the courthouse and all go in together. The question of what to wear was not one I had anticipated. The students were torn—there was a certain decorum expected in court, but over the last 3 years the young people had come to feel their full power and the court was not excepted from experiencing it. One young man was emphatic—vehement, even—that they should wear their black-fist t-shirts, and he had the backing of perhaps the most influential leader in the Project at that moment. On the other side, a young man and a young woman argued that if they were to be taken seriously, they needed to respect the court and dress appropriately.

There were just two adults in the room: Dr. Jay Gillen and myself. Jay founded the B.A.P., and I was working as a youth organizer alongside him. The B.A.P. uses a consensus decision-making model, so asking for our stances was often unnecessary. The process, though consistently frustrating for the youth, allowed for most of the ideas that we might offer to emerge naturally through the process of consensus-building. They had become highly skilled at analyzing decisions from many perspectives, poking holes in logic, forecasting consequences, and assessing personal and organizational risks. In this moment, though, they were truly at an impasse.

Most of the group seemed to be leaning toward those advocating for the t-shirts, but it still felt like it could go either way. They turned to Jay to ask his opinion and I was taken aback by his answer. I had been with Jay in nearly 100 meetings with youth by that time. I had never heard him do what he did in that moment; he responded by fully expressing his opinion on the matter and the logic behind this thinking:

> Judge Kaplan invited you to testify to represent the students of Baltimore. There are no other students who have been invited to speak and very few others at all. I would hate for him to think that you were showing him up after he invited you to testify. Also, people generally dress up in court. Of course, I'll support whatever you decide, but that's my opinion.

I expected to hear what I usually hear and what most successful organizers practice—answering a question with a question. My experience was that when Jay was asked to weigh in, he would do one of two things: ask a question that would help the young people grapple with the underlying tension or eventual roadblock, or present two or more sides of a decision to help clarify what was in tension.

As I was trying to understand Jay's move in the moment, I was caught off-guard again when one of the youth asked, "What do you think, Mr. Nik?" I wasn't expecting the question, partly because I was surprised by Jay's response but also because after Jay had made such a strong statement, I thought it would likely sway the room. First, it was logically sound; and second, because he so rarely brought his full voice to a discussion I thought they would take it as gospel. Not sure what move to make, I followed Jay's lead and gave my full and real opinion.

> I tend to agree with Mr. Jay—you have strong statements and important testimonies to give and I wouldn't want Judge Kaplan to be distracted by what you're wearing. But also as Mr. Jay said, I also support whatever you decide.

It was the first time I'd come so strong with them. With these two trusted adults making the case for one side I was surprised once more when the consensus at the end of another 20 minutes of discussion was to wear the t-shirts after all.

It wasn't until much later that I came to understand this moment was one of the clearest indicators that Jay and I had done an important part of our job as organizers. The youth-led rallies, marches, strikes, teach-ins, die-ins, street theater, and peer political education were exciting and gained the most attention, but for all those numbers of youth activated and media engagement, *this* moment was still a better measure for me! Jay and I had made strong and logical points, we offered them in full throat. The young people had considered them among all the other points made, and then they went against our recommendation. That is, they understood themselves as fully important, competent, and as valued as two adults whom they knew had their best interests at heart.

Sure, they had become accustomed to ignoring adults who were trying to bring them down or convince them they were wrong in their convictions or naïve in their tactics. At this moment, however, here were two adults who had been with them in the struggle, two people who they knew believed in them, two people with whom they had spent countless hours. To these two adults, they were able to say, "Thank you for your perspective, but we feel like this is the right thing." Going forward with this group, we could challenge them or offer them suggestions in ways we wouldn't have when they first joined the Project.

Conventional wisdom holds that in the early stages of building an organizing space with young people, adults need to support young people *more*. Young people often come in without knowing much about organizing, having "naïve" ideas about how to affect change, or limited analyses about structures in place to keep the status quo. Adults often have the instinct to move the young people along in these areas, rather than allowing the youth to make mistakes or "mess up" campaigns. But here I argue for flipping that script—that in the beginning it is important to say less and to give young people *less* direction.

Young people feeling their power is more important than guiding them through a successful action. When adults say too much, advise too much, steer too much, they miss opportunities for the young people to find their own power. That's not to say young people don't need support at the beginning. Many youth need a lot of early support in the form of rides, food, encouragement, but they also need space to find their voices, to build their confidence, and to build a culture with each other—ultimately, to build their power. I am offering the suggestion that when it comes to substantive matters, less is more.

The "Algebra" in B.A.P. refers to the fact that the B.A.P. does peer-to-peer math tutoring after school. The young people are able to utilize math as an organizing tool; that is, they are able to use math to bring young people together to build relationships, build knowledge with each other, and ultimately build power. When Jay created this after-school space, he intentionally designed a student-run staff meeting that took place directly after tutoring. This meeting time was designed to give space for political issues to arise organically. During staff meeting time, the young people might discuss snacks or paychecks, or they might work through some mathematics that came up during tutoring, or they might tackle an interpersonal issue at the site, or something happening at school.

I often found myself working with young people during one-on-one time to strengthen their ideas, but carefully—with the more important goal of them feeling ownership over their ideas. However, in group settings, like the staff meetings, where important discussions were playing out and decisions were being made, I would stay quiet, limiting myself to fielding questions about when the snacks would be refilled or when paychecks would be ready.

In my first few months working with students who were mostly new to the Project, I witnessed the magic of the staff meeting. They had been going along with their staff meetings, focused mostly on recruitment and the efficiency of the tutoring process, when word came that the school's security officers were being let go due to budget constraints. Many of the students had nice relationships with some of the security, and further felt that it was a signal that the school system did not care about their safety. Some of the most vocal students were incensed.

My personal stance was that the budget cuts were the problem—not the letting go of the security officers. My own political analysis of policing, in general, and policing in schools, in particular, led to some relief at their absence from school. Were it 2 years later, when the students were no longer new to the work, I would have shared this analysis, feeling confident that those students would think through my stance and weigh it against their own feelings and positions. In the moment, however, providing information that might dissuade them from action was not the move.

The students decided to write a letter of protest with the intent of having all the students in the school sign on. Despite my misgivings, I limited my contributions to the discussion to questions like, "Will you be telling the principal about your plan?" They were so fired up about the idea; they nominated someone to draft the letter which was to be presented at the next staff meeting in just 2 days (we had tutoring on Tuesdays and Thursdays). During the next staff meeting, they edited the original draft and asked me to check it for grammar. Over the next week, they were able to present it to the student body and get over 85% of the students to sign the letter. They felt so good about themselves.

While the citywide leadership of the B.A.P. was embroiled in a political battle about school funding, these particular students were new to it and had been on the periphery of the explicitly political work. But in this moment, they made their own move, ran their own action, and were proud to present their own political work to the citywide student leadership. Had I provided the "political education" that would have given them a more systemic analysis and in the process dissuaded them from trying to restore the security guards, we would have lost this important opportunity for growth.

There was also some loss in this approach—a missed teachable moment, maybe. But ultimately, I do not feel conflicted about this loss. I reconcile this by understanding that through this action, these nascent leaders had set themselves on a path to understanding themselves as people who matter. This understanding cannot be understated given that they live in a world that is constantly telling them that they don't matter. Campaign wins are important; they are evidence that a group of people has power, that is, they are evidence that the group can set out to do something and prove able to do it. But, at the same time, an organizing action that isn't "successful" in the sense of winning a clear victory is still powerful if the young people come out of it feeling their own power, affirmed in their mattering. The process of planning and creating the action can be powerful itself, even if the ultimate objective of the action is not reached.

When adults are too eager for young people to get it right, they take away the opportunity for young people to know their own power. The campaign win orchestrated by the adult does not evidence student power in the same way. When the adult can learn to trust the youth, to trust the process, they then get to see how far the youth can go.

Though I'm speaking here of an organizing context, there are lessons for people working with young people across many contexts. Building relationships of trust with young people, encouraging them to build relationships with each other, giving them the space to make mistakes, giving them space to grow their power, will pay dividends later. You will still get to offer your Marx, you will still get to teach them advanced campaign tactics, but these lessons might be more effective if we flip the script—offering less of our own steering up front, following where the young people's power leads us instead. When I hear about what amazing work the B.A.P. has done more recently in stopping the development of a youth jail, for instance, or their mass protests over standardized testing, or their work with the Baltimore Uprising following the murder of Freddie Gray, I think back to the great t-shirt debate in that classroom that summer, and I know that moment is as telling as any headline-grabbing campaign win.

ACKNOWLEDGMENTS

I would like to thank my partner, Carla Shalaby, who, as she is in all aspects of my life, was instrumental in this chapter from inception to final edits. I would also like to send a shout out to the too-many-to-enumerate young people in the B.A.P. who have been my greatest teachers. Thank you to the homie Jay. Finally, thank you to the editors of this volume who allowed me to take a reflective approach and share these ideas in an uncommon voice (for publication).

NOTE

1. The Baltimore Algebra Project is a democratic, youth-led, and youth-run organization, mainly focused on the one-on-one tutoring of math at the middle and high school levels. Their mission is to create a community of youth leaders committed to the education of those in need of advancements in their socioeconomic status, and to advocating for justice for all youth in the city of Baltimore. Learn more at batlimorealgebraproject.org

SECTION V

LOOKING FORWARD

CHAPTER 16

"AT OUR BEST"

Youth–Adult Partnership and the Struggle for Collective Well-Being

Gretchen Brion-Meisels
Harvard Graduate School of Education

Jessica Tseming Fei
Harvard Graduate School of Education

Deepa Sriya Vasudevan
Wellesley College

The purpose of this book has been to describe the power and possibility inherent in authentic youth–adult partnerships, identify a set of practices that enable these partnerships to exist, and grapple with the inherent tensions in this work. As defined by Zeldin, Christens, and Powers (2012), youth–adult partnerships are the practice of, "(a) multiple youth and multiple adults deliberating and acting together; (b) in a collective [democratic] fashion; (c) over a sustained period of time; (d) through shared work; (e) intended to promote social justice, strengthen an organization and/or affirmatively

At Our Best, pages 289–304
Copyright © 2020 by Information Age Publishing
All rights of reproduction in any form reserved.

address a community issue" (p. 388). The chapters in this volume help us understand what this type of work looks like in practice, by highlighting a set of principles and practices that make the work possible. These principles overlap with, and build upon, what Zeldin and colleagues (2012) consider the four core elements of youth–adult partnerships: authentic decision-making, natural mentors, reciprocal activity, and community connectedness. In so doing, they help us to imagine the types of relational and organizational practices that best enable authentic youth–adult partnerships to exist, and raise critical questions about the role of adults in the lives and the work of young people.

We conclude this volume by describing the principles outlined by the authors of this volume, which we define as foundational elements of effective youth–adult partnership work: *trust, problem-posing methodologies, democratic participation,* and *collective action.* Then, we use these foundational elements to amplify a set of practices that foster healthy intergenerational relationships, synthesizing learning from across the chapters of this book. By placing our authors in dialogue with each other, we hope to illuminate a set of useful next steps for the field.

THE FOUNDATIONS OF YOUTH–ADULT PARTNERSHIPS

Across the chapters of this book, four elements of youth–adult partnerships have emerged as foundational: *trust, problem-posing methodologies, democratic participation,* and *collective action.* These foundational elements are aligned with the four core elements of youth–adult partnerships advanced by Zeldin and colleagues (2012),[1] but also expand upon them. As such, they add nuance to our understandings about the types of relationships that best enable authentic decision-making, natural mentorship, reciprocity, and connection.

Building Trust

In many ways, the existence of trust underlies each of the four core elements of youth–adult partnership (Zeldin et al., 2012) as well as each of the chapters in this book. Griffith and Jiang's chapter (this volume) on trust formation in youth–adult relationships, highlights a set of contextual and relational factors that support the development of trusting youth–adult relationships. Describing strategies for trust-building that emerge from interviews with program staff, these authors articulate the importance of adults who foster feelings of respect, show genuine interest, and share personal information in age-appropriate ways. Program staff name the importance of consistency in fostering trusting relationships, as well as the unique mentoring role that many adults play. Building from this base, Griffith and Jiang describe a cycle of trust-formation that occurs over time, where youth observe trust-enhancing adult behaviors, engage more deeply with adults, and then are privy to deeper relationships with these adults.

A pillar of positive youth–adult relationships, trust is also built through these relationships. In other words, trust-building is both a necessary element in building youth–adult partnerships and a central outcome of the work. Griffith and Jiang highlight this process with their use of a cycle framework; they note the many ways in which responsive relationships nurture youth trust in adults. These insights are echoed in the other chapters of this volume, where youth and adults speak to the importance of respect, reciprocity, consistency, and responsiveness in cross-generational trust building.

Showing up in both interpersonal/relational and organizational/structural ways, the factors that enable trust appear central to the development of authentic youth–adult partnerships. Co-authored chapters on youth–adult relationships over time highlight the importance of consistency, reciprocity, agency, and co-creation in fostering trusting relationships. These stories speak to the explicit ways in which adults balance high expectations with high levels of support, as well as the less-spoken-about ways in which young people support the learning of their adult partners. Amplifying the importance of careful and caring adults, the youth authors in this section also highlight the power of trusted adults to support their individual and collective growth.

At the same time, chapters describing youth–adult partnerships in programming illuminate organizational structures that help foster trust: transparency, consistency, a commitment to honor the humanity of each individual, and a commitment to collective well-being, to name a few. Echoing many of the factors identified by Griffith and Jiang, these authors help us to see the ways in which organizational structures can nurture a cycle of trust-building between adults and youth.

Finally, many of the authors in this volume share examples of moments when trust has been broken and illuminate possibilities for rebuilding it. As editors, we are moved by the vulnerability of adults willing to share their own missteps in past partnership work through reflecting on feedback from their youth participants. We are also struck by the differing adult perspectives on how best to build and nurture trust in the context of youth–adult partnerships.

Using Problem-Posing Methodologies

Problem-posing methodologies underlie much of the work that occurs in authentic youth–adult partnerships. They are distinct from traditional forms of teaching and learning, which often presume that expertise lies on the side of the adult or designated professional educator. Instead, problem-posing methodologies hold that both adults and youth have critical questions and insights to share. In this sense, relationships and programs that draw on problem-posing methodologies often start with a set of goals and an accompanying toolbox, rather than a set curriculum or scope-and-sequence. Building together, the participants in these programs craft a set of activities that best promote individual and collective growth.

Problem-posing methodologies are woven through the chapters of this book. In his chapter on art education and problem-posing methodologies, Luis-Genaro Garcia draws on Freire's (1970) ideas about praxis and problem-posing methodologies. Freire writes that a problem-posing methodology "involves the constant unveiling of the socio-political realities which exist for students, pushes for the acknowledgement of limiting factors, and co-produces a resistance to those limitations" (Freire, 1970, p. 81). In this sense, problem-posing methodologies foster praxis—the process of acting and reflecting upon the world in order to better understand (and change) it. Garcia's piece helps us to imagine the elements of problem-posing methodologies—*dialogue, conscientization,* and *praxis* (Duncan-Andrade & Morrell, 2008; Freire, 1970; Solorzano, 1989)—in action. His work with students begins with active engagement regarding their personal and collective histories, providing opportunities for youth to both understand and question the effects of power structures on their lived experiences. In dialogue with youth, Garcia explores and questions the structures of power that often shape our lived realities. From there, Garcia engages with young people in the creation and production of public art, a process that deepens their understandings and allows them to act upon their world. By voicing and challenging some of the issues that impact their local communities, the young people with whom Garcia partners become active consumers and creators of the world's many texts.

In her writing about Youth in Action, Rahmanian outlines a complex way of considering individual and collective growth that includes identifying individual students' comfort zones, their need for support and agency, and the critical moments that will best shape their learning. Similarly, Van Steenis and Kirshner describe a responsive set of pedagogies at work in their chapter on Horizons Youth Services, where adults support youth in developing and building out projects motivated by individual interests and goals. But problem-posing methodologies do not just appear in the context of programmatic design; they also appear in the ways in which adults approach relationship-building with youth, as when Deb Bicknell asks Marcellina Angelo, "What do you want me to do?" And, they appear in the questions that are passed down across generations, as illustrated in the Highlander Center's powerful model of collective transformation across time.

The authors in this volume describe relationships and programs that are always in motion—always asking, critiquing, acting, and reflecting on themselves and the world around them. In so doing, these authors highlight problem-posing methodologies as a central pillar of building authentic youth–adult partnerships.

Prioritizing Democratic Participation

Reflecting Freire's (1970) concept of dialogue, the authors across this volume speak frequently about the importance of democratic participation in youth–adult partnerships. Democratic participation is typically defined as a set of processes through which citizens or constituents influence decisions that impact their lives, either directly or through representation (Verba, 1967; Verba, Schlozman & Brady, 1995). As Han (2014) suggests, this type of participation often includes "intensive, voluntary activity . . . that has the intent or effect of influencing decision-makers with power" (p. 32). Built upon a foundation of trust and nurtured by the problem-posing methodologies that Garcia describes, democratic participation requires that all members of a community have a voice and agency in decisions that affect their individual and collective well-being.

In their chapter on tensions in adult–youth partnerships, Medina, Baldrige, and Wiggins describe a set of sociopolitical constraints that make it difficult for community-based youth organizations to promote a "humanizing culture." They write:

> Like schools, CBYOs [community-based youth organization] are informed by the socio-political context in which they exist. Within this current context, CBYOs and the processes by which they are funded are linked to and shaped by market-based education reforms, neoliberal logics rooted in privatization, individualism and competition which impacts organizational culture and practices. (this volume, p. 75)

Medina and colleagues illuminate the importance of an "asset-based" culture in which young people and their communities are viewed as having important wisdom and gifts to share; this type of "humanizing culture" facilitates an understanding that youth are fully capable of participating in and contributing to the project of individual and collective growth. As a result, they center democratic participation in both organizational priorities and everyday practices. Thus, while they do not use the language of democratic participation directly, Medina and colleagues amplify humanizing, democratic practices as foundational for youth–adult partnerships.

Authors throughout this volume echo the importance of democratic participation. Zeller-Berkman and colleagues describe a set of practices that enable democratic participation through power-sharing, including the use of toolkits, scaffolding roles and responsibilities, being transparent about process and decision-making, and generating common goals for action. At the Highlander Center, organizers describe carefully holding space for voice and representation across different identities and life experiences. Building on their legacy of intergenerational activism and intersectional justice, the authors of this piece describe a process through which younger people are welcomed, supported, and given leadership opportunities over time. Authors also share examples of democratic participation in the context of interpersonal relationships, such as when Clark and Raynor describe an iterative process of program development that ensures both of their perspectives are held as equally important. As is the case with each of the other foundational principles, there are also several chapters that highlight barriers to democratic participation and propose strategies for overcoming these barriers.

Engaging in Collective Action

Perhaps most unique in its contribution to our current understandings of effective out-of-school time (OST) learning is the consistent role of collective action in this volume. Across these chapters, the authors describe processes of creating, building, writing, analyzing, and advocating; they talk about co-constructing understandings, actions, music and art, and hope. In this sense, the authors are careful to describe the praxis of youth–adult partnership work as involving some type of collective action. It is not enough to simply be in relationship; the youth and adults in this volume are in relationship around a set of collective goals and a commitment to collective action.

In their chapter on the Intergenerational Change Initiative (ICI), Zeller-Berkman and colleagues describe the influences of critical participatory action research on their work. They write:

> Critical participatory action research (CPAR) is an epistemology that engages research design, methods, analysis and products through a lens of democratic participation (Torre, Fine, Stoudt, & Fox, 2012). Regardless of whether one is working with adults or youth, a critical PAR approach invites members to collaborate at the more "participatory" end of the spectrum, be transparent about issues of power, and celebrate what differently positioned researchers bring to the knowledge-building process. Torre (2014) articulates how CPAR interweaves critical social science, feminist theory, queer theory, indigenous theory, and liberatory practice in order to interrupt injustice, democratize knowledge creation, and build community capacities.[2] (this volume, p. 163)

They go on to describe the critical role of action in this process, naming their "larger shared goal" of "using our research to take action" (p. 168). They add that their theory of change "includes adults and youth working together to change individuals, but also communities, institutions and societal perceptions of young people" (p. 174). Collective action provides a sense of hope and agency, a collective goal on which to work, and a new set of data on which to reflect. When done well, the actions that youth and adults take together can become a manifestation of their powerful work.

Many of the authors and organizations highlighted in this book describe a theory of change that includes collective action. In Section II, we read about the power of strong, trusting relationships to shape and catalyze collective action. The origins of RAW Talent, for example, seem to lie in a powerful relationship between a younger adult and an older youth, who co-create a space in which other youth can grow their writing. Both the form and the content of RAW Talent are shaped by this collective decision-making. Many of the youth pieces that appear throughout the volume describe similar co-constructions and collective actions. In Section III, the authors illuminate youth–adult partnerships that foster collective action. From youth organizing work (Youth in Action & the Highlander Center), to youth research (Intergenerational Change Initiative), to social justice artwork (Horizons Youth Services[3]), each of the settings described in this section builds on the power of youth–adult partnerships to create individual-, organizational-, and community-level change. While relationships are central to these actions, it is the power of collective action itself that often motivates the relational work. In fact, there are several moments when youth authors note that adults' willingness and commitment to take collective action enables the trust that becomes so foundational to their partnership. In Section IV, we are given a window into the complexity of collective action—especially in our current sociopolitical context. Here, adults and youth reflect on moments in which their actions were not collective, or where there was a collective that took no action, in an effort to continue to improve their partnerships. Sharing the feelings of mistrust, stuck-ness, inaction, hurt, and anger that accompany these moments, the authors share lessons learned and ideas reimagined.

Together, *trust, problem-posing methodologies, democratic participation,* and *collective action* lay a foundation upon which authentic adult–youth partnerships can be built. This foundation enables youth and adults to experience the types of trust described by Griffith and Jiang, as well as the four core elements of youth–adult partnerships, named by Zeldin and his colleagues (2012; authentic decision-making, natural mentors, reciprocal activity, and community connectedness). We describe these as foundational elements of youth–adult partnerships, because we believe that they must be intentionally built into the organizations and settings in which we hope youth–adult partnerships will grow (Figure 16.1).

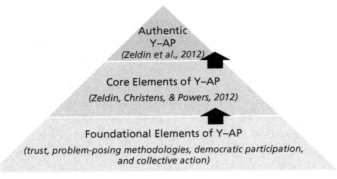

Figure 16.1   Foundational and core elements of youth-adult partnerships.

Promising Practices From the Field

Having provided an overview of the foundational elements of youth–adult partnerships identified in this volume, we now turn our attention toward the structures and practices that our authors named as enabling this work. Rather than nesting these structures and practices within the foundational elements named above, we describe them as distinct; this is because many of the structures and practices named below enable *multiple* foundational elements. For example, building the capacity for critical reflection and feedback in an organization or partnership helps to foster trust and democratic participation; at the same time, the practices used to build this capacity are often problem-posing methodologies, and using them supports the efficacy of collective action. Similarly, centering youth agency in organizations and relationships often facilitates trust and collective action; and, because centering youth agency is counter-hegemonic by design, it also enables the type of problem-posing methodologies that facilitate democratic participation.

In Table 16.1, we outline a set of broad strategies that the authors in this book shared with us. These broad strategies represent both values and organizational commitments; they are strategies because the organizations and individuals described in this volume draw on these values and commitments to nurture authentic youth–adult partnerships. Each strategy is defined in the table, using words that are often a mix of our authors and our own. Finally, for each broad strategy, we provide a list of the chapters in which they appear. Our hope is that this chart can serve as a useful reference tool for readers, who may want to revisit the more detailed and poetic descriptions that these chapters provide.

TABLE 16.1 Strategies, Structures, & Routines for Authentic Youth–Adult Partnerships

	Broad Strategy	Definition	Relevant Chapters
1	Building Capacity for Critical Reflection & Feedback	Structures and routines that enable individuals to reflect on their own practice, their relationships with others, and their contributions to the collective; as well as enabling the collective to reflect, critique, and appreciate their collective work.	• Hale, Ly, Lean-Nichols, & Mays • Luk, Schuettge, Catone, & Perez • Zeller-Berkman, Legaspi-Cavin, Barreto, Tang, & Sandler
2	Building Capacity for Transformative Conflict Solving	Structures and routines that enable individuals, dyads, and groups to identify conflict that is harmful in their relationships, communicate their needs and concerns in these moments, and work to build win–win solutions that address any harm that has occurred.	• Clark & Raynor • Hale, Ly, McLean-Nichols, & Mays • Kapadia, Kabani, & Chowdhury • Rahmanian
3	Building Capacity for Collective Action	Structures and routines that promote collective goal-setting, planning, organizing, and action, as well as the ability to reflect on and course-correct as new issues arise.	• Fei, Freeman, George, Henderson, & Maxfield-Steele • Griffith & Jiang • Hale, Ly, McLean-Nichols, & Mays • Luk, Schuettge, Catone, & Perez • Medina, Baldridge, & Wiggins • Rahmanian • Zeller-Berkman, Legaspi-Cavin, Barreto, Tang, & Sandler
4	Building Capacity for Dialogue	Structures and routines that enable equitable, inclusive dialogue among members of a community or individual in a relationship.	• Nikundiwe • Rahmanian • Zeller-Berkman, Legaspi-Cavin, Barreto, Tang, & Sandler
5	Centering Community/ Connection	Structures and routines that help members of a community honor and value each other's humanity and prioritize each other's needs; as well as build empathy and enable members of a community to feel connected to each other.	• Angelo & Bicknell • Clark & Raynor • Fei, Freeman, George, Henderson, & Maxfield-Steele • Garcia • Rahmanian • Torres & West • Zeller-Berkman, Legaspi-Cavin, Barreto, Tang, & Sandler

(continued)

TABLE 16.1   Strategies, Structures, & Routines for Authentic Youth–Adult Partnerships (continued)

	Broad Strategy	Definition	Relevant Chapters
6	Centering Creative Expression/ Creation	Structures and routines that bring creative expression into a space or community, and that allow members of the community to express their past, present, and future experiences through creative expression; as well as structures and routines that enable innovation and creation.	• Clark & Raynor • Garcia • Van Steenis & Kirshner
7	Centering Learning/ Growth	Structures and routines that support a growth mind-set in both adults and youth; as well as structures and routines that shift toward generative, co-constructed teaching and learning.	• Fei, Freeman, George, Henderson, & Maxfield-Steele • Luk, Schuettge, Catone, & Perez • Rahmanian • Zeller-Berkman, Legaspi-Cavin, Barreto, Tang, & Sandler
8	Centering the Experiences and Histories of People with Marginalized Identities	Structures and routines that bring in the sociopolitical history of individuals and groups, including opportunities to learn about the historical movements of these groups; as well as ensuring the voices of those most impacted are at the center of conversations about goals, processes, and actions.	• Fei, Freeman, George, Henderson, & Maxfield-Steele • Garcia • Kapadia, Kabani, & Chowdhury • Medina, Baldridge, & Wiggins • Rahmanian
9	Centering Youth Agency	Structures and routines that ensure youth are contributors to and leaders of every component of projects—from process to final product, everyday activities to big events.	• Garcia • Hale, Ly, McLean-Nichols, & Mays • Luk, Schuettge, Catone, & Pere • Medina, Baldridge, & Wiggins • Zeller-Berkman, Legaspi-Cavin, Barreto, Tang, & Sandler
10	Co-Construction	Structures and routines that allow youth and adults, or groups of youth, to jointly construct knowledge or understandings of the world or to co-create products or projects.	• Griffith & Jiang • Medina, Baldridge, & Wiggins • Van Steenis & Kirshner
11	Collective Visioning	Structures and routines that support adults and youth in generating a shared mission for their organization and a shared understanding about their ways of being in community.	• Griffith & Jiang • Rahmanian • Zeller-Berkman, Legaspi-Cavin, Barreto, Tang, & Sandler

(continued)

TABLE 16.1 Strategies, Structures, & Routines for Authentic Youth–Adult Partnerships (continued)			
	Broad Strategy	**Definition**	**Relevant Chapters**
12	Democratic Decision-Making	Structures and routines that enable equal voice and vote in organizations in ways that flatten traditional hierarchical power dynamics between adults and youth, and among individuals with different sets of life experiences.	• Griffith & Jiang • Luk, Schuettge, Catone, & Perez • Nikudiwe • Rahmanian
13	Dismantling a Culture of Adultism	Structures and routines that eliminate ageism and the dominant assumption that adult insights are more valuable than youth insights.	• Luk, Schuettge, Catone, & Perez • Nikundiwe • Zeller-Berkman, Legaspi-Cavin, Barreto, Tang, & Sandler
14	Explicitly Discussing & Analyzing the Role of Power	Structures and routines that explicitly bring structures of power into conversations and analyses; as well as that support individuals and groups in discussing the impact of power on their relationships.	• Kapadia, Kabani, & Chowdhury • Luk, Schuettge, Catone, & Perez • Zeller-Berkman, Legaspi-Cavin, Barreto, Tang, & Sandler • Medina, Baldridge, & Wiggins • Nikundiwe • Rahmanian
15	Healing-Centered Engagement	Structures and routines that ensure individual, dyads, groups, and organizations are strengths-based, advance a collective view of healing, and re-center culture as a central feature in well-being (Ginwright, 2018).	• Clark & Raynor • Kapadia, Kabani, & Chowdhury • Rahmanian • Torres & West • Hale, Ly, McLean-Nichols, & Mays
16	Integration with Families and Communities	Structures and routines that create space for families and community members to join in the work of youth–adult partnerships; as well as that create space for adults and youth to learn from families and community partners.	• Clark & Raynor • Torres & West
17	Joy	Structures and routines that provide opportunities for individual and shared joy, in its many forms.	• Clark & Raynor • Fei, Freeman, George, Henderson, & Maxfield-Steele • Rahmanian • Zeller-Berkman, Legaspi-Cavin, Barreto, Tang, & Sandler

(continued)

TABLE 16.1 Strategies, Structures, & Routines for Authentic Youth–Adult Partnerships (continued)

	Broad Strategy	Definition	Relevant Chapters
18	Natural Mentors	Structures and routines that provide opportunities for mentorship on the basis of shared interest and/or identity/background.	• Kapadia, Kabani, & Chowdhury • Rahmanian • Clark & Raynor • Van Steenis & Kirshner
19	Bridging Heart and Mind	Structures and routines that create space for emotions, emotional reactions, and emotional needs; as well as that explicitly acknowledge the role of emotion in knowledge creation and learning.	• Angelo & Bicknell • Clark & Raynor • Hale, Ly, McLean-Nichols, & Mays • Luk, Schuettge, Catone, & Perez • Torres & West • Zeller-Berkman, Legaspi-Cavin, Barreto, Tang, & Sandler
20	Providing Youth with Access to Resources	Structures and routines that transfer resources from adults to youth by enabling youth to access the financial, material, human, and temporal resources they need.	• Fei, Freeman, George, Henderson, & Maxfield-Steele • Hale, Ly, McLean-Nichols, & Mays • Medina, Baldridge, & Wiggins • Van Steenis & Kirshner
21	Supporting the Whole Person	Structures and routines that hold space and time for humanizing practices, such that both adults and youth feel seen and cared for as whole human beings.	• Clark & Raynor • Fei, Freeman, George, Henderson, & Maxfield-Steele • Zeller-Berkman, Legaspi-Cavin, Barreto, Tang, & Sandler
22	Transparency	Structures and routines that make the implicit workings of an organization (or relationship) explicit, such that they might be interrogated by those involved.	• Medina, Baldridge, & Wiggins • Zeller-Berkman, Legaspi-Cavin, Barreto, Tang, & Sandler
23	Youth in Leadership Roles	Structures and routines that transfer power from adults to youth by enabling youth to take on decision-making roles that are typically reserved for adults.	• Clark & Raynor • Fei, Freeman, George, Henderson, & Maxfield-Steele • Luk, Schuettge, Catone, & Perez • Zeller-Berkman, Legaspi-Cavin, Barreto, Tang, & Sandler

It is worth noting that the success of each of these strategies, structures, and routines is dependent on their appropriate use in context-specific, culturally-responsive ways. In other words, decontextualized, these strategies, structures, and routines may not be sufficient to nurture youth–adult partnerships. Rather, these strategies, structures, and routines should be considered to be "kernels of practice" (Jones, Bailey, Brush, & Kahn, 2017, p. 3) that—if studied more deeply—might provide critical nutrients for our individual and collective well-being.

WHERE DO WE GO FROM HERE? A CALL FOR COLLECTIVE TRANSFORMATION

At the start of this volume, we argued that authentic youth–adult partnerships are a core vertebrae of quality youth programming in OST settings. We noted that relationships between youth and adults are only truly authentic when they exist outside of traditional power hierarchies and negative constructions of youth; and, we suggested that constructing these types of authentic youth–adult partnerships are a critical capacity (or "what") for which effective OST programs must be held accountable (Pittman, 2017). Echoing the words of many, we noted the power and potential of OST spaces that resist dominant, neoliberal models of learning and, instead, provide context-driven, personalized learning. It is our belief that youth–adult partnerships may be one aspect of OST learning from which in-school educators might draw inspiration.

In this chapter, we have attempted to summarize some of the many insights that our youth and adult authors provide. Having placed our authors in dialogue around the foundational elements of youth–adult partnerships, as well as the specific strategies and practices that build on this foundation, we turn our attention now toward the future. What can the authors in this volume help us to understand about the future of out-of-school time learning? What fundamental assumptions about the *what* and *how* of OST practices do they challenge?

Perhaps more than anything else, the chapters in this book challenge a fundamental assumption that quality youth programming in OST settings should be measured based on the aggregated outcomes of individual youth. By illustrating the power of collective goal-setting, community-building, work, and action, the authors of this volume raise questions about the prominence of individual-level outcomes in definitions of efficacy, encouraging us to turn, instead, toward a more collective vision of well-being.

Collective well-being requires collective goal-setting; we cannot assume that the developmental outcomes or 21st century skills that the adult world has adopted fully reflect the needs and interests of young people today. Collective well-being requires paying attention to adult growth and wellness, both because adults are human beings, and because we know that the long-term well-being of young people is intertwined with the health and happiness of their adult caregivers. It means paying attention to the well-being of youth workers, educators, and others in the field, as well as paying attention to the collective well-being of the families and communities from which our youth come. Collective well-being requires that we not only explicitly learn and unlearn the impact of systems of power in our communities, but that we create opportunities for adults and youth to work together to dismantle these systems. Collective well-being means that we imagine and build a set of democratic, liberatory systems and practices to replace the status quo of yesterday. Reaching for collective well-being—rather than individual-level outcomes—requires that we seek transformation for ourselves, for each other, and for our communities; and, that we focus our attention on the critical work of healing.

The OST field is uniquely positioned to lead this critical shift. Although burdened by many of the same neoliberal constraints as schools, this field has been historically central to the push for context-driven, personalized learning. Creating learning spaces and opportunities that represent a wide range of artistic, athletic, technological, academic, and advocacy activities, OST programs are often tailored to meet the context-specific needs of the young people whom they serve. Unlike traditional schools, young people and adults are often drawn to OST spaces as a result of shared interests, commitments, or values. And, unlike traditional schools, OST spaces are often staffed by adults who reflect the geographic, demographic, and cultural identities of their youth. In this sense, despite persistent neoliberal socio-political pressures (Baldridge, 2019), many OST programs manage to carve out responsive, liberatory learning spaces for youth.

The OST field is uniquely positioned to lead the shift toward more liberatory educational processes and outcomes, and youth–adult partnerships are uniquely positioned to support this leadership. Youth–adult partnerships not only support effective youth work and youth development programming, they provide a model for collective well-being—an example of how adults and youth might work and exist together within the Beloved Community.[4] The authors in this volume help us to understand that youth–adult partnerships are not simply about *creating* effective OST programming, they are about *changing* the communities and contexts in which OST programs operate. In so doing, they inspire us to imagine a world in which youth–adult partnerships are a regular part of everyday teaching and learning—a world where *both* youth and adults are teaching and learning, inside and outside of school, in ways that build collective well-being.

NOTES

1. We believe that these elements (authentic decision-making, natural mentors, reciprocal activity, and community connectedness) are often outcomes of the more foundational elements we describe here.

2. See the Public Science website for more on the principles of CPAR: http://publicscienceproject.org/principles-and-values/

3. A pseudonym.

4. The phrase *Beloved Community* is credited to philosopher-theologian Josiah Royce, who founded the Fellowship of Reconciliation; however, many people (including each of us) know the concept as a result of the work of Martin Luther King Jr. As described on the King Center website, "Dr. King's Beloved Community is a global vision, in which all people can share in the wealth of the earth. In the Beloved Community, poverty, hunger, and homelessness will not be tolerated because international standards of human decency will not allow it. Racism and all forms of discrimination, bigotry and prejudice will be replaced by an all-inclusive spirit of sisterhood and brotherhood. In the Beloved Community, international disputes will be resolved by peaceful conflict-resolution and reconciliation of adversaries, instead of military power. Love and trust will triumph over fear and hatred. Peace with justice will prevail over war and military conflict" (para. 23; http://thekingcenter.org/king-philosophy/).

REFERENCES

Baldridge, B. J. (2019). *Reclaiming Community: Race and the uncertain future of youth work*. Stanford, CA: Stanford University Press.

Duncan-Andrade, J., & Morrell, E. (2008). *The art of critical pedagogy: Possibilities for moving from theory to practice in urban schools*. New York, NY: Peter Lang.

Freire, P. (1970). *Pedagogy of the oppressed*. New York, NY: Continuum.

Ginwright, S. (2018, May 31). The future of healing: Shifting from trauma-informed care to healing-centered engagement. *Medium*. Retrieved from https://medium.com/@ginwright/the-future-of-healing-shifting-from-trauma-informed-care-to-healing-centered-engagement-634f557ce69c

Han, H. (2014). *How organizations develop activists: Civic associations and leadership in the 21st century*. New York, NY: Oxford University Press.

Jones, S. M., Bailey, R., Brush, K., & Kahn, J. (2017). *Kernels of practice for SEL: Low-cost, low-burden strategies*. Cambridge, MA: Harvard Graduate School of Education. Retrieved from https://www.wallacefoundation.org/knowledge-center/Documents/Kernels-of-Practice-for-SEL.pdf

Pittman, K. (2017). Securing the future: Pivoting from where and when to what and how. In H. J. Malone & T. Donahue (Eds.), *The growing out-of-school time field: Past, present and Future* (pp. 293–308). Charlotte, NC: Information Age.

Solórzano, D. G. (1989). Teaching and social change: Reflections on a Freirean approach in a college classroom. *Teaching Sociology, 17(2)*, 218–225.

Torre, M. E. (2014). Participatory action research. In T. Teo (Ed.), *Encyclopedia of critical psychology: Vol. 3* (pp. 1323–1327). New York, NY: Springer.

Torre, M. E., Fine, M., Stoudt, B., & Fox, M. (2012). Critical participatory action research as public science. In P. Camic, & H. Cooper (Eds.), *APA handbook of research methods in psychology* (pp. 171–184). Washington, DC: American Psychology Association.

Verba, S. (1967). Democratic participation. *The Annals of the American Academy of Political and Social Science, 373, Social Goals and Indicators for American Society, 2,* 53–78.

Verba, S., Schlozman, K. L., & Brady, H. E. (1995). *Voice and equality: Civic volunteerism in American politics.* Cambridge, MA: Harvard University Press.

Zeldin, S., Christens, B., & Powers, J. (2012). The psychology and practice of youth–adult partnership: Bridging generations for youth development and community change. *American Journal of Community Psychology, 51*(3/4), 385–397.

ABOUT THE EDITORS

Gretchen Brion-Meisels, EdD, is a lecturer on education at the Harvard Graduate School of Education. Born and raised in Cambridge, MA, she feels lucky to have been brought up in a community of activist educators who pushed her to think carefully about her own identity, her relationships to others, and the complicated world around her. These early conversations nurtured Gretchen's commitment to challenging systems of inequity through dialectic learning and collective action.

Gretchen began her career as a middle school humanities teacher, working in Baltimore, MD; Cambridge, MA; and Berkeley, CA. The young folks with whom she worked honored her with their questions, stories, insights, and frustrations, providing generous opportunities for Gretchen to learn with—and from—their wisdom. In 2007, Gretchen arrived at the Harvard Graduate School of Education to explore successful models for holistic student support. Quickly realizing that she needed to go back to the source, she began learning and practicing participatory action research.

Over the last 12 years, Gretchen has studied adolescent development from the perspective of a developmental psychologist and a critical educator. Her research seeks to support educators and youth as they partner cross-generationally to improve school culture and climate. To this end, she has conducted two intergenerational critical participatory action research projects. Her courses focus on supporting positive youth development, creating loving educational spaces, and partnering with youth in educational research and practice.

At Our Best, pages 305–308
Copyright © 2020 by Information Age Publishing
All rights of reproduction in any form reserved.

Gretchen received her BA in American studies from Harvard College. She graduated from Harvard University with an EdM in prevention science and practice, and an EdD in human development and education. Gretchen is an editor of the volume *Humanizing Education: Critical Alternatives to Reform* (2010) and an editor of the publication *Planning to Change the World*, published annually by Rethinking Schools. Her work has been published in *Teachers College Record, Harvard Educational Review, Urban Education*, and *Educational Leadership.*

Jessica Tseming Fei leverages the tools of research, education, art, and activism to partner with youth and communities towards a more just world. Born and raised in Queens, New York, Jessica is proud to be a child of immigrants and a member of the Chinese diaspora. Since Jessica began her professional journey as an educator over thirteen years ago, she has worked with youth and young adults in a wide range of settings, including urban public schools, elite universities, arts agencies, and community-based organizations. Jessica is currently the director of programs at the Sadie Nash Leadership Project, a feminist organization that supports the leadership, activism, and college and career readiness of young women and gender-expansive youth of color. Her approach to education is deeply informed by her background as an English teacher and a teaching artist, and by the wisdom and visions of her former students in East Harlem and the Bronx.

Through her academic studies and various teaching experiences, Jessica has built extensive knowledge on critical, culturally-responsive, and place-based pedagogies. Drawing upon qualitative methodologies and frameworks of critical participatory action research, she investigates how social structures, culture, and geography shape the identities, lived experiences, and civic participation of young people in cities. As a Presidential Scholar and a New Civics Early Career Scholar at Harvard University, Jessica conducted research on young people's neighborhood narratives and completed a portraiture study of the youth programs in an urban community art studio. Her work has been published in *Educational Researcher* and *Toward a Positive Psychology of Relationships: New Directions in Theory and Research.*

Jessica collaborates closely with other researchers, educators, activists, and artists on initiatives that foster equity and inclusion, and that center youth and communities of color. In the Boston area, Jessica has worked with community members to develop place-based curriculum for high school students, conduct case studies on a teen recreation center, research issues of inequity in their schools and communities, and plan conferences on topics at the intersection of arts, education, and justice. As an advisor for Harvard College students, Jessica has led programs that cultivate social consciousness, foster healing and reflection, and build connection and community.

She has won numerous awards for her work with undergraduates, including the 2018 Star Family Prize for Excellence in Sophomore Advising. Jessica currently works at the Sadie Nash Leadership Project, an organization that supports the critical consciousness of young women and gender-expansive youth of color in New York City and Newark, New Jersey.

Jessica received her BA in literature and ethnicity, race, and migration from Yale University. She graduated from the Harvard Graduate School of Education with an EdM in human development and psychology, and an EdD in culture, communities, and education.

Deepa Sriya Vasudevan began her career as a youth worker and researcher in Philadelphia, where she engaged with and worked in support of a vast and vibrant landscape of youth programs across the city. She first worked with young people at a student program center at Parkway Northwest High School for Peace and Social Justice. Subsequently, she worked at the Out-of-School Time Resource Center, a professional hub for youth workers that offered program tools, training opportunities, and evaluation services. Deepa has served on the board of Seybert Foundation since 2011 and was previously the board chair of the Philadelphia Wooden Boat Factory, a nonprofit focused on experiential and apprentice-based maritime learning for youth.

As a scholar, Deepa's research is guided by sociological and cultural inquiry into issues of educational opportunity and inequality. In particular, she explores the experiences and meaning making of youth workers and adolescents in community-based organizations through qualitative methods. Through the lens of narrative inquiry, she has examined the occupational identities and persistence of experienced youth workers in a field fraught with issues such as financial precarity and social undervaluation that typically lead practitioners to exit organizations and the career altogether.

As a graduate student, Deepa served as an editor for the *Harvard Educational Review* and co-chair for the Student Research Conference. She has developed and taught courses on youth work and community-based youth programs. Additionally, she researches and writes about the experiences of undocumented youth through the National UnDACAmented Research Project. Deepa has work published in volumes such as *The Changing Landscape of Youth Work: Theory and Practice for an Evolving Field, Dilemmas of Educational Ethics*, and *Toward a Positive Psychology of Relationships: New Directions in Theory and Research*. She was the 2018 recipient of the Emerging Scholar Award from the Out-of-School Time Special Interest Group at the American Educational Research Association and the John Schmitt Award for Outstanding Graduate Research from the New England Educational Research Organization.

Deepa is currently a visiting lecturer at Wellesley College, where she teaches courses on the social dynamics of schooling and community-based youth programs. She completed her EdD in culture, communities, and education as well as an EdM in educational policy and management at Harvard Graduate School of Education. She received her BA from Haverford College with an English major and cultural anthropology minor.

ABOUT THE CONTRIBUTORS

Marcellina (Marcy) Angelo, although originally from the country of South Sudan, is a longtime resident of Portland, Maine. Marcy has been working as an organizer and youth advocate in the community for over ten years. She truly believes in the importance of empowering young people to use their influential voices, partnered with guidance from strong adult figures. Marcy has worked with a broad range of organizations such as Seeds of Leadership, Make it Happen, Maine Seeds of Peace, and the local NAACP's youth program, the Martin Luther King Fellows. She is also a coach for TEDx Dirigo, a writer and a spoken word artist. Throughout all her work, there is one message that has stayed of constant importance to Marcy: The community we build is a shared responsibility, whether or not you're a youth or an adult.

Bianca J. Baldridge is an assistant professor in the Department of Educational Policy Studies with affiliations in Afro-American Studies and Sociology at the University of Wisconsin, Madison. Her scholarship explores the sociopolitical context of community-based youth work and afterschool education. Bianca's research critically examines the confluence of race, class, and gender, and its impact on educational reforms that shape community-based educational spaces. Her book, *Reclaiming Community: Race and the Uncertain Future of Youth Work* (Stanford University Press), examines how neoliberal education reforms, with its emphasis on privatization and accountability, undermines Black community-based organizations' efforts to support comprehensive youth development opportunities. Some of Bianca's research has been published in the *American Educational Research*

At Our Best, pages 309–320
Copyright © 2020 by Information Age Publishing
All rights of reproduction in any form reserved.

Journal; Review of Research in Education; Teachers College Record; and *Race, Ethnicity, and Education.* Bianca's experiences as a youth worker continues to inform her research in profound ways.

Jessica Barreto is an afro latina college student at CUNY Baruch College, where she intends to finish with her bachelor's degree in public affairs, and continue to attain a master's degree in public administration. She aspires to work for the child welfare system in hopes of contributing positive changes to future children who may have to come across these agencies. She is an adopted child who has been in foster care and has had multiple experiences with multiple child welfare agencies. As a senior in high school, she began working with—and still works with—the Intergenerational Change Initiative as a youth researcher, where she is able to use research to advocate for the youth in her community.

Deborah Bicknell is a Portland, Maine-based global citizen with a wide heart, deep thoughts and big questions. She is a professional facilitator, curriculum and program designer and runs her own international consulting business with concentrations in creative facilitation, conflict transformation, leadership development, youth empowerment and advocacy, school and community engagement, multiculturalism and equity, multi-stakeholder change and organizational strategic systems thinking. Her work centers around truth, expression and evolution. Deborah helped to start an intergenerational youth advocacy organization in Maine and now works within a wide range of educational and community contexts. Some of her clients include Seeds of Peace International, American Councils/Kennedy-Lugar YESProgram, Americans for the Arts, Saalam Institute for Peace and Justice, the Eurasia Foundation, AMP Global Youth, Illinois Global Scholars, Muskie School of Public Service and many other local, national and international organizations. She is a TED talk coach, youth mentor, wedding officiant, and published writer and poet.

Keith Catone is executive director of the Center for Youth and Community Leadership in Education (CYCLE) at Roger Williams University. Previously, he served as associate director for Community Organizing and Engagement at the Annenberg Institute for School Reform and adjunct assistant professor of education at Brown University. He was the project director for the Youth 4 Change Alliance in Providence, RI and co-founded the New York Collective of Radical Educators, a citywide grassroots teacher activist group, while teaching high school social studies in the Bronx. Keith serves on the board of directors for the Education for Liberation Network and has authored numerous research and opinion pieces. His first book, *The Pedagogy of Teacher Activism: Portraits of Four Teachers for Justice,* explores connections between pedagogical purpose, power, and possibility in the context of working with teachers, youth, families, and communities to change the world. Keith holds an EdD from Harvard University.

Nudar Chowdhury is a sociology and anthropology student at Stockton University in New Jersey. She is currently the vice president of Students for Justice in Palestine at Stockton.

Donté Clark, a native of Richmond, California, reigns as one of the most prolific writers and voices out of the Bay Area arts community. Donté is not only eclectic in the art of storytelling through the spoken word, his body language and musical presence in performance is poetry in itself. He captures the complexities of what it feels and looks like to be vulnerable within Black masculinity while governed by a society of White supremacy and hyper violence among Black youth. Graduating high school in 2008, he co-founded an arts collective called RAW Talent (Richmond Artist With Talent). Based in his hometown, Donté engaged young people in writing and performance workshops, securing space for the youth to process their trauma and rewrite the narrative that has surrounded their community. October 2018, 10 years after co-founding RAW Talent, Donté published his first collection of poetry *KnowFreedom*, which is now available on Amazon.

Nayir Vieira Freeman is a trans, nonbinary, afro-latinx artist, activist, and organizer, concerning themself with the work of justice based in equity and reparations. They consider themselves a southerner, midwesterner, and islander, but are currently based in the South Central/Gulf Coastal region in central Texas, as well as along the Texas-Mexico border. Vieira's work is based around community, advocacy, and youth organizing, and general education on issues of queer- and transness, immigration justice, the prison industrial complex, and socialism. Their latest involvement has been with the #TXSTSitIn, a resistance by and for marginalized students demanding accountability from their administration at Texas State University. Vieira currently stands on the executive board for Transcend at Texas State as the VP of community, as well as the YDSA chapter at Texas State as co-chair. Vieira is currently majoring in studio arts with a concentration in painting at Texas State.

Dr. Luis-Genaro Garcia is an artist and professor of art education at Sacramento State University. He previously taught art for 14 years at his former high school in the Los Angeles Unified School District. His research draws on critical education frameworks such as the funds of knowledge, critical pedagogy, and critical race theory in art education as tools for social consciousness. His experience as a Los Angeles based artist, art educator, and scholar has developed opportunities for students to draw on their historical, cultural, and personal experiences and use their home based knowledge to collaborate with families, students, educators, professors, and artists, in their own communities.

Rush George uses written and spoken word to bring awareness to and advocate for necessary change on issues that are important to me and often directly impact her (gender inequality, racial injustice, prison industrial complex, mental health resources for youth, reentry into society, poverty, and food justice). She works with the Deep Center's YPAR (Youth Participatory Action Research) group to strategize and act on issues affecting youth (i.e., school to prison pipeline and affordable mental health resources). Rush also participates in Deep's Block by Block program, Action Research Team, and Policy Action Committee. She is affiliated with the Highlander Center for Research and Education's Seeds of Fire program as a member of their advisory committee. She has been published in several anthologies with the Deep Center since the age of 12 and enjoys performing using various art forms.

Aisha Griffith is an assistant professor in the Department of Educational Psychology at the University of Illinois at Chicago. Her research focuses on the development and function of supportive relationships between adolescents and non-parental adults within informal and formal learning contexts. She is particularly interested in the critical role of trust within youth–adult relationships and how these relationships support positive adolescent development. She has discussed the role of trust in out-of-school time (OST) settings in a number of publications: "Building Trust: Reflections of Adults Working With Youth in Project-Based Programs," "How Trust Grows: Teenagers' Accounts of Forming Trust in Youth Program Staff," "Why Trust Matters: How Confidence in Leaders Transforms What Adolescents Gain From Youth Programs," and "Trajectories of Trust Within the Youth Program Context." More broadly, she is committed to connecting research and practice on OST programming. In order to generate a comprehensive understanding of trust across learning contexts, her scholarship is expanding from researching OST settings to exploring trust within formal school contexts.

Samantha Rose Hale (they/them) is a music therapist, performing artist, educator, and independent consultant in group facilitation and leadership in Boston, MA. Supported by a BA in music therapy from Berklee College of Music and a MEd from Harvard Graduate School of Education, their career has coalesced a broad range of experience. Samantha has designed, implemented, and managed music therapy and arts-for-justice programs for diverse populations in age and background in therapeutic, educational, and nonprofit settings. They have also served as adjunct faculty, instructor, and supervisor for undergraduate and graduate programs. Central to their work is creating environments that empower others to realize and act on their individual and collective potential. Their facilitative approach is human-centered and emphasizes a culture of equity and inclusivity. Formerly the assistant director of Boston Programs at the Center for Teen Empowerment, Samantha co-designed and co-directed TE Studios (originally B4 Studios), a youth-run and adult-supported project that aims to challenge the status quo by producing and showcasing socially conscious and progressive content in the performing and visual arts. A seasoned musician, Samantha has performed throughout the United States and abroad over the past fifteen years. Samantha continues to collaborate with youth and adult activists and performing artists to deconstruct harmful narratives and amplify the voices of those who have been historically and systemically oppressed.

Ash-Lee Woodard Henderson is the first Black woman executive director of the Highlander Research & Education Center, a social justice leadership training school and cultural center founded in 1932. Through popular education, language justice, participatory research, cultural work, and intergenerational organizing, they help create spaces—at Highlander and in communities—where people gain knowledge, hope, and courage, expanding their ideas of what is possible. Ash-Lee is a longtime activist working against environmental racism in central and Southern Appalachia. She serves on the governance council of the Southern Movement Assembly and is a nationally recognized leader in the Movement for Black Lives. Most recently, Ash-Lee was featured on the 2019 Frederick Douglass 200, a list of 200 individuals who best embody the spirit and work of Frederick Douglass, one of the most influential figures in history.

Xue Jiang is a doctoral student in educational psychology at the University of Illinois at Chicago. Her research interest focuses on the socialization of attachment and its relationship with children's learning in different cultural contexts. Specifically, she studies the caregiving relationships within migrant families in rural China. By examining the conceptions and interactions between children and their multiple caregivers, Xue hopes to better articulate different cultural conceptions of childrearing and learning and extend current assumptions of attachment theory. Xue is also interested in various research methods. She has particularly engaged in several projects that apply observational assessment, measurement development, and interview strategies to discover and explain individuals' development trajectories across age groups. She is currently obtaining a master's degree in measurement, evaluation, statistics, and assessment. Her latest manuscript is a meta-analysis of teachers' socioemotional teaching and young children's socioemotional competence.

Anika Kabani is an Islamic studies graduate student in London at the Institute of Ismaili Studies. Previously, she worked at a migrant and gender justice non-profit in New York City. She received her undergraduate degrees in international and area studies and anthropology from Washington University in St. Louis in 2017.

Melissa Kapadia is a radical educator/organizer from Philadelphia, who organizes with the Radical Asian American Womxn's Collective (RAAWC) and Philly South Asian Collective (PSAC); she was an East Coast Solidarity Summer (ECSS) organizer for 3 years. She is currently a lecturer in the University of Pennsylvania's Critical Writing Program, and serves as a community advisor for Asian Arts Initiative (AAI). Melissa's areas of expertise include workplace literacy; race, gender, and power; reading/writing/literacy education; adult education; and Asian American Studies.

Ben Kirshner is a professor of education at the University of Colorado Boulder. In his research Ben collaboratively designs and studies learning environments that support youth development, activism, and civic participation. Projects include design-based research in action civics classrooms, measures of youth policy arguments, critical participatory action research, and ethnographies of community-based youth organizing groups. His 2015 book, *Youth Activism in an Era of Education Inequality*, received the social policy award for best authored book from the Society of Research on Adolescence. Ben is editor for the Information Age press series on adolescence and education. He got his start as a youth worker in the 1990s in San Francisco's Mission District.

Mia Legaspi-Cavin is a program associate with Vera's Center on Youth Justice, where she works with prisons to transform conditions of confinement for young adults. Prior to working with Vera, Mia spent nearly five years running young adult mentoring programs. Mia's interests are in systems change by means of impact-led and rights-based advocacy, youth adult partnership development, and implementation of healing practices in traditionally toxic environments. She is a strong believer that those who are most impacted by the systems should inform and shape policy, and program development. Mia received a BA in Spanish and law, societies and justice at the University of Washington. She received her MA in youth studies at the CUNY School of Professional Studies.

Kristy Luk got her start in youth work while in college and ran a youth leadership and social justice program after graduating. She is currently a consultant at TCC Group, where she supports funders in strategizing ways to create more opportunities for community-based, participatory models of grantmaking. Previously, she was a program manager at the Center for Youth and Community Leadership in Education (CYCLE) at Roger Williams University. In her role, she supported a portfolio of youth and parent organizing groups in New England, from creating research scans to providing critical thought partnership, and designing and facilitating workshops. Kristy believes that all powerful social movements begin with young people, and continues to ground her activism in the belief that people most impacted are the ones who have the brilliance, creativity, and lived experiences to shape the solutions our communities need. Kristy received a BA and an MPP from Harvard University.

Heang Guek Ly is an expert in the field of youth development, group facilitation, and nonprofit management with 20 years of experience organizing, teaching, and consultation around a variety of community and social justice issues. In her former role as director of consulting and training at the Center for Teen Empowerment, she provided technical support and skills training for nonprofits, businesses, foundations, schools, and city departments to ensure successful organizational and program development. She currently continues this work through her independent consulting practice using a facilitative leadership framework with a diversity, equity and inclusion lens. Ms. Ly holds a bachelor's degree in psychology and education, a master's degree in administration, planning, and social policy and a certificate in nonprofit management. Her short story "The Lotus Gift" was published in the award winning book, *Troubling Borders: An Anthology of Art and Literature by Southeast Asian Women in the Diaspora*, incorporated nationally in higher education courses.

Rev. Allyn Maxfield-Steele grew up in Texas, Germany, and North Carolina. He once had the opportunity to live and learn alongside human rights organizers and community leaders from the Assembly of the Poor in Northeast Thailand. That experience transformed Allyn's understanding of the power and purpose of education. Since 2002, Allyn has worked as a school teacher, a college educator, a neighborhood organizer, and a pastor. Allyn is an ordained minister in the Christian Church (Disciples of Christ), and he has served congregations in Alaska and Tennessee. He pays a lot of attention to pastoral care, institutional change, dystopian science fiction, the problems of historical memory, and sculpture. He currently serves as a co-executive director of the Highlander Research and Education Center.

Carrie Mays is a 19-year-old freshman at UMASS Boston, majoring in business management with a concentration of marketing and minoring in political science. For the past four years, she has been a youth organizer at The Center for Teen Empowerment (TE) and an artist manager at TE Studios. Carrie has both witnessed and internalized a lot or discrimination during her childhood and teenage years and is committed to being a social justice activist warrior for herself and her community. She has facilitated large-scale racism dialogues, voter registration parties, community cookouts, and movie nights. She has spoken at national conferences and academic institutions throughout the United States on topics of racial equity. As an artist, she has created and performed original dance, spoken word, and music pieces, and was the lead actress for an original theater production at The Paramount Center in Boston. Carrie plans to pursue an MBA and give back to her community similar to how TE did for her.

Nathaniel McLean-Nichols is an artist activist who has worked for 4 years contributing to the advancement and uplift of Black culture/society. Currently, through his work with Teen Empowerment (TE) and the arts-based programming that TE offers (TE Studios), he works to empower youth of color by solidifying their understanding of systems and institutions that uphold oppression. As an artist, Nathaniel understands how crucial it is for youth to have many different outlets of expression at their disposal in order for them to find their creative niche and feel as empowered as possible through their time, work, and art. Nathaniel currently attends the University of Massachusetts Boston and is studying to receive his Bachelor of Arts in English.

Juan Carlos Medina is a doctoral candidate in educational policy studies at the University of Wisconsin, Madison. His scholarship examines Latinx education and racialization, the dynamic intersections of race and language, and the potential of community-based spaces to holistically support the development of Latinx youth. Further, Juan's work centers around youth voice to examine how they make meaning of the ways race and language intersect to inform their educational experiences and identity development. As a credentialed classroom teacher, historian, and youth worker, Juan is passionate about creating equitable opportunities for youth via the use of culturally-sustaining practices within community-based contexts. Juan's work on community-based spaces as sites of resistance and vulnerable places under the weight of neoliberal dominance has been published in *Review of Research in Education*. His work also seeks to examine the developing practices of preservice teachers and youth workers, and what they might learn from each other.

Thomas Nikundiwe is the executive director of the Education for Liberation Network. Thomas started his career teaching secondary mathematics in the Baltimore City Public School System and then serving as a Peace Corps volunteer in Uganda training primary school teachers. Following his time in Uganda, Thomas worked as a youth organizer for the Baltimore Algebra Project. Convinced of the power and promise of organizing as a tool for personal, institutional, and community transformation, Thomas decided to further study youth and community organizing at the Harvard Graduate School of Education (HGSE), where he earned a doctorate. While at HGSE, he was on a team of researchers that published *Match on Dry Grass: Community Organizing as a Catalyst for School Reform*. In his last year in Boston, Thomas served as the coordinator for the Youth Organizers United for the Now Generation (YOUNG) Coalition. Thomas now lives in Detroit with his partner and two boys.

Catalina Perez is a program manager at the Center for Youth and Community Leadership in Education (CYCLE) at Roger Williams University. Catalina's current work supports the development, coordination, and implementation of key technical assistance and training opportunities for youth and parent organizing groups all over New England. Previously, she worked with young people and parents in Rhode Island supporting college access for middle and high school students. Catalina received a BA from Rhode Island College and a Community Interpreting Certificate from Boston University's Center for Professional Education.

The daughter of Iranian immigrants, **Pegah Rahmanian** spent most of her childhood with one foot in the American Midwest experience, and the other foot deeply rooted in the post-revolution Iranian experience. Suspended between worlds provided a language with which she navigated both her small town and rural upbringings, and later her life and work in urban settings working within frontline communities. Rahmanian's work has included youth-centered HIV prevention in post-Katrina New Orleans; community-based school in Emeryville, California; digital media arts programs that bridge to the silicon valley era; and backpacking with 300 urban youth. Recently, Rahmanian has shifted her gaze to higher education equity and justice work as the director of Rhode Island College's Intercultural Resource Center. Rahmanian holds a BA from Oberlin College in anthropology, gender and women studies, and comparative American studies; and an MA from Wright State University in applied behavioral sciences and sociology.

Molly Pershin Raynor is a poet and educator. She has facilitated poetry workshops in prisons, halfway houses, high schools and teen centers, and traveled coast to coast performing spoken word. Molly co-founded RAW Talent (now the RYSE Performing Arts Program) in Richmond, California. Her work is highlighted in the documentary film on Netflix, "Romeo Is Bleeding," which follows her co-founder Donté Clark and their students as they fight to address gun violence through spoken word and theater. She won a Jefferson Award for public service and a Teachers 4 Social Justice award. Molly just moved back to her hometown of Ann Arbor, Michigan, to serve as the literary arts program manager at the Neutral Zone Teen Center. Her poetry has been featured on NPR and published in several literary magazines including *Vinyl*, *The Rumpus*, and *Porkbelly Press*.

Asha Sandler is a student at Hunter College High School. She volunteers at Mount Sinai Beth Israel's Pediatric Emergency Department and at New

Sanctuary Coalition, a pro se clinic which helps undocumented immigrants apply for asylum. She is also a mentor at her school's writing center and is co-president of the Hunter chapter of the grassroots political activist organization Indivisible. She has been on the Star Track cycling team since she was eight, and now mentors younger members of the team. Having struggled with PTSD, depression, and anxiety, she understands the difficulties of falling behind in school due to extenuating circumstances. She has been working at the Intergenerational Change Initiative as a youth researcher for 2 years, helping to conduct focus groups and develop their app Amplify.

Noah Schuettge currently seeks to cultivate relational cultures of interdependence in social movements and organizations as a consultant and trainer with Relational Uprising and was formerly a program associate at the Center for Youth and Community Leadership in Education (CYCLE) at Roger Williams University. Noah is an educator and organizer with experience in community building, facilitation, training, and youth-led education spaces who believes that young people will lead our communities in the direction of justice. Noah is committed to building and supporting social movements, currently organizing within his American Jewish community as a leader of IfNotNow and Never Again Action. Noah holds an EdM in learning and teaching from the Harvard Graduate School of Education and a BA in English literature from the University of Wisconsin at Madison.

Jennifer Tang is a PhD candidate in the environmental psychology program working on issues related to the promotion of children's rights to participation and participatory democracy, focusing on young people's participation in community and municipal level governance. She is also a research fellow with the Intergenerational Change Initiative and a research associate with the Children's Environments Research Group. Jennifer has worked in the promotion of children's rights, child-centered community development, and participatory research with children and communities.

María Elena Torre, PhD, is the founding director of the Public Science Project and faculty member in critical psychology and urban education at The Graduate Center of the City University of New York. She has been engaged in intergenerational critical participatory action research nationally and internationally for over 20 years with communities in neighborhoods, schools, prisons, and community-based organizations seeking structural justice. Co-editor of *PAR EntreMundos: A Pedagogy of the Americas* (Peter Lang) and co-author of *Echoes of Brown: Youth Documenting and Performing the Legacy of Brown v. Board of Education* (Teachers College Press), her work looks at how democratic methodologies, radical inclusion, and solidarity can inform a justice-based research praxis for the public good.

Amanda Torres is a queer, Mexican-American writer, educator, and strategic dreamer who has been working since 2003 to grow the field of justice oriented arts in education. She is the co-founder and former director of MassLEAP, a statewide youth arts and social justice non-profit. She's served as a teaching fellow at the Harvard Graduate School of Education, artist-in-residence at the Institute of Contemporary Art, and spoken word and community collaboration fellow at AIRSerenbe. Torres has led professional developments for educators at The Poetry Foundation, The New Museum, Andover Breadloaf, the National Council of Teachers of English and Community Word Project. Currently, Amanda works as a creative content writer for HarperCollins and directs programming for community engaged poets through the Poetry Foundation & Crescendo Literary in Chicago. As a chronically ill aspiring curandera, Amanda is committed to creating accessible spaces for all her people to make art towards collective liberation.

Erica Van Steenis is a doctoral candidate in learning sciences and human development program in the School of Education at the University of Colorado, Boulder. She holds a Master of Science in community development from the University of California, Davis and a Bachelor of Arts in history from the University of California, Berkeley. Erica has extensive teaching experience with undergraduates, which includes her continued development on an adolescent development and educational psychology course. Motivated by 15 years of experience as a youth worker, her dissertation explores youth practitioners at different stages of the profession across three contexts of inquiry. Her research interests include making a case for the value of youth work, pedagogical approaches to developing youth practitioners, and positive youth development in out-of-school contexts.

Anna West is the executive director of Humanities Amped program in Baton Rouge, Louisiana. Anna founded Forward Arts, a youth writing organization; she co-founded Louder than a Bomb, the country's largest youth poetry slam festival, and she is a co-director of the Andover Bread Loaf Summer Teacher Workshops. She holds a PhD in English education from Louisiana State University where she was awarded the 2018 Distinguished Dissertation Award in Arts, Humanities, and Social Sciences for "'In the School, Not of the School': Co-Performing Critical Literacies with English Amped" (2017). She holds a MEd from Harvard Graduate School of Education where she received the 2011 Arts in Education Intellectual Contribution Award. She co-authored "Call and responsibility: Critical questions for youth spoken word poetry" in *Harvard Educational Review* (2012) and is co-authoring a forthcoming chapter in the *MLA Social Justice Pedagogy* volume (2019).

Dr. Tanya Wiggins has over 20 years of experience as an educator, during which she has supported youth through middle school instruction, professional development, nonprofit leadership, and higher education. Tanya currently serves as clinical assistant professor of Foundations and Adolescent Education in the School of Education at Pace University. Her research seeks to bridge the worlds of research and practice by exploring the triumphs of community-based youth organizations as well as challenges they face. In this work, Tanya also examines the role of these organizations as educational spaces.

Sarah Zeller-Berkman, PhD is the director of Youth Studies Programs at the CUNY School of Professional Studies. At CUNY SPS, she oversees the MA and Advanced Certificate in Youth Studies programs and directs the Intergenerational Change Initiative (ICI), a youth participatory action research project involving tech and participatory policy making. Dr. Zeller-Berkman has spent the last 2 decades as a practitioner, researcher, evaluator, and capacity-builder in the field of youth and community development. Trained in social-personality psychology, she has worked in partnership with young people on participatory action research projects about issues that impact their lives such as sexual harassment in schools, incarceration, parental incarceration, and high-stakes testing. Her publications include articles and chapters in the *Journal of Community, Youth and Environments, The Handbook of Qualitative Research, AfterSchool Matters, New Directions for Evaluation, Globalizing Cultural Studies*, and *Children of Incarcerated Parents*.

CPSIA information can be obtained
at www.ICGtesting.com
Printed in the USA
JSHW021229130520
5631JS00002B/2